CAREER REFLECTIONS OF
SOCIAL WORK EDUCATORS

To Wendy
I'm very flattered
that you like my book.
You are the future of
Social Work!
Happy Reading.

Also available from Lyceum Books, Inc.

Advisory Editor: Thomas M. Meenaghan,
New York University

WOMEN IN SOCIAL WORK WHO HAVE MADE A DIFFERENCE
edited by Alice Lieberman

COMPLEX SYSTEMS AND HUMAN BEHAVIOR
by Christopher G. Hudson

CRITICAL MULTICULTURAL SOCIAL WORK
by Jose Sisneros, Catherine Stakeman,
Mildred C. Joyner, and Cathryne L. Schmitz

SOCIAL WORK PRACTICE WITH LATINOS
edited by Rich Furman and Nalini Negi

ESSENTIAL SKILLS OF SOCIAL WORK PRACTICE:
ASSESSMENT, INTERVENTION, EVALUATION
by Thomas O'Hare

STRAIGHT TALK ABOUT PROFESSIONAL ETHICS
by Kim Strom-Gottfried

USING STATISTICAL METHODS IN SOCIAL WORK
PRACTICE WITH SPSS
by Soleman H. Abu-Bader

RESEARCH METHODS FOR SOCIAL WORKERS
edited by Cynthia A. Faulkner and Samuel S. Faulkner

SOCIAL WORK EVALUATION:
ENHANCING WHAT WE DO
by James R. Dudley

HOW TO TEACH EFFECTIVELY
by Bruce Friedman

CAREER REFLECTIONS OF SOCIAL WORK EDUCATORS

SPENCER J. ZEIGER, PHD

Foreword by
MARSHALL L. SMITH

LYCEUM
BOOKS, INC.
Chicago, Illinois

DEDICATION

To my mother, Syril Harriet Zeiger
To all social work educators—past, present, and future

© 2010 by Lyceum Books, Inc.

Published by
LYCEUM BOOKS, INC.
5758 S. Blackstone Avenue
Chicago, Illinois 60637
773–643–1903 fax
773–643–1902 phone
lyceum@lyceumbooks.com
www.lyceumbooks.com

6   5   4   3   2   1   10   11   12   13   14

ISBN 978-1-933478-39-5

Book and cover design by Tim Kaage, Laurel Graphx.
Printed in the United States of America.

Library of Congress Cataloging-in-Publication Data

Zeiger, Spencer J.
    Career reflections of social work educators / Spencer J. Zeiger.
        p. cm.
    Includes bibliographical references and index.
    ISBN 978-1-933478-39-5
    1. Social work education. 2. Social service—Vocational guidance—United States. I. Title.
HV11.Z43 2010
    361.3071'173—dc22
                                                        2010001240

Contents

Foreword

Spencer Zeiger has made a significant contribution to the understanding of the social work educator's academic life. Many of our colleagues, myself included, entered social work education quite naïvely, without having initially aspired to become an academic. We knew nothing about the demands of academic life, other than the classroom personas projected by our own teachers, professors, lecturers, lab assistants, and recitation section leaders over the years. It was clear to me, for example, that one had to "be prepared" before entering a classroom, but how to confidently walk into a room filled with social work students was not initially obvious. I remember my graduate MSW student days at the University of Michigan and the insanely-more-than-copious notes I took from the lectures and discussions given and led by the likes of Rosemary Sarri, Bob Vinter, Frank Maple, Edwin Thomas, and Charles Wolfson. Intense study was also required in my undergraduate psychology student days, my engineering student days, and even my high school days. I was blessed with teachers who always seemed to walk into classes with excellent preparation under their belts. At least I had absorbed the basics from their examples before I ever stepped into a classroom and faced my own students.

There is so much more to becoming a social work educator than just being prepared to walk into class. In *Career Reflections of Social Work Educators,* Professor Zeiger and his colleagues have illustrated this fact. I certainly wish I had known about academic politics, grant writing, the process of achieving tenure, strategies and requirements for promotion, and the need to spend time in the community recruiting new students. I also wish I had known about limited resources, dealing with mercurial administrators, and the shift from teaching to research that occurred after the time I was hired. And of course, knowing about the incredibly complicated process of accreditation and reaffirmation *before* I began my career in social work education would have been invaluable. In fact, apart from social work education, professionals from *other disciplines* who wish to enter the academy will find Professor Zeiger's insights beneficial in launching an academic career.

Career Reflections of Social Work Educators takes a giant step toward preparing the fledgling practitioner-turned-social-work-educator for the career adventure ahead. It brings to the forefront the importance and long-lasting effects of hiring well, from the perspectives of job seekers and search committees. We all try to put our best foot forward during search processes, but perhaps more than any other time, this is the single most significant occasion for going the extra mile. Both candidates and search committees are engaged in a decision that will potentially affect the professional and personal lives of everyone involved for long periods of time. Hiring decisions will likely shape social work education integrity and the future of professional social work.

Perhaps the greatest value of *Career Reflections of Social Work Educators* is that it will help novice academicians enter the academy with eyes wide open and avoid, or at least face, the inevitable bumps in the road with their sense of humor firmly intact. It is the closest we have to a global positioning system (GPS) for navigating the career of the social work educator.

Marshall L. Smith
Professor Emeritus, Rochester Institute of Technology
Professor (Retired), University of Hawai'i at Mānoa

Acknowledgments

First, everlasting gratitude to my colleagues who shared their career reflections: Lynne Adkins, Sally Alonzo Bell, Brenda Armstrong Clark, Freddie Avant, Jackie Azzarto, Frank Baskind, Gerald Berman, Luther Brown, Pamela Brown, Kathy Byers, Mary Campbell, Graciela Castex, Barbara Chandler, Vivian Dames, Judith Davenport, Virginia David, Eddie Davis, Tammy Faux, Jerry Finn, Jody Gottlieb, Kay Hoffman, Jane Hoyt-Oliver, Ruth Huber, Grafton Hull, Mitch Kahn, Karen Kirst-Ashman, Connie Kledaris, Rebecca Leavitt, Twyla Lee, Alice Lieberman, Donna Macintosh, Cheryl Mathews, Carl Mazza, Ann McAllister, Aaron McNeece, Ann Meyers, Emily Meyers, Linda Moore, Murali Nair, Larry Ortiz, Michael Patchner, James Piers, Jean Quam, Tim Rehner, Robert Rivas, John Rogers, Alvin Salee, Joe Schriver, Jack Sellers, Brad Sheafor, Paula Sheridan, Debbie Simpler, Elizabeth Sirles, Marshall Smith, James Stafford, Andrea Stewart, Paul Stewart, Anne Summers, Mary Ann Suppes, Mary Swigonski, Billie Terrell, Rebecca Turner, Katherine VanWormer, Sue Wein, Linda Williams, and Jackie Winston.

Second, my thanks to those who provided valuable assistance and support: Kevin (K.C.) Carr, my cat Chance, Ralph Courtney, David Follmer, Elaine Lockhart, Lyn Lockhart-Mummery, Henry Maier, Tom Meenaghan, Mary Parker, Lyn Rosen, Diane (Di) Shelburne, Marsha Tarr, Barbara Zeiger, Henry Zeiger, Moses Zeiger, and Richard Zeiger.

And finally, I wish to acknowledge my amazing "stealth" editor, Myrna Robinson.

Introduction

"Social Work Educator Longevity and Engagement" was the original title for this project. I planned to interview educators from around the country who had ten or more years' experience teaching social work. I anticipated forty to fifty subjects. The response to my study was far greater than I imagined. What began as a project that looked at the advantages and disadvantages of faculty longevity turned into something more personal and complex. I began to see that my subjects were eager, even *hungry* to reflect upon their careers as social work educators.

CONCEPTUAL FRAMEWORK

In my twenty years of academic experience, I have almost annually been involved in a faculty search. Faculty searches require time, energy, and money—and, for some programs, there is fierce competition for qualified applicants. Nationally, in social work education, demand far exceeds the supply. An explosion of new social work programs (especially MSW programs) translates into a need for more faculty, yet the number of PhDs who *want* to teach social work remains flat (Anastas, 2006; Karger & Stoesz, 2003). Baby boomers have either begun to retire or are nearing retirement (Winter & Kjorlien, 2000; Mahroum, 1999).

Searches take away from time otherwise spent. Red tape (writing and posting a job announcement, securing administrative approval, publicity, references checks, interviewing, faculty discussions) consumes program and faculty resources. Searches often come with a hefty price tag (Childress, 2001; Logan, 1997; McBride, Munday, & Tunnell, 1992; Brown, 1967). Transportation, accommodations, and meals can be expensive—and costs multiply when looking for more than one candidate.

Program success requires time and a sustained commitment from at least a core of faculty and administration (Kanter, 2006, Beckerman, 2002; Childress 2001; Cartledge, Gardner III, & Tillman, 1995). Identifying factors that contribute to stable and productive faculties, and educational, professional, and commu-

1

nity needs is important. *Career Reflections of Social Work Educators* gives voice to the wisdom of veteran social work educators from across the nation.

METHODOLOGY

Interviews for subjects averaged 57½ minutes in length, with most subjects willing to talk well beyond the scheduled fifty to sixty minutes. Interviews were scheduled seventy-five minutes apart, allowing time for short breaks for introductions and setup. Many respondents were willing to share beyond the allotted time.

The interviews were conducted at state, regional, and national social work education conferences (in Mississippi, New York, Texas, and Illinois*) with the goal of gathering information from a wide range of programs and geographical areas. To meet study parameters, subjects had to be current social work educators who had been at the same department or school of social work for ten years or more, or social work educators who had "moved around a bit" (i.e., taught at three or more locations [for at least ten years] during their career). I recruited subjects from a variety of sources, primarily Listservs and word of mouth. As an incentive, I offered, and later presented each subject with, a genuine Alaskan Moose Calendar.

All respondents were self-selected. The response exceeded expectations. I conducted fifty face-to-face interviews and another sixteen interviews over the telephone, for a total of sixty-six interviews. The telephone interviews were necessary because I literally ran out of time slots during the conferences. In order to avoid overrepresentation of individual states and institutions, I declined to interview twelve willing subjects. Another eight scheduled interviews did not occur owing to logistical problems. When all interviews were completed, sixty-six subjects representing sixty-two different institutions from thirty-five states and Guam provided data.

DESCRIPTION OF SUBJECTS

Some subjects have a national reputation among their peers through their service as present or former leaders of social work education organizations such as the Council on Social Work Education (CSWE), the Association of Baccalaureate Social Work Program Directors** (BPD), and the National Association of Deans

---

* Originally, I had planned to interview subjects at the 2005 Midwest Social Work Education Conference in Michigan, which was billed as drawing social work educators from nine states. As numbers began to rise, I considered the volume of data analysis that lay ahead and decided against adding more subjects.

** The name Association of Baccalaureate Social Work Program Directors is clearly a misnomer, as half the members are *not* program directors, though some have been so in the past. A more fitting name that

Years in increments of 10

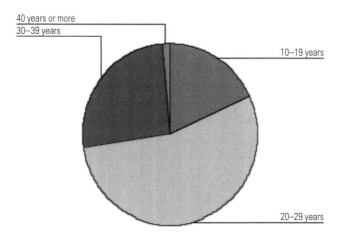

and Directors of Schools of Social Work (NADD). Others were equally committed but not as well known.

Ten years or more of experience proved to be a conservative estimate for yielding enough subjects. The average length of experience as a social work educator was 25.58 years with a breakdown as follows:

10–19 years	12	(18%)
20–29 years	36	(55%)
30–39 years	17	(26%)
42 years	1	(2%)

Small (two to six full-time), medium (seven to fourteen full-time), and large (fifteen or more full-time) faculties were well represented:*

Program Size

Small (2–6)	Medium (7–14)	Large (15+)
n = 30	n = 20	n = 16

---

accurately reflects the composition of membership would be the Association of Baccalaureate Social Work Program Directors and Educators.

    * I have not come across reasonable standard size ranges. CSWE divides faculty size by increments of ten, resulting in a sizable bulge at the lower end (programs with < 10 = 250 out of 417 [Council on Social Work Education, 2007]). After consulting with several colleagues, I developed increments that seem more useful. Extrapolating from CSWE's ranges, my sample appears to be fairly representative of small, medium, and large program sizes nationwide.

Twenty-six men (39%) and forty women (61%) participated in the study. Subjects were categorized as those with less experience (10–26 years) and more experience (27–42 years). A statistically significant relationship between age and gender (X = .020) was revealed. Women in the ten-to-twenty-six-years range outnumber men three to one. Perhaps a wave of job announcements encouraging women to apply, and an eye toward gender equity, have influenced this shift in demographics.

	Male	Female	Total
10–26 years	8	24	32
27–42 years	18	16	34
Total	26	40	66

Forty-six subjects were from public institutions, and twenty subjects were from private institutions (70% and 30%, respectively). More women than men teach in private institutions by a ratio of four to one (16:4). Seventy-nine percent (n = 52) either taught at BSW-only programs (n = 36; 55%) or combined BSW + MSW programs (n = 16; 24%). The following pie chart illustrates the distribution among BSW-only, BSW + MSW, MSW + PhD, and BSW + MSW + PhD programs.*

Program type

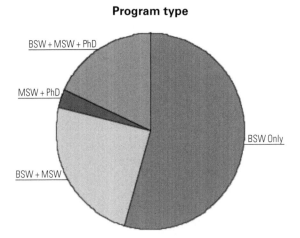

Examining the mobility patterns of subjects led to the following conclusion: most (n = 45; 68%) long-term social work educators spend the majority of their

* These proportions are close to the proportions listed for CSWE accredited social work education programs according to their most recently published data (Council on Social Work Education, 2007). CSWE data leave a margin of error, due to an overall response rate of 77 percent (i.e., 23 percent of all programs did not report data).

career—either their entire career (n = 29; 44%), 90 to 99 percent of their career (n = 8; 12%), or 60 to 89 percent of their career (n = 8; 12%) in one place.

Exceptions to the above include "Hybrids," social work educators who alternate between short and long stints throughout their career (n = 9; 14%), and "Academic Nomads," those who have taught at four or more institutions and "seem to get an itch to relocate every four to six years" (n = 12; 18%).

	Frequency	**Percent**	**Cum. Percent**
One place only	29	44	44
90–99% at one place	8	12	56
Settled at one place	8	12	68
Hybrid	9	14	82
Academic nomad	12	18	100
Total	66	100	

Mobility

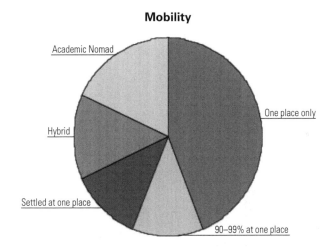

BRIDGE TO RESULTS

My research examines how faculty longevity is related to worker satisfaction, continued productivity, and ongoing professional stimulation. Secondarily, these factors are likely to play a key role in the overall quality of social work education. Goodness of fit (how well a social work academic program meets the needs of a faculty member, and how well program needs are met by a faculty member) is paramount for faculty satisfaction and program stability. Data analysis has revealed the following themes:

Factors leading respondents to enter social work education;

Factors that have sustained them in various institutions of higher learning;

Events (unexpected and positive) that occurred during their careers;

Events (unexpected and negative) that occurred during their careers;

Knowledge of academic politics prior to career entry;

Availability of faculty resources;

Advice subjects would give to those wishing to become social work educators;

Advice subjects would give to search committees; and

Pros and cons of longevity.

At the beginning of this introduction, I remarked upon the intensity and passion of the life stories my colleagues shared with me. The timing was fateful for two reasons. First, I conducted these interviews, about sixty-five hours' worth, while on sabbatical—a time I had envisioned as one for self-renewal and reflection; a golden opportunity to evaluate where I've gone, where I am now, and how I wish to live in the future. Hearing the sagas of sixty-six career social work educators certainly intensified my ruminations. Second, my mother died shortly before I began my sabbatical, intensifying the perennial questions: What am I accomplishing in my life? Am I doing what I want? and What matters most? Professional social work educators talk about their professional life journeys as they answer these pivotal questions.

THE AUDIENCE

Career Reflections of Social Work Educators is intended to satisfy the needs and curiosities of several audiences. Students enrolled in a social work or social welfare doctoral education program, and considering a career in academia, may obtain valuable insights and information from the stories of seasoned social work educators provided in this book. You may be inspired or have second thoughts, but you will have a clearer notion of academic life before you make an employment decision.

Current social work educators, whether at the beginning, middle, or twilight stages of their careers, may also benefit. One of the unexpected outcomes of conducting sixty-six in-depth interviews was to provide the subjects an opportunity—one they had never taken before—to review the meaning of their life's work. Considering their wealth of experience, and considering that many of the subjects played key roles in social work education programs throughout the nation, their stories may inform and inspire future generations of social work educators.

Career Reflections of Social Work Educators is also written for faculty search committee members and college/university administrators. "Hiring well" is paramount. Most (if not all) search committee members and administrators have stories of hiring mistakes that have drained time, resources, and productivity. Synchronization is key; when professional development of faculty blossoms, and institutional missions are realized, both social work education and the profession of social work grow stronger.

Perhaps you are a social work practitioner looking for a career change. It may surprise you to learn that most social work educators began their professional careers as practitioners, never intending to become academicians! As you will see in the first chapter, for some it was the teaching element of clinical work that set their minds to wonder: Why influence an individual, couple, or family, when I can teach twenty students per class who will in turn empower so many clients? Drawing upon practice experience strengthens pedagogy.

Just as "You don't have to be Jewish to love Levy's [rye bread]," you don't have to have a particular interest in social work or social work education to appreciate this book. While interviewees were social work educators, most of the vicissitudes of academia—including the elements of a successful job search, academic politics, professional development, collegiality, and tenure—are relevant to *all* fields in the academy, from accounting to zoology. If you are interested in becoming a professional educator or want to reflect on your current (or past) academic career and social work is not you bailiwick, relax and enjoy a slice of rye.

RESEARCH LIMITATIONS

All research is conducted within the bounds of limited time and resources. My goal was to have at least one subject from as many U.S. states as possible. Thirty-five states and Guam are represented from a sample of sixty-six subjects. I was unable to interview subjects from Oregon, Montana, Wyoming, Idaho, Nevada, Arizona, North Dakota, Nebraska, Oklahoma, Maine, New Hampshire, Connecticut, Rhode Island, Delaware, and Georgia.

Though imperfect (the thoughts of those who *didn't* participate are not included), I believe my sample is fairly representative of seasoned social work educators in the United States. I consciously sought to attain a sample that mirrored the proportions of CSWE accredited institutions in terms of faculty and program size, faculty gender, regional representation, program auspice (private vs. public), and program type (BSW-only, BSW + MSW, BSW + MSW + PhD, and MSW + PhD). Although I can say that my sample is in the ballpark, so to speak, my claim to its reliability must be tempered by its small size.

I have no doubt that I could have interviewed a hundred subjects or more. I made a conscious decision to stop at sixty-six, based upon the criteria listed below. Staying true to these criteria resulted in my turning down many potential subjects who wished to participate.

No more than two individuals were interviewed from the same program.

I made a deliberate effort to interview a proportionate number of subjects from any one state, region, and auspice.

I made an educated, albeit intuitive, estimation that to conduct more interviews would result in a volume of data too large to manage.

I reached a point of saturation (i.e., I sensed a reduction in new information).

A final limitation is worth noting. The interviews for this book were conducted in 2005 and 2006. From approximately 2007 to the present, the United States has been experiencing a sharp economic downturn—affecting perks and benefits offered by most academic institutions (see pages 43–44). The validity of data in the present study should be viewed in temporal context.

Paths to Social Work Education

WHY SOCIAL WORK?

What leads people to become social work educators? Doctoral students majoring in social work or social welfare (or a related field), social work practitioners considering a career shift to academia, and current or former social work educators wishing to reflect upon their careers may find this chapter of interest. The paths of those interviewed vary—from a temporary teaching position that grew into a long-term career to needing a change from social work practice to being inspired by a mentor. For example:

> I majored in group work, got steeped in the literature, worked in a residential treatment center. It was difficult employment. I looked for another job, and was offered a one-year replacement gig at a state university—I stayed for seven years. I always wanted to get into education, and that was my big break. I was director of the field for the undergrad program, struggled through reaffirmation, and became BSW director after that. I [also] taught group work in the MSW program. [But] I couldn't be on tenure track without a PhD. Then, a college that had employed me as a consultant, made me an offer in 1981. I was hired as program director, to begin the BSW program. I was offered job security (tenure), a good salary, and the opportunity to launch a BSW program from scratch.

> I started off working at a women's prison in New Jersey. This grew out of an MSW field placement. I then worked as a dialysis social worker for five years, then two years in a hospital as a medical social worker. Part of going into teaching was just burnout from the death and dying work. But it was a growing dissatisfaction with social work education. I had the arrogance to say, "I can do this better." When I was practicing [social work] I felt like I didn't know enough. All my friends had PhDs and I wanted one too. I received my PhD at [a Northeastern] university and then went into teaching.

A mentor picked me out of the crowd—spoke to me about the importance of getting a PhD and the future of social work education. I never had an inclination at all to do that. I saw myself as getting an MSW, being a practitioner, and being happy with that. I found I did not derive sufficient satisfaction from being a practitioner. I became bored because I like the world of ideas. Meanwhile, my wife received a faculty appointment at a state university. Then we both decided to go after PhDs at the same time. This produced tension, stress. Neither one of us was going to "go first." To save the marriage, we did it at the same time, with a toddler and an infant. I first taught in an unaccredited social work program, attended a couple of APMs [Annual Program Meetings of the Council on Social Work Education], and decided this is what I wanted to do. Even though my PhD was in sociology, I clearly identified myself as a social worker.

Subjects were asked what led them to become social work educators. Responses are divided into the following nine themes:

Answered a calling/committed to social change;
Influenced by social work education;
Inspired by a mentor/taken under someone's wing;
Disenchanted with practice/needed a change;
Perceived schedule flexibility;
Inspired by the teaching element within practice;
Entered by chance and became infatuated;
Provided with a ground floor opportunity/chance to build a program;
    and
Motivated by family needs and family history.

Answered a Calling/Committed to Social Change

Being naturally drawn to the profession of social work education was a frequently voiced theme. A corollary to this notion is that being an effective social work educator, one can effect social change for future social work practitioners, the clients they will serve, and the social systems in which they live.

When asked to be guest speaker in a class taught by her mentor, one respondent recalled:

I remember feeling this calling, this vocation, and this sense of "this is what I'm supposed to be doing." When a position opened up on the West Coast, it felt like an affirmation of a hunger—which could only be satisfied by going into social work education.

One subject voiced a love of the profession beginning in high school. She added: "It's a deep calling—challenging, interesting, a good life to be in social work academia. We're lucky to get paid to do these things; it's one of the best jobs in the whole world."

A strong tone of commitment and conviction—more than earning a paycheck—came through loud and clear. When asked to describe what led him to become a social work educator, one subject was definitive and articulate:

> Commitment to the profession. Commitment to the values. I think of social work as a calling. It's more than a simple job or occupation; it's a life. You commit yourself to a lifestyle; it's a set of values. I'm passionate about the profession. I'm very protective of people we have in it. I'm as excited about teaching as I was eighteen years ago. It's really a basic commitment to the profession.

Another subject, who had been a social work practitioner for eight years, noticed an ad in the *NASW* (National Association of Social Workers) *News* for a faculty position at a local state university. They were recruiting someone to develop a BSW program in her home community. She had even been a former student, but switched to another school that offered an accredited social work program. She reflected:

> I knew I had a mission to develop the BSW program that was missing when I was a student. That's what got my foot in the door. I knew immediately that that's where I needed to be. I knew it from the beginning. That was the right place and the right work for me.

A quarter of a century later, she proudly holds title to social work educator at the same institution.

Subjects spoke of fulfilling a sense of purpose, of "not just being here for the hell of it." To empower clients to achieve their goals, and to alter societal structures to improve social justice among the oppressed and disenfranchised; this is what matters in life.

For one participant of color, the lack of diverse faculty she experienced while receiving her social work education had a strong influence on her career aspirations:

> There was a lack of professors who represented who I am. There is a lack of Latino men and women who go into social work and teach. I wanted to be able to close this gap, to influence institutions to hire people who represent the student body.

Regarding teaching social work instead of being engaged in direct social work practice (which all subjects did prior to entering academia), subjects expressed an initial dilemma: "I had a difficult time reconciling the fun I was having teaching—the fact that I wasn't out working with clients." Seven years into teaching, this subject knew she was going to stay. She tried to resign and return to practice, but her department really needed someone to teach policy. She found herself at the library, studying the roots of poverty and realizing that teaching really excited her:

> I had the opportunity to make a difference in the world, in people's lives. I had to decide how to make a difference. I decided I could teach students how to make a difference in the lives of others versus making a difference with individual clients. I just multiply the gift.

Some subjects spoke of always wanting to teach social work, as early as high school. Exposure to academicians may have made a difference. When asked how she got into social work education, one subject said that she "grew up around universities. My mother was assistant dean of women, and I saw universities as really cool places to be and work." Another subject knew many faculty and administrators through well-established church connections. It was not uncommon for subjects to have mothers, fathers, or both parents involved in higher education. One subject reflected that she was married to an academic and had "always lived in an academic setting. I've always felt inclined toward education."

Influenced by Social Work Education

One positive aspect of quality social work education is intellectual stimulation. Rather than supplying cookbook instruction, quality education stimulates critical thinking and provides an opportunity for students to grapple with ways to improve the quality of service to consumers of professional social work. For some, it is a life-changing experience; they become empowered to see the world differently, and develop the capacity to empower others.

For better or worse, students enrolled in social work education programs are exposed to role models of what it might be like to teach social work classes. They are exposed to the world of academia, surrounded by students, professors, and an institutional atmosphere dedicated to improving the quality of life through higher education. Being in an academic milieu may become a source of satisfaction and comfort. Some subjects praised the quality of the social work education they received, while others concluded they could (eventually) do a better job. Based upon their educational experience, becoming a social work educator themselves provides an opportunity to emulate heroes, find their own voice as a professor, and perhaps do things differently. It is also a chance to return to (or extend) the world of academic stimulation: "I was disappointed in the social work education I received. It was intellectually thin. I thought I could broaden the minds of social work students. I wanted to make social work students smarter."

Some subjects voiced strong satisfaction with the social work education they received. But for others, a motivating factor for their entry into social work education was a desire to improve upon social work education for the next generation of students: "Sitting in college classrooms when I was young [in her BSW program], brash, and not very humble, I was thinking: 'I can do this better.'"

Social work educators are role models, giving students a sense of what it might be like to teach social work, or stimulating thought about how social work education might improve. One interviewee was first inspired to teach while enrolled in an MSW program, more specifically, while he was in field practicum and seminar. At that point, he knew he wanted to become a social work educator. From there, it was a logical progression. After receiving his MSW, he became a field instructor, and "I internalized the message: 'You might be a good teacher.'" He has been teaching social work for the past twenty years.

When asked to describe a marker event that influenced the career choice of social work education, one respondent noted that while working on her MSW, she persuaded her academic advisor to allow her to take a doctoral class on social work education as an elective. She learned about curriculum, accreditation, and kindled an interest in academia. She thought: *"I might want to do this someday."*

And do it someday they have. Today's social work educators are strategically positioned to influence future social work practitioners. It's an awesome responsibility. As one respondent noted: "I can affect people who effect change." And another, bewhiskered, subject noted: "My former students are now running agencies, making a positive impact on the community."

A woman of color, who has taught at a private university on the West Coast, noted:

> I can never succeed or fail as an individual. I succeed or fail as a representative of my people—Latinos. I feel an obligation. Twelve percent of the student body is now people of color. That's the flag I have to fly.

Inspired by a Mentor/Taken under Someone's Wing

Mentors inspire future educators (Barnett, Gibson, & Black, 2003). Subjects reported being encouraged to teach either by their social work professor while they were enrolled as social work students, or by their supervisors while they were practitioners. One subject, while working with delinquent youth, was encouraged by her supervisor to enroll in graduate school. She reported having an epiphany: "I should teach; this is a sign from God—out of the blue—helping people understand social work. I was influenced by my supervisor, who was committed to quality social work education."

To many respondents, pursuing their doctoral studies meant becoming socialized to social work education. In the words of one subject: "I went in as a clinician, and came out as a social work educator. It was the socialization among faculty and fellow doctoral students. Faculty were models for me of what it would be like to teach." And in another example:

> I was influenced by M. at [a state university]. She encouraged me to go for a PhD. She was starting up a BSW program and two classes needed coverage: Introduction to Social Work and Field. I liked everything about it. The seed was planted. I went to [another state university], worked as a social worker for three years, and had an offer to teach again; this time it was full time. M. told me: "If you really want to teach, this would be a good way." I jumped in, just trying to stay two weeks ahead of the students. I applied to five or six places for a PhD, and [one school] offered me a full ride for three years. M. felt if social work was to be a strong profession, people needed a PhD.

Other subjects reported being singled out and inspired by a professor whom they held in high regard. One spoke of the influence of a highly regarded faculty member, who, impressed by his in-class presentation, recommended him for a teaching position. He remarked: "I don't know if I ever would have gotten into teaching without my mentor's suggestion."

Disenchanted with Practice/Needed a Change

"I worked as a medical social worker for seven years. Part of going into teaching was just burnout from the death and dying work."

It is rare for social work students, particularly at the BSW and MSW levels, to aspire to become social work educators. They are more likely to be focused on becoming practitioners. It is fair to say that practically all subjects of this study aspired to become practitioners, with no intent of teaching in a social work program. A common journey involved being a practitioner for a number of years after graduation, and then becoming bored, frustrated, and realizing that becoming an educator would be a better fit. It would be a more satisfying application of their talent, skills, knowledge, and energy. One subject related the following tale:

> I started off working in child protection, burning out due to the intensity and the caseload. The situation was so bad at my agency that a kid who needed placement couldn't get placed. So I contemplated taking her home

with me. That's when I knew I probably needed a different perspective and a different job. A position came up at a neighboring university. I always said I wanted to be a teacher in social work; I told that to my professors in graduate school. I decided I could work with thirty families or I could teach thirty students who could [each] work with thirty families—and affect—nine hundred families.

The refrain of being able to influence many was a common one for leaving practice. In another example:

After struggling through my first year of teaching, I decided it was better not to be just one social worker attacking social problems, but [*sic*] having the ability to influence lots of people to become ready to go out and attack structural problems, so that individuals, families, and communities could function better.

In another scenario, a subject had been working with emotionally disturbed adolescents for a number of years and was feeling stuck and hungry for change. She was in a dead-end position within her agency. She applied and was accepted into a PhD program. A tuition waiver and a part-time teaching position sweetened the deal. She has now been a social work educator for more than a quarter of a century.

In most cases, an advantage of working in an academic setting, as opposed to an agency setting, is greater opportunity and support for conducting research. One subject, who spent years engaged in hospice social work, decided that direct practice felt limited ("It was claustrophobic."). She decided she would change systems that cause problems. She saw the power of research in an academic setting as the best vehicle. She would become a source of information for frontline practitioners. Eventually, she obtained a grant to establish an innovative hospice program.

As the reader will see, a recurrent theme is for social workers to "fall into" social work education. Few began with the intention to become a social work educator some day. People are drawn into social work with the best of intentions: a desire to help society. Social workers are advocates, activists, and catalysts for social change. They work for the greater good of individuals, families, organizations, and communities. Working long hours with challenging populations and large caseloads (sometimes with minimal "payoff") may lead to a feeling of depletion and a desire for something different.

Perhaps a by-product of human development, people become less idealistic and more realistic regarding their goals as they progress through their life span. Priorities may change. They may become less willing to sacrifice time. They may be ready for a career shift that will allow more time for family and recreation. Like movements in a symphony, perhaps their pace and rhythm in life is no longer the same. Entering social work practice was akin to the overture offering a sampling of "movements" to come and clarifying life's possibilities. Or perhaps they entered social work practice as a "wounded healer," accomplished sufficient healing of their past wounds, and are now ready to walk away from practice and enter academia.

We have seen a shift from practice to academia. Do academicians ever return to their practice roots? Or is it good-bye and perhaps good riddance? One subject worked in mental health services, medical social work, and child and family services for seven years before moving into academia. When asked what motivated her transition, she stated that work morale wasn't high, the turnover rate was high, and that practice was no longer exciting. Today, she has found, in over twenty years as a social work educator, that she prefers interaction with students, though she has been able to maintain some practice ("to stay fresh, to stay connected") and is an active consultant to agencies.

Perceived Schedule Flexibility

"You mean I only have to work nine months out of the year?! I get summers off, and a spring and winter break too? Someone pinch me!"

One subject, who had been working year-round as a medical social worker, was attracted to the "flexibility" of an academic schedule. "I started having children, and realized this would allow me to spend more time with them. I jumped at the chance."

While there is some schedule flexibility, social work educators with a "nine-month contract" will tell you that their academic work rarely comes to a halt in May or June. Frequently, there are "incompletes" to complete, evaluations and letters of recommendation to be written, and numerous loose ends to tie up. In the words of one nine-month subject: "I think the last time I really had a full summer off, was—well never, actually." And another noted:

> On paper, I do have a nine-month contract. But there are always extra demands, like needing to work on an accreditation self-study, or preparing a tenure file. Or getting around to all the stuff I never had time for during the year, like writing and curriculum development. We have summer classes too, and they need to be covered. And to be honest, I need the extra income. So yeah, I don't really have much free time in the summer. Nine months is a myth.

Inspired by the Teaching Element within Practice

"I headed a field unit while I was practicing, so there was an element of teaching while I was a practitioner for four years."

When asked what led them to become social work educators, subjects revealed that the part they enjoyed most about social work practice, be it child protection, work with refugees, or medical social work, was the teaching element of group work and educational presentations.

The students of today will become the graduates of tomorrow. And graduates become eligible (usually after two years of postgraduate practice experience) to become field instructors and assume a teaching role. Some supervise two or more students within an academic year. This experience is often pivotal, inspiring a future role. In the words of one subject who has now been teaching at the same small program for more than thirty years:

> I was a social worker in a hospital and had a remarkable field placement student. This experience [as a field instructor] made me extremely interested in social work education. I remember the student was from the same social work program where I teach today.

Entered by Chance and Became Infatuated

"It wasn't my goal."

"I fell into it by chance."

"I didn't go out looking for a job in education, it just fell into my lap."

"It was by accident; it really was."

"My story's atypical because I never planned to go to college. I went for lack of anything better to do. I stumbled into mental health, with no aspiration to academia."

Are social work educators drawn to the profession by some inexplicable force, like people to the mountain in *Close Encounters of the Third Kind*? It was a rare subject who set out to become a professional social work educator. The following scenario was typical:

> I stumbled into it. I was originally an employee of the state department office of public welfare—a food eligibility worker. A faculty person offered me a training coordinator position as part of a Title XX [twenty] grant, and I was able to move into a faculty position when the grant ended. I never intended or desired to teach.

Having, as he put it, stumbled into teaching, he has stayed with the same social work program for over twenty-five years.

Another example of a chance entry into the profession came from a subject working in alcohol rehabilitation:

> I came to social work education in an odd way. [I was] teaching people who
> had been convicted of DUI, as a hospital social worker/alcohol counselor.
> Someone slid a job notice under my door. It was serendipitous; I'd never
> been serious about anything to do with education. But I thought, "If I can
> teach [people] who don't want to be here, I can teach people who really
> want to learn!" I'm an adventurer; it was a developmental process. I never
> thought I would be a teacher.

That subject has now been a social work educator for almost twenty years.

And in another example of a chance occurrence leading to a career in social
work education:

> I did not intend to be a social work educator. I worked with mentally re-
> tarded adults after earning my MSW. I was a case manager. I got a call [from
> a social work program] to fill in as a field director. I thought, "Sure, I'll
> do this for a year or so"—and the next thing I knew they put me on hard
> money. I just stayed [twenty-seven years and counting]. It was just that
> phone call.

Do professional social work educators discover their vocation by pure
accident? A chance phone call at the right moment? Having an inspirational
mentor? A genetic predisposition? Or is it something in their academic preparation, their application of skills and knowledge in professional practice, or
perhaps a force beyond their power that has led them to where they are today?
Forces that contribute to entering a career may be multiple and complex. I believe there is no one reason people become social work educators. For some,
there may be rational reasons for doing so, for others the reasons are more eso-
teric. My favorite social work professor of all time, Henry Maier, once told me:
"Chance favors the prepared mind." While few subjects would have predicted
they would one day become social work educators, they would probably agree
that the goodness of fit is real, and certainly enduring.

If happenstance was a common refrain, "catching the teaching bug" was
equally common. Once they gave teaching a try, they were hooked. Here's a
vivid description:

> I did not intend to be an educator. I was content being a clinician and I was
> a damn good clinician. I was asked to be an adjunct at a school on the West
> Coast. I came home and told my husband: "Now I know how these rock
> stars feel when they have a stadium and all the energy comes at them." I
> hit the front of the classroom and I strutted. I love it when I teach!

It may be comforting for those considering social work education as a career that teaching enthusiasm can be long lasting. According to one veteran

educator: "[After more than thirty years] I still have that same sense of exhilaration when I finish teaching social work education theory. That sense of being fired up is still there."

Provided with a Ground Floor Opportunity/Chance to Build a Program

> In 1971, I interviewed for a position as a psychiatric social worker at a mental health center. During the interview I met an academician who wanted to start up a social work program. After the interview I spoke with him by phone, and it was more than a social call. It was a defining moment. I received an offer two weeks later. I never thought about teaching very much. Being able to start a program from the ground up attracted me. I spent three years building the program.

Many social work educators began their academic careers in the 1970s when programs, especially BSW programs, were being launched. They were hired as program directors for programs that did not yet exist. Part of the attraction, for one colleague, was her "professional choice to control my fate by writing a self-study, creating a program from inception to product, feeling loyalty and ownership—versus joining someone else's program." They had the opportunity to build a program from scratch, to be in on the ground floor. A sense of pride comes through as a veteran of thirty-four years tells a story:

> I often thought of returning to practice, but then a new opportunity would arise at the university, such as supervising or mentoring students in field practicum, administrative opportunities, or directing the Aging Families and Intergenerational Studies Program. I began a Community Service Learning Program in 1987. I had the opportunity to build our BSW program [approved but not accredited when she came on board]. I've sustained a personal drive to make the program the best it can be through accreditations and reaffirmations in '77, '84, '91, '99, and I'm writing for 2007 now. I've watched the program grow and gain recognition on campus and in the community.

As a researcher, I was struck by the level of dedication, sense of commitment and passion, and long hours these pioneers gave of themselves. One participant who was hired to join an amalgam of young social scientists spoke of his early professional days:

> I was initially hired to develop field programs for the entire campus. I was working seventy to eighty hours a week. I hired two other social work faculty who were committed to work closely with the community. It was 1974;

the BSW program was just getting started. We submitted our first self-study in 1977 and were fully accredited in 1979. The self-study was only fifty or sixty pages!

As we will see later, being in on the ground floor is a factor contributing to longevity at a single institution. Twenty-five years or more for a "founder" is not unusual.* One veteran of three and a half decades had this to say:

I feel program ownership—no desire to leave. I've been department chair since 1975. My position itself is a reason for staying. I'm just a year and a half from retirement. It's where I should be. I've never interviewed anywhere else. It's home. I like the students, the community.

Motivated by Family Needs and Family History

Social work has often been described as a profession that attracts so-called wounded healers. A common refrain voiced by my colleagues was the occurrence of personal or family experiences that had a powerful influence on their career decision: to become a social work educator. For one person, it was the history and experience of mental retardation among his relatives. For another, it was the influence of his mother lobbying for a local adult rehabilitation center. Here's another example:

My mother was a kidney patient. She lost her hearing when she was thirty because of a medicine overdose. We had the kidney machine at home; my sisters were nursing students. My mom had kids, had to quit her job and go on disability. I asked a college faculty person what I could do to help my mom. She suggested going into social work. I took courses; I liked the nonjudgmental attitude. It felt right; it would help my mom to find resources. I chose to teach because of the major impact teaching would have on my mom.

A marker event for another subject was having a daughter born with "lots of physical problems—lots of trauma for us." He thought a university community would be more accepting of a child with special needs. In another scenario:

My entry into social work education developed out of being a macro thinker. It stemmed out of my mother's death and the "hospice job" my

---

* Forty-one of the sixty-six subjects have twenty-five years or more of longevity (i.e., experience in social work education). Among the forty-one, sixteen (39%) have spent their entire careers at the same social work educational program, and twenty-three (56%) have spent 90 percent or more of their careers at the same program.

family did. My mother died at home; I did peritoneal dialysis at home for a year. I came to realize I'm not just here for the hell of it. I need to use my gifts for humankind. What can I do to make a difference? I fell in love with research in my MSW program. I did hospice social work but decided that direct practice felt limited, claustrophobic, that I'd rather change systems that cause problems. I saw the power of research—the informant for practitioners on the front line. I got a grant to set up a hospice program.

Is it important to know how or why people become social work educators? Maybe. Perhaps reading other people's journeys will stimulate a higher level of consciousness regarding career choices. Perhaps the stories of professional social work educators will evoke a better understanding of personal and professional needs, which may or may not include becoming a social work educator. Launching a new career is a major life task, with tremendous potential impact for social work educators, their families, students, communities, and institutions of higher learning. Given the pressing need for more high-quality social work educators, it is hoped that learning about the journeys that have led some to long-term careers in social work education will inspire others to follow a similar path.

Chapter 1 has explored the paths taken to enter the career of social work educator. While the journeys vary, one thing most subjects shared in common was that they did not initially aspire to become social work educators. Their entry was serendipitous. Nonetheless, for the sixty-six subjects in this study, their impact on social work education is real and enduring.

Now that we have an idea of how they entered into social work education, let's explore what happened next. What indicators confirmed their career choice? Was there a turning point when they knew they had made the right choice in becoming a social work educator?

The Defining Moment

WHEN DID YOU KNOW?

After describing a path that led subjects into social work education, participants were asked to identify a marker event, a turning point, or a definitive moment when they *knew* they were going to remain in social work education as a career. What makes this identification important? Anything that enhances self-awareness, that makes us more conscious of the choices we make in life, is positive. Being able to recognize marker events, and tune to the attendant gut feelings, is a valuable source of heightened consciousness. When it comes to making a career choice—a choice that may have a profound impact on family, colleagues, students, and the future of social work—I believe that it is important to pay attention to our deepest instinctively felt emotions and responses, in addition to our sense of what is rational or logical.

A defining moment is likely the result of multiple factors. Any major decision in life is influenced by practical considerations such as salary and benefits, cost of living, geography, life-span development stage, career stage, extended family obligations, and work conditions (past and potential future). Similarly, emotional factors come into play such as readiness for change, what it feels like to walk around campus, the way students and faculty respond to your colloquium, a spiritual connection of being in the right place at the right time, or any combination of the above. And while it's rarely a single factor that lets us know "this is it," the decision of knowing that social work education is "where I belong" was often captured by an event or feeling that merited subjects' attention.

Definitive moments can come at different times in different ways for different people. And there is not always a single definitive moment. Subjects' responses to the request to identify a marker event, a turning point, or a definitive moment when they knew they were going to remain in social work education as a career are divided into the following eleven themes:

Love from the beginning;
Mystical whispers;

A better fit than practice;

Achievement of tenure and promotion;

Receiving a PhD;

Positive teaching evaluations and awards;

Validation at national conferences;

The challenge of program building and the fight for recognition;

Successful accreditation experience;

Family circumstances; and

Steady satisfaction/no one point in time.

Love from the Beginning

Instant positive attraction to the field of social work education was a common refrain. For many, adoration began on the first day of teaching. As one subject noted: "The first couple of minutes of the very first class I taught, I loved it. When I started seeing the light bulbs go on, I thought: 'This is cool; this is for me.'" Other subjects agreed:

> I knew it right away. There's something special about teaching social work. I love the discipline. I love working on behalf of those who are disenfranchised. I love the liberal orientation of changing society. From the very beginning, I've been excited about inspiring others to effect change.

> It happened in my first year. [At twenty-eight] I was the youngest member of the faculty. I received a warm reception from the faculty. We had mutual ties to the African American community. Seasoned professors befriended me. I felt wanted and needed, accepted. I looked upon older faculty as mother figures. It was a definitive moment to feel accepted. I knew I could use my knowledge and skills.

For some subjects, that sense of knowing came even before formally joining academia. This connects with the sense of answering a calling cited in the previous chapter. One veteran of thirty-one-years' experience commented:

> [I knew social work education was right for me] the day I had the interview for my first job. I *love* to teach. They knew I was new but they wanted me anyway. I truly believe that I am called to be in social work education. When I came for the interview, it was like I was home.

Subjects spoke of how teaching social work was a source of satisfaction and a boost to their ego. One subject who has taught in the same social work program for twenty years grinned with animation as she explained: "That first class I taught as an adjunct, the bug hit me. My narcissistic side enjoyed the attention, the energy, and I was good at it. It felt right." Another noted, with a twinkle in her eye:

> At [my university] right away, from the beginning, I've enjoyed the variety and challenge of working with students, helping them find their niche. The students have taught me a lot. It affirms this is what I should be doing. [As social work educators] we have a sense of wanting to be needed; feedback is really important. The most profound feedback you get is unsolicited. A student walks in a couple of years later, unannounced, and lets you know how grateful they are.

Mystical Whispers

Gut instincts. They may be challenging to describe, difficult to quantify, and beyond the realm of traditional research. Yet many subjects, when asked to describe a defining moment, described a powerful sensation of knowing they were in the right place at the right time, and confidence they were about to make an intuitive decision they would not regret (Goleman, 2006).

One story from a social work educator with twenty-five years of social work education experience stands out. The director of a school of social work of a combined BSW/MSW program described her pivotal moment. It came while she was away from home, on a sabbatical, conducting a needs assessment for a nascent MSW program in Alaska. She heard what she termed "mystical whispers," and subsequently leapt at the opportunity. It happened, as she recalled, late at night.

> I saw an apparition of Raven in the Girdwood sky. The northern lights were going nuts. And Raven said: "I thought you were smart enough to figure out how to stay here." The next day, I saw an ad in the paper, hiring faculty for the new MSW program in Anchorage. I even bought land *before* I had the job. I felt an emotional and spiritual tie. I knew I would be coming back [after sabbatical]. I sent in my application the next day.

And the rest is history. And while not everyone will hear Raven whispering, or peer into the late night sky and view the aurora borealis dancing, I believe many of us experience meaningful and powerful visions that rivet our attention as we make career decisions. To be sure, a mystical whisper is likely one component among many (and not one that we freely admit to aloud) in considering one's life work, but I suspect it is closely aligned to long-term job satisfaction.

A Better Fit Than Practice

A common sequence of events for social work educators in this study was to obtain a social work education and receive a BSW and/or an MSW degree, move into social work practice, perhaps obtain a DSW or PhD (while still in professional practice), then move into social work education full time (sometimes continuing practice on a smaller scale). One might assert, as many subjects did, that practice experience serves as a solid foundation, and sets the stage, for teaching social work. One subject stated:

> When I was in my MSW program, I learned the skills and values of the profession. I was able to apply those somewhat in my internship, but where my education really came alive was when I began to work full time (and be paid a decent salary). I was really making a difference in people's lives. Today [as a social work educator] I can call upon my practice experience as a valuable resource, from success stories to ethical dilemmas, as I teach the next crew of social work practitioners.

Why change jobs? If practice is so rewarding, why shift into teaching? As many subjects noted, it was the teaching element within practice that influenced their entry into academia. It often began with an adjunct or part-time opportunity that "happened by chance." A veteran of thirty-four years of social work education experience voiced a common scenario:

> I began teaching part-time while I was working in mental health with adolescents, but I realized it was the teaching component in my practice that really interested me. I was asked to become full-time faculty but I turned them down. They hired another person who didn't work out, so they asked me again and I took it. I instantly *knew*. I connected with the women's college nonhierarchical structure. I connected with the social justice mission. It was a natural next step after practice.

Another subject had been teaching for six years as an adjunct while working in the field of child welfare before he applied for a full-time academic post. The move from practice to academia was a logical progression related to dissatisfaction with professional practice. When asked about marker events, he responded:

> Three things happened: One, I became increasingly frustrated with administrative bureaucracy. I was becoming more certain I did not want to spend the rest of my career as a child welfare administrator. Two, I began to realize I received much more satisfaction from teaching. And three, I received my PhD in child welfare [which increased his marketability in academia].

Although some subjects have sustained ties to the social work practice community, and some have engaged in part-time practice, none of the subjects stated regrets for having made the move from social work practice to social work education as their primary career. In fact, one colleague stated:

> The more time I spend [in social work education], the harder it would be to go back to practice. I don't miss worrying about how we are going to make payroll each month. There's no nine to five. I probably work just as hard, but [now] there's schedule flexibility.

While these scenarios may be representative of current social work educators, they do not speak to the thoughts of former (not retired) social work educators who have either entered or reentered practice after academia. Perhaps this is the topic of a future publication.

Achievement of Tenure and Promotion

Two marker events for many academicians are the achievement of tenure and promotion. Tenure and promotion may occur simultaneously, as in the case of being promoted from assistant to associate professor and being granted tenure status as a by-product of the same process. "Promotion" for some meant becoming a department chair, with or without a change in academic rank. Promotion is frequently accompanied by an increase in salary. Tenure *and* promotion are perceived as an increase in professional status, and are often accompanied by new opportunities and responsibilities, such as serving on a tenure and promotion committee. Tenure is often viewed as a symbol of acceptance, recognition, and validation. It can provide job security, and may relieve anxieties related to self-worth.* Both tenure and promotion were cited as significant events for the following subject:

> The marker events were tenure and promotion. That really sealed the deal. I knew I was going to stay here a long time [in fact, twenty-five years and counting at the same place]. I still hold out possibilities for moving related to my wife's family in [another state]. But when tenure and promotion came, I decided that [X College] was a good place to work for the rest of my life.

And from a subject with a somewhat different perspective:

> Earning tenure was the beginning [of a turning point] but not the glue. It was being asked to serve as [department] chair when I was promoted to

---

* The topic of tenure as it relates to longevity will receive additional attention in chapter 12, "Keeping the Grass Green."

associate professor. I thought, "This feels like people value me and want me. I don't need to go anywhere else. I'm doing fine." That was the turning point. That was when I decided to stay.

And he did—for thirty years. (A potentially "darker" side of tenure will be discussed in chapter 13, "The Pros and Cons of Longevity.")

A common marker event in deciding to stay in one place, and contributing to a sense of purpose and direction, was assuming a leadership role. In another example:

I started out on tenure track. I had no clue about writing, publishing, or doing research—just farted around, did my job, didn't do any research. My department chair suggested I move into an administrative position and I did. It was a much better fit. It was my sixth year. *That* was a real turning point. I knew that I could stay [and did, for twenty-one years to date].

Focusing specifically upon tenure as a marker event, the following comments were recorded: "I felt I was in the right place all along, but getting tenure clinched the deal. I knew I could cut it. The weight hanging overhead was gone." And two more examples on the impact of tenure:

I knew I would stay when I was granted tenure. I had flirted with returning to practice before that. Even though I had already been tenured [at another social work program], when the certificate came in the mail that was the marker event.

It had to be tenure. I did consider leaving as I was going up for tenure. I've never seen social work education as many of my colleagues, hopping around to advance myself. I see [social work education] as a last career. After tenure, I thought, "Why do I need to look around?" It was at this point in my life when I was ready to make this a permanent career.

Receiving a PhD

Twenty-five years ago holding a PhD (or DSW) was far less common for social work educators entering academia. And while holding the advanced degree today is more critical than ever for entry into social work education, most academicians would agree that a doctorate has always increased employment options. For some subjects, attaining their PhD proved to be a marker event, and a vital step in career enhancement. For example:

Three or four years into teaching, my mind got hungry and I began exploring PhD programs. This was before we became rigorous, as a profession, about hiring PhDs. [University X] set humiliating requirements. I played the game and even got asked to teach a policy class. Being in the doctoral program motivated me to enter, and stay in, teaching.

Positive Teaching Evaluations and Awards

I'll go out on a limb: social work educators crave affirmation that our life's work is making a positive contribution to society and the field of social work. We welcome sincere recognition. We need to know that we are effective in training the next generation of social work practitioners, researchers, and policy makers.

A story I heard repeatedly was that social work educators frequently enter academia with little or no teaching experience and minimal, if any, training in how to teach at the college/university level. Some spoke of "early success" in teaching, others told a tale of struggle and on-the-job training in learning the art of pedagogy. One subject noted: "I got negative feedback after six weeks of teaching, but by the end of the semester, I was getting the highest ratings. I realized I had a talent for teaching." In contrast, another subject reflected: "The first good teaching evaluations didn't come until I had been at it for almost ten years." She is still "at it" after twenty-three years, with consistently positive feedback from her students.

Amazingly, six of the sixty-six colleagues I interviewed, with an expression of pride, stated that a defining moment, a point when they knew they were going to stay, came when they were awarded institution-wide teacher-of-the-year awards. Being chosen professor of the year out of hundreds of faculty is a tremendous validation. It's amazing what dedication, passion, and a measure of natural ability can do. Despite these achievements, and the ability of social work educators to rise to the occasion, there is a clear message here that as a profession, we need to do a better job at training social work students who aspire to become social work educators *how* to effectively teach *before* they begin.

Validation at National Conferences

The Association of Baccalaureate Social Work Program Directors (BPD), the Council on Social Work Education (CSWE), and the relatively new Society for Social Work Research (SSWR) hold annual meetings where social work educators from around the country share research findings, exchange ideas and experiences with curriculum development, discuss ways to strengthen the image of social work, and recruit social work educators. With attendance ranging from one to three thousand, these venues provide an opportunity for colleagues to learn about social work education programs in other parts of the country, compare notes, and engage in stimulating discussions. It is a time to receive validation and to experience professional solidarity. As one subject with nineteen years of social work education experience recalled:

> My first year of teaching was enjoyable. But then I began attending national conferences. I saw I could measure up. I felt I could cut it. It gave me validation and confidence to say, "This is me."

Another social work educator, with more than forty years of experience, weighed in:

> After the first year, I considered going back to practice but felt loyalty and commitment to developing a BSW program. Then I attended a BPD workshop in Nashville: "Social Work as a Profession." That event turned things around and renewed my commitment.

And one more quote on this topic:

> When I attended my first CSWE conference there were about two thousand people—maybe more. Coming from a small program [four faculty], I was floored. Social work education is a big deal! Teaching social work is not just some abstract notion; there are people here just like me, struggling with the same issues, sharing the same joy. For a naïve person, new to academia, it opened my eyes to a powerful network.

The Challenge of Program Building and the Fight for Recognition

Thirty of the sixty-six subjects that participated in this study came from what I have termed small programs, those with two to six faculty (see page 3). Equipped with little more than passion and determination, in the 1970s and 1980s, many of these subjects bore primary responsibility for the creation and development of new BSW programs. Often they faced significant hurdles in explaining the value and credibility of social work and social work education to academic colleagues, community members, state legislators, and boards of directors.* They "just fell in" to the right place at the right time.

They were answering "the calling." They were more preoccupied with what needed to be accomplished academically than they were with earning a decent wage. Often beginning with only one or two faculty, they were pioneers with a mission, and as one subject put it, "working my ass off."

Realization that they were either making a positive contribution to the quality of an existing social work education program, or building a program,

* Subjects who helped launch MSW programs in the last twenty-five years with medium (7–14) and large (15+) programs experienced similar problems.

one that would have lasting value, was a true marker event. Here are a few stories that speak to the spirit of determination that has forged the shape of social work education:

One subject conducted a needs assessment to measure the viability of launching a new BSW program in the central region of the United States. She started from scratch. Being in a rural community, there were no social work programs for hundreds of miles that might serve as models. Yet she was assigned to be the "chief architect." To top it off, she was making a twelve-hour round-trip commute every week in order to complete her MSW degree. And by the way, she had six foster children at home at the time. Yet the program was successfully launched!

Another subject began building a BSW program in the late 1970s and didn't add a second faculty member until four years later. She organized and rallied students, community members, and local practitioners. She diligently toiled to facilitate a partnership between academia and community. All the while, she was teaching five classes and developing field placements!

Another veteran, with sixteen-years' social work education experience, cited her turning point as occurring in the late 1990s, when she became a social work program director. She spoke eloquently of the struggle of her social work program to survive within a research-oriented institution:

> Becoming a director in 1998 was a defining moment. Nobody [in the social work department] was tenured. We were the bastard children. We were given the message: "You guys are expendable; prove that you shouldn't be done away with." I mounted a campaign to save the program; I rallied the state, alumni, and the community. The lesson I learned was: "Never turn your back on the fact that this [program dissolution] could happen at any time."

Successful Accreditation Experience

Accreditation and reaffirmation of accreditation from the Council on Social Work Education is rigorous; for most, if not all, social work programs, it is a time-consuming, arduous task. The stakes are high, perhaps even more so for a program's initial accreditation. Futures are on the line. Stakeholders include faculty and their families, students and their families, administrators, social services agencies and the clients they serve, and the profession of social work.

Receiving that call or letter from the Commission on Accreditation announcing a positive outcome is good news. It is validation, a sense of relief, and a sign of respite from living in the culture of accreditation (Zeiger, Ortiz, Sirles, & Rivas, 2005). For many, successful first accreditation was a marker event. One subject with more than thirty-five years of social work education experience at the same program reflected that one of the key reasons he has remained in one place so long was because "I didn't want to start over somewhere else." His initial accreditation and first reaffirmation, he added, were genuine turning points.

Another reason accreditation is important is that, at least for some subjects, it reinforces a sense of pride, ownership, and responsibility. For one subject, the combination of establishing community roots and receiving strong institutional support for the social work program was significant in his decision to stay in the same institution for over three decades:

> I was putting down roots, solidifying my professional life, establishing political connections. I founded a [statewide] citizen's action committee. I got involved in major community organization projects. At this time [1984], our social work program was undergoing reaffirmation. We had the backing of the college. I felt program responsibility and ownership. We were one of the first programs in the country to have a macro practice course. We had six-hundred-hour [BSW] field placements. Teaching never got dull. I secured internship money. It was always exciting. Staying ahead of the curve, I was able to play a major role in shaping the program.

Family Circumstances

However we define family, our career decisions are influenced by our relationships with those we hold dear, and with those for whom we feel a sense of commitment and responsibility. Beginning a new job, perhaps with attendant relocation, and sustaining a career in a given locale will likely have a major impact on our significant others. Family circumstances are crucial when considering the goodness of fit between people and their environments.

One subject recalled looking for alternative job opportunities in different parts of the country, then decided: "The grass really wasn't greener . . . The turning point came when my daughter married and came to live here [the same city where the subject was teaching]." Another subject wanted to be close to her mother, who was undergoing dialysis treatment.

One subject, who has been at the same institution in the central region of the country for the past thirty-three years, noted that the marker event was his wife completing her master of science degree:

> She was offered a job locally. She began a lucrative professional career. Then we added to our debt load by buying a house. Now we're both in secure positions. I considered a PhD, but didn't want to pursue it. I [already] knew the system here. I knew the community.

Some subjects spoke of not wanting to disrupt the relationships that their mates and children had with friends and to forfeit knowledge and use of community resources. Here's an example:

> I had been teaching nine years when I received my doctorate. I was disgruntled, looking around for other places and opportunities. A friend warned me I was living in a dying community. But uprooting the family (my kids were five and ten at the time)? In the end, I was the only one who wanted to move. I decided: for the good of the family, everyone's happy here, let's stick it out. I considered [another state], but was told I'd have to foot the bill [for a visit] if I didn't take the job.

He's now been at the same university for over twenty-five years.

Whether it be services for special needs children, health care needs of aging parents, or a desire to remain physically near loved ones (regardless of their health), family circumstances may exert a strong influence on career satisfaction. They may also impact the decision to stay in one location for an extended period of time.

Steady Satisfaction/No One Point in Time

Subjects were asked to identify a marker event or definitive moment when they knew they were going to remain in social work education. This assumes that such a moment exists and is identifiable. From a methodological standpoint, being asked to recall a marker event, even if none rose to the surface, may have made some subjects feel like they were on the spot. Pinpointing a defining moment may be a valuable exercise in self-reflection, but it is not necessarily a measure of professional competence, nor should it be seen as a requisite exercise.

One subject, who had just completed her twenty-ninth year of social work education at a small program in the South, when asked this question stated that there was no one point—no marker event. Rather,

> ... it was a steady satisfaction over time. Overall, it's been challenging intellectually, emotionally, and the community support has been good. As I got older, I knew I would be here until I retired. But there wasn't a specific time or event.

Another subject, an Academic Nomad with twenty-nine years of social work education experience in five different institutions, searched her mind for a defining moment and then commented:

> I never had a defining moment. I wish I did. I figure I'll stay with [social work education]. I really enjoy it. It wasn't a conscious or passionate decision. I'm grateful for the opportunity in life to give back. It's a privilege to share ideals.

So far we have identified factors that have drawn people to the profession of social work education, and explored marker events when they realized the profession was a good fit. We now turn to factors that have influenced our group of sixty-six academicians to remain in social work education for an average of more than twenty-five years.

In for the Long Haul: Why They Stay

So far we have examined forces at play that influence people to choose social work education as a career. Remarkably, our sixty-six subjects have on average sustained their career choice for more than a quarter century. Further, 56 percent (37) have spent 90 percent or more of their academic careers at only one institution.

What has kept them in one place? Is it loyalty to the profession? The institution? The students? The good humor of colleagues? Is it the perks of academia, the ambience of ivy-covered walls, or the view from their office? Or maybe it's their inner constitution. Perhaps it is kismet that has led subjects to the occupation of social work education. Likely, it is a combination of two or more of the above—such is the complex nature of human behavior.

This chapter will explore factors that have influenced the longevity of forty women and twenty-six men in their social work education careers. Factors are divided into three categories: job-related, environmental, and personal drive.

IT'S THE JOB

What we do for a living is an integral part of our identity. If we are lucky, what we do to earn a salary brings us personal satisfaction, lends purpose to our lives, and makes the world a better place.

Subjects discussed twelve job-related factors* that have influenced them to remain in social work education for an extended period of time:

Enjoyment of students;
Supportive administration;
Professional autonomy;

---

* Subjects were not asked to rank these factors, nor has the author ranked them.

34

Career success/professional growth;

Challenges/stimulation;

Loyalty/pride/ownership;

Collegiality;

Perks and benefits;

Salary;

Schedule flexibility;

Small department size; and

Limited mobility without a PhD.

Enjoyment of Students

When asked to discuss factors that had sustained long careers in social work education, virtually all subjects mentioned the positive influence of students. The following comments speak to this satisfaction:

> I enjoy the students. They keep me honest. They keep me fresh. They bring compassion, love of people, and this helps reinforce what *I* believe. Watching them develop over the course of a semester, or the time in our [social work] program, and seeing the final product: their contribution to the practice community after graduation—that's rewarding.

Students, with their energy, enthusiasm, and hunger for social justice, provide a stimulus for social work educators to remain fired up, hopeful, and optimistic about effecting social change. For example, one subject viewed her classroom as a venue—an outlet for her to express concerns to a receptive audience—regarding poverty issues. She noted: "I think I'd be a little too cynical, a little too angry, if it weren't for the students sharing the load."

There is a myth that professors are "stuffy old people with PhDs, set in their ways." The implication is that they stop learning once they begin teaching. In a sense, quality educators remain receptive *students* during their entire academic careers. Without preconceived notions, they listen carefully and openly to their students. They never cease learning from their students. Teaching challenges educators to think clearly and communicate effectively. Students energize professors. When asked to address factors that have kept him in social work education for a sustained period, one subject with thirty years of experience spoke with passion regarding his experience teaching deaf students:

> The impact of my deaf students is the biggest single factor. I knew nothing about deafness when I began teaching. The first day, the [department]

> chair said: "I'll walk down to class and introduce you to the interpreter."
> Interpreter? Do we have a lot of Spanish-speaking students? My experience
> with deafness has had a profound effect on how I teach, how I evaluate my
> teaching, how I pay attention to people, my communication skills, how
> I organize and present material such as visual images. The deaf commu-
> nity communicates with each other in a powerful way. Communication is
> *very* efficient. They support each other. It's amazing to see how strongly
> connected the deaf community is—more powerful than with the hearing
> population.

Students eventually become former students. As professional social workers, they are able to apply the skills, knowledge, and competence they gained
while matriculating. Course evaluations from students at the end of the semester, when students may be feeling burnt out and anxious about exams and
grades, reveal a limited view of student learning. Measuring how well students
perform as professional social workers helps to complete the picture. Subjects
spoke of a delayed gratification, and a sense of pride in seeing the professional
blossoming of former students.

> On those days when you think you just can't do it again, I watch my alumni.
> I watch them out in the community doing such wonderful things—heading
> up agencies, advocating for client rights in the state legislature—and I'm
> so proud of them, and I know I can continue doing my work.

As noted in chapter 1, many educators worked as social work practitioners
prior to entering academia. One subject spoke enthusiastically of having
worked in the 1960s as a practitioner in Southern California against the back-
drop of the antiwar movement, on issues of social justice and human rights. He
was able to put social work values into action. For the past twenty-six years, he
has been a social work educator. In our interview, I was compelled to ask: "What
does teaching do that practice cannot?" He said it was a matter of focus and a
lifestyle issue. He didn't want to continue seeing six clients every day, six days
a week. His focus shifted from influencing clients one at a time, to influencing
the minds of many students.

Social work is a noble profession. It is a challenge to teach bright, motivated students. It is an awesome responsibility to prepare students to have a
positive impact upon clients' lives. It is a rewarding experience, whether students are nineteen, thirty-nine, or sixty-nine, to see the light come on, make an
impression, and give them a vision of the world that can be. The enjoyment of
students influences social work educator longevity. One subject with more than
four decades of experience said it well: "Forty-two years later, I can still see the
light in their eyes."

One advantage of conducting a live interview is that the researcher experiences more than words. When subjects spoke of their love of students, I could see it in their body language and in the brightness in their eyes. I could hear the passion in the tone of their voice.

Supportive Administration

Without strong administrative support, educators are less likely to be productive, and more likely to seek employment elsewhere (Beckerman, 2002; Mahroum, 1999). With academic support, which includes consistency of reasonable expectations and requisite resources, an educator is likely to experience greater job satisfaction, and is more likely to stay. Quality administrative support requires a blend of promoting social work programs and creative autonomy, while navigating sometimes-turbulent political waters within the campus and local communities. In the case of public colleges and universities, lobbying at the state legislature may be part of the process.

When asked to discuss factors that have influenced them to stay in one academic setting for an extended period of time, subjects spoke of being presented with new challenges and obtaining administrative support to accomplish new goals. The recent historical trend of adding MSW programs to existing BSW programs at departments and schools of social work (Zeiger et al., 2005) is a good example. In the words of one subject:

> Launching the MSW [program] really got me fired up, and the rest of the faculty as well. But without strong administrative support, we would have been dead in the water. They helped us make the case. It's definitely a reason for my longevity here. We're responding to the need in the community for practitioners with advanced skills and leadership capabilities.

Another example of administrative support is the provision of opportunities for professional growth and development. This may include generous funding of conference and workshop travel, including lodging and registration fees. It may also include investing time and encouragement in a faculty member's future. One subject with a quarter century of social work education experience at the same university noted:

> I've had support of the dean from the beginning—support to get my doctorate [which included academic leave]; needed resources to develop our BSW program as we grew from two to ten faculty. My professional development has been supported. I was asked to be program director, department head, and associate vice president. They recognized my talents before I did. I realized I could do more.

Her current role is vice president for academic and student affairs. She now uses her position and influence to ensure that faculty have the resources they need to do their jobs well. She is "returning the gift" by affording faculty with opportunities like the ones she received.

Effective administrators are accessible and approachable. They have credibility that extends from the campus to the local community. Effective administrators do not exist in every institution where there is a social work program. But where they do, they strengthen social work education and contribute to the longevity of social work educators. The following quote illuminates this point:

> I really feel I could walk up to the chancellor and say, "What the hell are you doing?"—and nowhere else that I've worked could I really be that candid with anybody—all the way up the academic chain.

Finally, it was noted that administrators who genuinely care about social work educators as people—not just performers of work—ultimately influence longevity, and likely the overall quality of work. A quote from a veteran of over thirty years at the same university illustrates this point:

> I've had support around the deaths of my father and my husband, and my breast cancer. That kind of support really makes it hard to leave. These are my friends; they are my family. I've talked to others and I've really got it good [at my university]. Perhaps it's like Lake Wobegon, where everyone's a bit above average. Is this place great by itself, or did I help make it great? People who have "successfully aged" within the institution do make a difference. If you are rewarded for the contributions you make, you want to make more.

And if you are not rewarded and supported by the administration, you may move on, or remain—with a degree of cynicism and subpar job performance.

Professional Autonomy

Related to administrative support is the notion of professional autonomy. There is definitely an autonomy component of being an educator. Beyond the basic standards of a course content guide or a syllabus, the principle of academic autonomy gives educators the freedom to be creative and unique in the classroom. For example, current events may be infused into classroom activities. Learning objectives may be stated up front, but *how* those objectives are achieved—including a wide range of assignment possibilities, ever-changing community opportunities and resources, and dynamic local and national political developments—gives social work educators wide latitude in influencing student learning. Further, learning objectives are dynamic. They are subject to review. Faculty, working individually or in collaboration with curriculum groups, which may include students, may alter course content to better suit student learning needs and respond to the needs of the practice community. One educator with nineteen years of experience noted: "I feel good about the way I've been able to influence changes in the [social work] program. I have the autonomy to make changes in the wider community. The administration supports our autonomy."

Career Success/Professional Growth

Who among us does not revel in workplace achievements? Educators may discount positive student evaluations, and teaching awards, but I suspect they really enjoy being praised, especially for performing a job for which they feel passion. One subject admitted what I suspect are the thoughts of many: "This sounds kind of narcissistic, but I think if you're a good teacher, you become a hero to your students; you become a role model. It strokes your ego." And another noted:

> I've had career success. I've made a positive impact on the university. I've created opportunities for myself and for the community. I've brought in two and a half million dollars in grants, working with community-based agencies. I've established [positive] relationships with local and state government—and that just takes time to develop. I'm not sure I want to go someplace else and start over. I can make more of a broad difference here [in the deep South] than I could in Boston.

Although this is primarily a qualitative study, it is worth noting that seven of the subjects interviewed mentioned (without solicitation) that they had received an institution-wide teacher-of-the-year award. Whether it is being chosen to give a commencement address, receiving tenure, being promoted to associate or full professor, or being selected to become department chair, subjects expressed strong satisfaction with being validated and needed. Being responsible for the development and maturation of social programs was mentioned repeatedly as a source of pride. To know that one's knowledge and achievements are respected and acknowledged institution-wide contributes to a sense of belonging and self-worth. It influences faculty longevity.

Subjects were driven by a deep sense of commitment and passion for social work. Time and again, they spoke of how interaction in the classroom and enthusiasm for the profession have propelled them above and beyond expectations. One subject spoke with a tone of passion and pride of her role as a program builder:

> I love to create programs. The university is young and growing—lots of op-
> portunities to impact the institution. We are constantly looking for ways to
> improve the curriculum, to use the strengths of faculty and staff. It's a chal-
> lenge to meet [our state's] social work needs. Social work is different here
> than anywhere else in the U.S. I can't imagine another university where this
> kind of social work expansion could occur—lots of work, creativity—it's
> kept me awake. I really feel we're making a difference. It's not a nine-to-five
> job for me; it's a life.

As programs grow and make positive contributions to the social work practice community, social work educators gain validation. Likewise, the profession
of social work gains credibility.

Challenges/Stimulation

What sustains social work educators? What keeps them returning to academia every fall semester? In part, it's a passion for the profession. In part, it's
a devotion to prepare students to have a positive impact on clients' lives. In
part, it's a driven commitment, an internal force. It's the richness of educating
students who want to make a difference. For experienced educators, it's a commitment to nurture junior faculty through the maze of tenure, promotion, and
academic success. It's professional growth and development, and, fostered by
an academic environment, the drive to add to the knowledge base. Boring moments in academia are few and far between. Annual conferences such as those
hosted by CSWE and BPD afford social work educators the opportunity to share
information with, and learn from, colleagues on a regional, national, and even
international level.

Feeling challenged is a strong factor contributing to faculty longevity. One
social work educator, with twenty-seven years of experience, and currently a
program director, commented that she has remained at one program so long
because:

> Enough new things are happening: diverse faculty hires; improved [of-
> fice/departmental] space; nurturing faculty through tenure. I keep finding
> challenges. I'm rooted. I continue to see new things I can do (for example,
> starting a distance program). I need challenges. I'm hungry for them. I'll
> create them if they're not there.

Whether building a BSW program or adding a new MSW program to an
existing program, being in on the ground level, creating a new curriculum, hiring
new faculty, and acquiring grants all provide stimulation. As one veteran of over
twenty-five years stated: "There's always something new and challenging that

keeps me from leaving. If you ask why I stay, growth is a factor. Seventy percent of our student body are first-generation college students. I see the potential."

Social work education is a dynamic field. Social problems ebb and flow with a changing environment. If educators are to project a sense of hope in combating societal ills, they must stay current. As one subject related, "If I'm teaching stuff I learned twenty years ago, my students aren't going to be ready to work with today's clients." The message is clear: always move ahead; always update.

For twelve subjects, the Academic Nomads (those who have taught social work at four or more institutions), the challenge and stimulation are in part due to a change in location and academic atmosphere, including a different administration, new colleagues, and different students. However, for one subject, a self-described "trailing spouse" with over a quarter century longevity, there were threads that connected his five appointments: "There's been a continuity across all my academic appointments: commitment to information technology in human services, and intellectual stimulation that comes from teaching and research."

Loyalty/Pride/Ownership

Eyes open wide, beaming smiles, leaning forward with animated hand gestures—I'm not an expert on body language, but I can detect pride when I see it. Whether it's the influence of a service commitment in the Franciscan tradition, allegiance to a Historically Black College or University (HBCU), or the appeal of being in a state-funded institution training students to work in the public sector, long-term educators consistently expressed loyalty, pride, and a sense of ownership in their social work education programs.

This was especially true for those who were in on the ground floor, and those who played a major role in launching social work programs twenty-five years ago or more. To some extent, social work educators control their career trajectories when they create a program from scratch and author accreditation self-studies. Ownership, pride, and loyalty are by-products. And these elements contribute to faculty longevity. More than one subject observed that she had outlived several university presidents.

> I feel program ownership. In thirty-four years of teaching at the same university, I've never felt a desire to leave. I've been department chair since 1975—that's more than thirty years. It's where I should be. I've never interviewed anywhere else. It's home. I like the students and the community.

One subject who has taught at an HBCU for close to thirty years offered the following thoughts:

> We have acceptance and strong support for our social work program—
> the first nationally accredited program on campus. There are many
> first-generation college students here; I see eyes open and wings spread.
> Our students don't have a problem getting jobs. Our program is very strong
> and stable. We have a good reputation. We have the highest percentage of
> students going on to graduate school compared to any other program on
> campus. Here I am, shaping young minds. They come in as rough rocks and
> go out as diamonds.

Another subject, who has taught at the same institution for thirty-five
years, spoke in glowing terms of how his college's nonhierarchical structure
has enabled his personality to flourish. At one point in his career, he visited
another social work program twenty-five hundred miles away on the other side
of the country and received an attractive offer. In the end, he decided to stay
put. The grass wasn't greener, but the offer helped him clarify his "current position of privilege."

Perhaps it would be a healthy exercise to shop around every five years or
so—just for a reality check. Goodness of fit is paramount. It all boils down to
making an impact on society, and working in a setting where one's potential is
optimized.

Collegiality

Here's a poser. Consider Academic Nomads, social work educators who
move from one institution to another every five years or so. They sometimes
lament about the "difficult" people they leave behind, and say their newer colleagues are so much better. Yet, in another five years. . . . Are there really *any*
social work programs free of personalities colleagues would consider to be difficult? As this book demonstrates, there are a wide range of reasons educators
stay in one place a long time, or change jobs. But a consistent factor influencing
longevity and mobility is the nature of collegial relationships. How we function
as social work educators is strongly influenced by our colleagues. Interaction
may occur within a department, or across campus with faculty in related disciplines such as nursing and justice. Whether our workmates are collaborative
or competitive makes a difference. If they have a genuine interest and faith in
seeing all department members succeed, it makes a difference. It matters if you
look forward to seeing your colleagues on campus, or dread attending faculty
meetings because that problem person will be in attendance.

Although most subjects acknowledged that they had worked (or still do
work) with "difficult" people, for the most part, subjects expressed strong satisfaction with the nature of their collegial relationships.

Collegiality may reveal itself in time of need. One subject with a quarter century of experience spoke of "the incredible affection of colleagues" she experienced while living through two life-threatening illnesses. She was bedridden for a five-month period, yet she was provided with a computer and secretarial services.

> I truly like the people I work with. They're my colleagues and my friends—and that's been almost thirty years. We party together; we scream at each other about Marxism and social justice—but it's always intellectually stimulating.

> We have an extraordinarily sane department. We respect and appreciate one another. We don't let things go unresolved. We have conflict in a very healthy way. We articulate concerns and work toward resolution. It's a real healthy place to work. We laugh a good deal; we have fun. We're constantly educating one another.

> Our department is small—lots of student contact, close relationships with colleagues. I wouldn't want to be at a large university. I have humor with my colleagues. We feed off each other. We are all dedicated to an excellent program.

Interestingly, the above three quotes come from social work educators who are faculty members in small departments (two to six faculty). Does department size influence the nature of collegiality? Are smaller departments more likely to have a fun atmosphere? Perhaps. Within this sample of subjects, positive comments about one's colleagues were relatively rare for those representing medium- to large-size departments or schools of social work. But one cannot conclude that their collegial relationships were less satisfying compared to those faculty who were part of smaller programs.

Subjects spoke glowingly of how great their colleagues were in their programs, especially compared to other social work programs across the nation. They'd heard stories of dysfunctional departments. Only one out of sixty-six subjects spoke of poor collegiality within her program. However, despite my attempts to establish an atmosphere of trust and rapport, some subjects may have felt uncomfortable airing their dirty laundry, so to speak. Or, perhaps, programs with poor collegiality are rare, or underrepresented in this sample.

Perks and Benefits

A "start-up" package; a new computer every three or four years; the latest software; opportunities for professional development, including travel expenses, lodging, and per diem to attend conferences and exchange state-of-the-art professional knowledge and build a national network of colleagues; sabbatical leave; domestic partner benefits; release time to further one's research agenda. And let's not forget those free "examination" copies of the latest textbooks. Granted, start-up packages do not exist everywhere, and travel expenses are limited for many social work programs (especially the smaller ones), and course releases to pursue scholarship are not available to all, but most subjects were quick to point out that the perks of being a social work educator are a factor contributing to their longevity. According to a veteran of twenty-eight years:

> There are lots of perks to this job. You go to the mail, and you have books. You didn't ask for them; they just come. And the books are wonderful, books about the subjects I love. There are travel perks to attend conferences. I've learned about social work and cultures in different parts of the country. I've visited an Indian reservation outside of Portland, Oregon. I've traveled abroad, taking students to England, France, Prague, and Berlin.

Several subjects made note of fringe benefits such as health care, life insurance, and retirement plans. One subject noted that as her service increased in years, as an incentive for longevity, her contributions toward benefits actually decreased while the university's increased.

One subject with over thirty years of experience spoke of a serious medical diagnosis that influenced her decision not to seek an academic appointment at another location:

> I had to reevaluate my priorities. In my case, the personal reasons trumped the professional reasons for staying. I have excellent health care services here. I would never want to venture very far from a place that has the kind of health care services I need and value.

Retirement benefits are important, perhaps of greater concern to those in or nearing the twilight stages of their careers. How does this influence social work educators' choice to leave or stay when they are in their fifties or sixties? Most colleges and universities, especially under public auspice, have a system of investiture. After a certain minimum number of years of service, say ten, they are eligible to retire with a guaranteed income, a percentage of their salary, for the remainder of their life. For example, retirees with ten years of service might receive 20 percent of their yearly salary (for some, an average of their three highest-paid years), but retirees with twenty-five years of service in the same state system might receive 75 percent per year. Thus there would be an incentive to stay, and a deterrent to seek employment elsewhere.

Salary

Perhaps it is not politically correct to say that salary plays a major role in determining whether or not one wishes to work in a given social work program. Nevertheless, subjects consistently downplayed the influence of salary. For many, the concept of negotiating for a better salary at the point of hire (especially the first academic appointment) was entirely foreign.

The strongest statement recorded was: "The money's good." No one offered a specific amount, nor did I as a researcher deem it appropriate to ask for subjects' salaries. Yet some subjects did mention that their starting salary strongly influenced their future salary, because they became locked into minimal, or in some cases nonexistent, cost-of-living raises. Many suggested that a surefire way to increase salary (despite the possible decrease in retirement benefits) was to move to another institution and come in at a higher starting level.

One subject, when first hired, was thrilled to be offered a salary five thousand dollars higher than he had been previously receiving. But what he didn't know was that salaries had been frozen for the previous four years and future raises would be minimal. It never occurred to him to ask.

Schedule Flexibility

Ah, the sweetness of academic life! Those of us in academia know that teaching a twelve-credit load translates into far more than twelve hours of work per week. And for those with a nine-month contract, the notion of having summers off is largely a myth. The number of hours may easily exceed forty, fifty, or more in a given week. But unlike traditional jobs, there is a fair amount of schedule flexibility. If you are not an eight-to-five person, to some extent, you can set your own pace. For those with children, schedules are flexible enough to manage child care or take your daughter to a dental appointment. "Time off" to attend conferences is acceptable, even encouraged. Sabbatical leave for most long-term social work educators is part of the package. One subject with twenty-three years of experience made the following comments regarding a flexible schedule:

> This is the ideal job for me. I basically set my own schedule, which includes part-time during the summer. During the regular school year, I am able to pick up my kids at 3:00 p.m. I can go to a school play; no one has asked me any questions. I can go to conferences, building a national network of colleagues and friends. I can spend more time with my kids by working while they're asleep if I want.

Small Department Size

A small department was defined as having two to six full-time faculty. Thirty of the sixty-six subjects identified themselves as being members of small departments. A crosstabulation was run to examine the relationship between program size (with values of small, medium, and large) and stability/mobility (stability was defined as serving in one program for 90 percent or more of one's academic career; mobility was defined as holding four or more academic appointments over the life of one's career).

Faculty Size

Stability/Mobility	Small (2–6)	Medium (7–14)	Large (15+)	Total
Relatively stable	27	13	7	47
Relatively mobile	3	7	9	19
Total	30	20	16	66

Person Chi-Square Value = 11.43, Sig. = .003

These results suggest that faculty who join small programs are more likely to spend most, if not all of their careers at one place. In fact, 90 percent of those teaching in small programs had little or no movement. In looking at the stability/mobility of medium and large programs, one can see that the larger the program size, the more likely people are to move. Is it better to be working in a small department? For some the answer will be yes, for others, no. Longevity at one location and faculty size cannot guarantee worker satisfaction. Likewise, these factors are not predictors of productivity. Again, goodness of fit is paramount. But one thing is clear: less formal structures and closer relationships—getting to know one's colleagues well—are more often found in smaller departments. For many that is an attraction; for others it is a distraction.

Limited Mobility Without a PhD

Twenty-five years ago, with an MSW degree in hand, an aspiring social work educator would have a reasonable chance of landing a job as an assistant professor. In contrast, today, while CSWE does not require all social work faculty to hold a doctoral degree (CSWE, 2008),* a job seeker looking for a social work faculty position without a PhD in hand will be far less marketable.

Likewise, today a current faculty member with an MSW but without a

---

* The latest *Curriculum Policy Statement* states that for faculty teaching primarily MSW curriculum, there must be four PhDs for every two non-PhDs. No parallel requirement exists for those teaching primarily BSW curriculum. However, individual programs and institutions may have separate requirements.

PhD will find it difficult to move to another institution. Lack of a doctorate renders one less mobile. For those educators who have already been teaching for twenty-five years or more, the notion of pursuing a PhD in order to become more marketable, or to improve their knowledge and skills, may not be compatible with family obligations or be in sync with their current stage of life. Pursing a PhD requires a significant investment of time, energy, and resources. As one subject with twenty-seven years of experience noted:

> At the time I began teaching, an MSW was enough. Now I'm sort of trapped. It's a nice trap, a velvet trap, but I don't think if I wanted to move anywhere else I would be marketable. The payoff for pursuing a PhD would not be enough. At this point in my life, I don't like change. Going on the open market doesn't interest me.

EXTERNAL FACTORS (ENVIRONMENTAL FORCES)

Social work educators discussed five external factors that influenced them to remain at one or more institutions for an extended period of time. External factors are operationally defined as environmental elements not directly related to academic positions. The factors, which were not ranked, fall into five categories:

Family roots/family needs;
Community resources;
Geographic location;
Cost of living/housing; and
Physical environment of the college or university.

Family Roots/Family Needs

Bear in mind that the average length of time subjects have spent as social work educators is more than twenty-five years. The definition, composition, and influence of one's family may be quite different for subjects at their current stage of life, compared to the perceptions of social work educators in nascent stages of career development. Faculty with more career experience might be more concerned with educational needs of their children, career satisfaction of their spouses or partners, and, especially true for those with aging relatives, proximity to their kinfolk.

It could be a benevolent consideration such as the high quality of public schools in Hattiesburg, Mississippi; a partner's family living in nearby Mobile, Alabama; a mate having a great job in the same community of College Town,

U.S.A.; or the fact that "My children were born in the same hospital where I was born." Family roots and family needs do matter. Families become "established" in the area; academicians become anchored in the community. The following quote comes from a subject with more than thirty-years' experience at the same institution near the geographic center of the United States.

> My wife's job [in the same community] was a major factor. Not having a PhD, I wasn't very marketable. My parents lived in a nearby city and I needed to care for them; my brother lives five hundred miles away. My wife's family is local. We have good friends in the area. We have established a certain quality of life that would require a significant increase in salary for both of us in another location. And then there's the family.

Kids make a difference. Parents want stability for their children. They don't want to disrupt their children's schooling, community activities, and social networks. Many have purchased property. They've set down roots. They are committed to staying in the area because of family ties.

One's definition of family may include "the people I grew up with," whether they are related by blood or not. For one subject, with thirty years of teaching experience in the South, the decision to teach at an HBCU meant moving back to her hometown, a community of six thousand. She is now with her extended family, and they are proud to have her home as a professor.

Here's another example of family ties, from an educator who has set down roots in Virginia for thirty-five years:

> My husband's job as a minister in the same area has kept us here. And I stay because of aging parents and wanting a consistent community for my children. The Shenandoah Valley is a wonderful location; we have made a commitment to a nonurban area. My husband grew up in one location. I want my family to repeat that. Our grandchildren will likely be tied to the same area.

Some subjects, as in the case of a thirty-three-year veteran, have taught social work in various parts of the country, only to return to their hometown:

> I came back to Missouri because of family. I'm originally from Jefferson City. My parents and my husband's mother all live in Missouri, fifth generation from Springfield. That's a big, big influence. My husband was able to get the job he wanted in the area. Three of my siblings live here.

The happiness of a partner, or what one subject described as a "trailing spouse," is paramount. Assuming a move from one geographic location to another, hundreds or even thousands of miles away, the physical environment, social community, employment opportunities, and proximity to family may change dramatically. A decision to work in one place versus another will likely have a major impact on partners, spouses, children, and other relations.

The importance of family cannot be overestimated as a component of a social work educator's career decision making and employment satisfaction. A veteran of more than a quarter century of experience in the Upper Midwest was articulate on this point:

> The number one reason I've stayed is family. My partner does not want to leave [this state]. Her mother and father live nearby. Both are in their nineties. There's frequent communication. Our kids are in grade schools. We live in a good neighborhood where any parent on the block would feel fine parenting our kids if we're not there—very accepting of us, a lesbian family. We have domestic partner benefits. My partner works at home; she's there when the kids get home from school.

Social work is a profession of giving. Social work educators not only give knowledge and tools to their students, they are committed to providing a good life for their families. And it's a reciprocal arrangement; families are a major source of support for educators. A career in social work education is not a bed of roses each day. A reliable support system may be vital to longevity. In reviewing his career, an educator with thirty-five years of experience made the following observation:

> What sustains me is the support of my wife—putting up with the crap and the misery I bring home. If I didn't have a commitment to family, I would have left [my job] years ago. Having disrupted the family to move here, the real focus was: Make it work. I really have to say, in my heart of hearts, it's a commitment to not disrupt the lives of other people.

Community Resources

Social workers foster linkages between clients and community resources. Social work educators have a keen awareness of community resources, in part, because they are consumers of these resources. Awareness and utilization of community resources affect life quality. It can provide comfort and security.

Examples of resources mentioned by subjects include:

Quality and proximity to health care;
Places to experience recreation, relaxation, and beauty;
Public school systems;
Safety/low crime;

Opportunities for political involvement;

Entertainment and arts;

"Manageable" community size;

Access to a variety of foods and restaurants;

Quality of public transportation;

Clean air; and

Shopping.

What factors contribute to a "great place to live"? For some, it will be a rural setting with less automobile traffic, noise, and pollution. For three subjects, it was the availability of disability support services for their children. For others, being able to live in the community where they were raised was a source of comfort. And manageable size was mentioned more than once. One subject described the small town of Bethany, Pennsylvania, as a good, safe environment in which to raise children, especially as a single mother. Another subject noted:

> Canton, Ohio [population 90,000], has a strong community spirit. If we have a problem, we can solve it and we have the energy to do that. It's a good place to do social work—without the multilayered complications of a large city like Cleveland.

Dwellers of large metropolitan areas need not be dismayed. One subject described the Twin Cities (the adjacent cities of St. Paul and Minneapolis, which constitute the major population center of Minnesota) as being "very livable." Nevertheless, subjects cited rural pluses far more often than urban attributes.

As stated earlier, the typical career path for social work educators includes professional practice experience prior to an academic appointment. It is logical for someone who has established good relationships with local agencies to want to teach in the same community. It makes sense because of the networks they have established. This is particularly true for field coordinators who facilitate matches between students and local agencies.

One subject with nearly thirty years' experience mentioned his commitment to the community, not because of its amenities, but because it was poor, one of the poorest communities in one of the poorest states. He was able to identify with the community needs of Arkansas.

Geographic Location

How much does geographic location, independent of family proximity and community resources, influence a person's decision to stay at one job?

Not much, perhaps, although "ideal" locations are often touted in social work educator job announcements.

Certainly, some locations, such as Hawaii and Alaska, are more geographically distant than others (try driving from Anchorage to Seattle for the weekend!). But distances are relative. For one subject, New York City was "only two hundred miles away." Another subject told a story of when he was first married. His wife lived eighteen hours away in Canada. Then he moved to Indiana, which was "only" seven hours away. One person's dream geographic location may be another person's nightmare. What one person conceives of as "too isolated" may be paradise for another.

Again, an urban setting is a good fit for some. It's where the needs of deserving students can be met. As one subject with thirteen years of experience related:

> We're in the middle of the Bronx [a borough of New York City]. Most of our students are not only the first ones in their family to go to college; they are the first ones to get a high school diploma.

One subject reported that he lived in a rural cabin on a lake just twenty-five miles from New York City and only a fifteen-minute drive to his social work program in New Jersey. Another, with a smile on her face, told of living on the banks of a river in a small Wisconsin town. And subjects spoke of the beauty of seasonal variation—refreshing to this native of Southern California, where there is basically one season. Examples included Fort Worth, Texas, where "we have spring in February"; the Ozark Mountains of Arkansas and the Shenandoah Valley of Virginia, where the autumn colors are spectacular; and the grandeur of Alaska. A representative of our northernmost state commented:

> I live in paradise. I live where my heart connects with my home. I commute along an incredibly beautiful scenic highway, which gives me a chance to separate myself from work and renew myself. Beluga whales, Dall sheep, it's all there.

Cost of Living/Housing

Where is the cost of living greater, Hawaii or Kansas? How about Cedar Rapids, Iowa, versus San Francisco? Manhattan versus Florence, Alabama? Cost of living varies greatly from state to state, and from one city or town within a state to another in the same state.

Where to live is often a trade-off. One subject, who has lived and worked in the country's heartland for over thirty years, noted that he was able to live in a nice house, go out to eat whenever he wanted, and travel to Europe—a lifestyle that would be a financial stretch were he living in a different part of the country.

While Dorothy in *The Wizard of Oz* found herself "not in Kansas anymore," another subject, who grew up on the East Coast, found herself living *in* Kansas twenty-three years and counting. She came unwillingly, but learned to love it. In her words:

> The best thing I ever did was come to Lawrence, Kansas—a great place to raise kids and a lot of house for the money. And it's a place where you can insinuate yourself into the center of anything you want—not at all like New York City.

Physical Environment of the College or University

For many academicians, campuses provide an ambience, a certain je ne sais quoi that is a source of comfort: ivy-covered walls, quadrangles, libraries filled with academic journals, stadiums, lecture halls, book-lined faculty offices, auditoriums, perhaps a signature campanile. The campus may be a public square, a cultural hub, and an intellectual center of the town or city.

Aside from physical amenities, many subjects expressed satisfaction in working at relatively small campuses. One commented: "I am able to be a big fish in a small pond. I don't think I'd have that opportunity in many other settings." Another offered: "The president knows who I am. I can get elected to academic committees. I'm respected. I have credibility. I know who to talk to in order to get things done."

The above comments come from social work educators at smaller institutions with small social work departments. Some boasted of small class sizes ("just 8–10 students!"), where they get to know the students, and even the students' families, well.

PERSONAL DRIVE

Aside from the job itself, and the aforementioned external factors, there is the factor of personal drive. Personal drive is influenced by priorities that individuals hold, such as the desire to improve society through education. Personal drive is closely woven with one's individual constitution and worldview. As discussed by interviewees, elements fueling personal drive may be divided into five categories:

Professional pride/identity;
Sense of obligation to the profession;
Enjoyment of a leadership position;

Stability of staying in one place; and

Not wanting to "start over."

Professional Pride/Identity

"Who I am as a person is a social worker." In chapter 1, subjects described their entry into social work education as an answer to a "calling." Now, as they describe those factors that have sustained them as educators, it becomes apparent that the strength of that calling has endured. The fire of passion still burns. Painting a composite picture of a social work educator from this sample, she (forty of the sixty-six subjects are female) would be one who is a social worker at heart, sensitive to those who have experienced exploitation and discrimination. She would value the redistribution of wealth. She would have an affinity for the poor, the downtrodden. As an educator, she would work collaboratively and tirelessly with peers and students, fueled by energy, vitality, and enthusiasm. She would project a sense of hope for a better world. She would be proud of her profession. She would delight in the growth and development of others. Such would be the nature of her moral fiber.

Subjects spoke optimistically about the future of social work, and what they could do to make improvements. One subject with thirty-three years of teaching experience reflected upon his selfless attitude and his commitment to his continuing education:

> Every day I ask: "What good did you do for others?"—not for yourself. Don't jump out of bed immediately; reflect on what you can do for others. It is my breeding that I always find something positive in others. I always project positive energy to others. Listening to students, I get more energy because I learn [from them]. I've never felt [that] by earning a PhD I have learned everything.

One of the Academic Nomads, with twenty years of experience in five programs, gave a powerful articulation of his professional pride:

> It's commitment to the profession, commitment to the values. I think of social work as a calling. It's more than a simple job or an occupation; it's a life; you commit yourself to a lifestyle; it has a set of values. I'm passionate about the profession. I'm very protective toward the people we have in it. I'm as excited about teaching now as I was when I first began. It's really a basic commitment to make a difference.

As he spoke, I could see the pride in his body language. I could sense the passion in his voice and in his eyes. I felt fortunate to experience a powerful presence that transcended the written word.

Sense of Obligation to the Profession

Related to the notion of commitment is the sense of obligation to the profession of social work. It could be the influence of role modeling by "incredible grandparents," the inspiration of a charismatic professor, or being assisted by a social worker in a time of need. Many subjects described themselves as being "incredibly loyal" and needing to "give back to society" in exchange for the gifts they received. Here's an example from a veteran of nearly twenty years:

> At the point of hire, I was given the message: "we believe in your ability to succeed," not just to achieve tenure or promotion, but to enrich the social work program. The university made an investment in me, and I feel a sense of obligation to give back. And it's one I can own. There's nothing more gratifying than teaching students and seeing the light come on—giving them a vision of a world that can be—making a difference in their lives.

As stated earlier, many subjects were in on the ground floor of launching a new BSW or MSW program. This, too, contributes to longevity, a sense of ownership, and a loyalty to their "baby." For some who have assumed leadership roles within social work schools and departments, there is a sense of obligation toward junior faculty: "I need to stay until all new faculty achieve tenure—to see them through, to be successful."

Enjoyment of a Leadership Position

Today there is a severe shortage of academicians aspiring to become leaders of social work programs. This was acknowledged by the Council on Social Work Education, which sponsored two conferences in 2007, one in South Carolina, the other in Arizona, entitled "Building Leaders in Social Work Education." A wave of program coordinators, directors, and deans have recently retired or are planning to do so within the next five years. Add to this equation the dramatic rise in new MSW programs (Zeiger et al., 2005) and one can see the pressing need for new leaders in social work education.

Although no questions regarding leadership roles were asked directly, it is telling that among all subjects interviewed (the majority of whom were either in leadership positions, or had been so at some point in their academic careers), only two subjects spoke of the satisfaction they derived from serving in a leadership role. For one, it was a brief mention: "I like to coach, help people develop, and nurture faculty." For another, a veteran of over three decades in seven different programs, there was a refreshingly candid admission:

> It's a personal thing; I like being in charge. I like to make decisions, develop programs, and create things. That's why I've been a director/program head

for a gazillion years. I know I can have an impact on my environment. I enjoy being in a position to influence events and people. I've learned along the way that that's the way I am.

Social work is said to be a noncompetitive sport. We disparage any sense of hierarchy. People often assume leadership roles by default rather than aspiration ("They asked for a volunteer and I was the only one who didn't take a step backward."). It's not "cool" to say "I want to lead" in an egalitarian world. Yet, this author suspects that many social work educators do aspire to leadership roles or relish the ones they currently hold, even if they don't say so aloud. Perhaps the words of the subject in the previous quote will inspire others to rise to the occasion and fill a vital need.

Stability of Staying in One Place

"I've never been one who loves change."

In the introductory chapter of this book, two definitions of longevity were offered: being in the field of social work education for an extended period (ten years or more), which may occur at one or more social work programs; and being an educator primarily (90% or more) or exclusively at one social work program for an extended period of time. This section focuses on the latter group.

Why stay in one place? The author proposes that social workers remain in one place for an extended period of time because it is, at least in part, in their nature to do so. For some, it is the magnetic pull of where "home" is—whether it is Nashville, Tennessee, or Newport News, Virginia.

There is another possible explanation. Again, remembering that most interviewees were in the latter part, if not the twilight stage of their career, subjects have become more settled. They may be at a stage in their life span when the desire to change residency is no longer appealing. Here are a few reflections:

I like the idea of long-term commitment. I am the product of growing older and settling down in one place. I like to stay put—building community connections. After going through the hoops of tenure, I can't imagine walking away.

We've already settled in the area. We don't want to move around. Both families are within two hundred miles. We've bought property, built a house, and planted roots. I've made a professional choice to control my fate by writing a self-study, creating a program from scratch, and there's a loyalty versus not being part of someone else's program. I do not give up easily. I'm not a cut-and-run-type person. I've outlasted several university presidents.

The comfort, security, and predictability of staying are weighed against the uncertainty and risk of leaving. It comes back to individual comfort zones and the best fit. Tolerance levels vary.

> I'm a rooted person. I'm not one who will move around for a job. My family and community are always within a twelve-mile radius of my job. I could have moved around; I was getting calls, but I've always wanted to stay.

> Colleagues have been difficult, but I'm able to compromise. I was ready to quit three years ago, but what else would I do? There's unpredictability in leaving. Even now we have an abusive faculty member, and I'm in a grievance process. But I like what I do. Why should I have to leave because there are crazy people? There might be crazy people wherever I go.

Not Wanting to "Start Over"

Related to the desire to stay in one place for an extended period of time is the lack of desire to "start over"* at another institution. Beginning a new academic appointment often requires building campus and community networks, and learning to adjust to a different academic culture. It may also necessitate the discovery of health care providers, transportation options, and other community resources. Relocation often results in distancing from friends, relatives, and support systems. Moving may be a risky business, especially if you have "burned bridges."

Again, keeping life-span development issues in mind (Erikson, 1997), a veteran of more than twenty-five years as a social work educator noted that at his current career stage (with retirement on the horizon), he lacks the energy and impetus to look for other jobs, noting: "There's no need to leave; I'm very comfortable."

As mentioned in the introductory chapter, subjects not only shared their perceptions on faculty longevity, they reflected upon their careers as social work educators. Their thoughts ranged from "Have I done the best I can?" to "Are my contributions of value to the profession?" to "With the time I have left, could I do better?" One veteran of over twenty years, and on the threshold of turning sixty, offered the following thoughts in regard to her professional longevity:

> It makes you think. I've probably *made* most of my contributions. All right, what do I still want to do? I want to make a mark, leave a legacy, and this desire keeps me here. Why would I want to start over somewhere else?

---

* "Start over" is placed in quotes because moving from one academic setting to another, while involving acclimatization to the new setting, does not imply learning about the academic life without experience. Movement may, however, involve repeating the processes of tenure and promotion, albeit sometimes on an expedited schedule.

Unexpected Pluses

"Thinking over your career as a social work educator, what positive things (things or events that have made your job more desirable) have happened that you didn't expect or anticipate?"

One of the target audiences for this book is people considering social work education as a career. This chapter, chapter 5, "Bumps in the Road," and chapter 6, "I Wish I Had Known . . ." will give the reader a better vision of what to expect from a long-term commitment to academia.

In part, subjects' responses to the topic of unexpected pluses serves to check the validity of their responses to the question: "What has enabled you to sustain a career in social work education for a long period of time?" as covered in the previous chapter. In fact, many items mentioned by subjects as factors contributing toward longevity were also cited as unanticipated positive aspects of their academic careers. These include the ability to inspire student growth and development, administrative support, workplace autonomy (especially compared to social work practice), opportunities for professional growth, a positive collegial atmosphere, perks and benefits, and a flexible work schedule. Positive factors new to this chapter will be divided into three categories: career benefits, mezzo and macro benefits, and personal benefits.

CAREER BENEFITS

Fulfilling a Leadership Role

Recalling the beginning of their academic careers, few subjects remembered aspiring to assume a position of leadership within social work education. Their entry into an administrative role was more often by default rather than by design. Yet today, many hold leadership titles such as dean, director, or coordinator, and are enjoying their roles. Tasks such as launching a lecture series, implementing off-campus or distance-delivered programs, chairing a statewide committee for ethics in social work, becoming chair of the college faculty senate, and becoming a site visitor for the CSWE are other examples of unanticipated leadership roles that social work educators have assumed over the course of their careers.

Often, especially in the case of social work educators playing critical roles in nascent social work programs, the leadership role was assumed shortly after beginning an academic career. A thirty-three-year veteran recalled:

> I was offered a BSW chair position after my first year. I had never been an administrator. I didn't know if I could do it. I had been critical of one previous chair, and had admired another. I began with trepidation, but found it rewarding. I found I really enjoyed it.

The above words may be helpful to those considering entering administrative roles. Those educators who assume leadership positions are afforded opportunities to become involved in areas beyond their department, such as chairing a search committee for a new college president, or serving on the board of directors of a national social work organization such as the BPD or CSWE. Subjects spoke of how taking advantage of such opportunities has given them challenges, sharpened their administrative skills, and given them the chance to "associate with amazing, visionary people."

Longevity as a social work educator provides time to establish a positive reputation within one's department, school, institution, community, state, and in some cases, nation. As we will later see, longevity can be for better or worse. But, as one subject, in pondering her thirty-one years as a social work educator, noted: "People who have 'successfully aged' within the institution do make a positive difference. If you are rewarded for the contributions you make, you want to make more. That has been my experience in leadership roles."

In another example, a program director recalled how the state director of Family and Youth Services had sought out her School of Social Work to train child protection workers, resulting in a two-million-dollar-per-year training academy that has become a national model. This positive relationship between the state and the School of Social Work took time to cultivate. Trust, rapport, and demonstration of integrity do not come overnight.

Statewide and National Connections

The opportunity to attend conferences was mentioned in the previous chapter and is worthy of elaboration here. Social work is a profession that is taught in classrooms and social service agencies throughout the nation and throughout the world. Yet without meaningful communication among colleagues in other departments and schools, social work educators would limit their opportunities to share information with their peers, expand their horizons, create a national (if not worldwide) community, and optimize their professional skills and knowledge. Building statewide and national connections and a sense of universal community was cited repeatedly as one of the benefits of being a social work educator for an extended period of time.

Over time, social work educators take advantage of opportunities to become involved with people and organizations beyond the scope of their own departments and schools. This can occur at a statewide or regional meeting of the NASW. For example, the first five subjects were interviewed at the 34th Annual Mississippi-Alabama Social Work Educators Conference in Tunica, Mississippi—attended by over three hundred social work educators.

Depending on budgetary fluctuations and financial support from their home institutions, most social work educators regularly attend one or two national conferences, giving them the opportunity to network with their colleagues and build a national circle of friends. Many are able to attend state and regional conferences. Occasionally, international travel is possible. One subject noted: "I've spent a summer in New Zealand and a year in China on a faculty exchange program. Over the years, I've been able to build close relationships with colleagues nationwide." Another seasoned educator offered the following advice for those considering an academic career:

> In our program you're likely to receive financial support if you have a paper accepted, or you've been formally asked to speak on a panel. But not all proposals are accepted, and you need to make travel plans in advance. What to do? Well, if possible, at the point of hire, I'd do some negotiating. Request as a "benefit" that you be funded to attend X number of conferences per year. Attending conferences is vital; it's how we mature as a profession. We need to look beyond our home programs for ideas.

More will be said in chapter 10 regarding recommendations for the savvy future academician.

Scholarship Support

Expectations for and definitions of "scholarship" vary widely among programs and institutions. For social work educators at so-called Research I institutions, the expectations will be greater and may include a consistent pattern of peer-reviewed journal publications (perhaps one to three articles per year), book chapters, textbooks, and the procurement of externally funded grants. Professors at these institutions tend to teach less compared to colleagues who work at an institution where teaching loads are higher, and research agendas are less ambitious.

"Publish or perish" is a classic phrase heard in academia. It applies to social work educators who are seeking tenure and promotion. Briefly stated, it means that without a clear and consistent record of scholarly production (and definitions vary from one institution to another), employment may be terminated and/or promotion denied. There are several problems with the system of tenure and promotion in academia.

The definitions of scholarship are often muddy and subject to the whims of evaluations review committee members. They may also change over time, so candidates may chase a moving target. The expectations upon entry may not be honored five years later. Without a time machine, it would be difficult to reconstruct one's past achievements to conform to the latest requirements.

The element of service, a time-consuming yet vital part of social work education, often holds little value in the consideration of tenure and promotion. Countless hours spent in student advising, attracting new social work majors, devoting personalized time to students, and time spent in preparation of accreditation documents are discounted.

Scholarship expectations may be high, but there may be little or insufficient support in terms of reduced teaching loads and secretarial services. Instead, educators may feel they must publish "in their spare time." This can result in exhaustion, cynicism, lower-quality work, and lower quality of life outside work.

Fortunately, there are authors who are motivated more by the desire to share important information that enhances the knowledge base of social work, and less by the need to expand their curriculum vitae. And fortunately, there are authors whose scholarship is supported by their programs.

Not all academicians begin their jobs with the expectation or confidence that they will become published authors. But seeing their name in print and gaining respect, praise, and admiration from their colleagues become a welcome surprise. A twenty-five-year veteran of a small program commented:

> Publishing journal articles and a book—I didn't foresee this before coming to [my college]. I've always been given a great deal of support for scholarship, even though demands [for publication] have not been huge. I receive workload release; the department has done well with resources and equipment; the faculty turnover rate is low here.

Another subject, with over thirty years of experience, who teaches at a large program in the South, had this to say:

> The support I've received for research and professional development has been far greater than I expected—more generous than anywhere I've taught [including a Research I university]. The dean's been very supportive of my scholarship and professional accomplishments.

Clearly, the preceding two quotes don't represent all social work educators. In the early stages of their careers, not all academicians realize they are capable of producing articles and texts that their peers will find useful in strengthening the profession of social work. Nevertheless, scholarship, especially when supported by release time and secretarial assistance, can be a rewarding element of a successful academic career, and a contributing factor to faculty longevity.

Appreciation of Support Staff

Who *really* knows what's going on in a social work program? Who is the first point of contact for students and out-of-town visitors? Who really holds the place together?

Subjects who have remained in social work education a long time often had words of praise for their professorial colleagues. They also had compliments for their support staff. The quality of human interaction at the workplace contributes to longevity and employee satisfaction.

Social workers care about the quality of human relationships. And for social work educators, relationships with secretarial or support staff are of prime importance. Support staffs are sources of information. They often possess institutional history. They know whom to contact on campus to access resources, cut through red tape, and avoid running around in circles. They are goodwill ambassadors. They are often sources of encouragement and moral support. It is difficult to imagine a day at work without them.

I recall writing one of my first articles for a major peer-reviewed journal. My research involved contacting 182 subjects from twenty-six institutions nationwide. I set out to gather information (for each institution) from program coordinators, field coordinators, school/department deans or directors, local community members, support staff, faculty, and students. With an epiphany, I realized: Who better to coordinate subject contacts and boost my response rate than my secretary!?

My BSW program secretary contacted other staff persons at participating schools (her peers), sent questionnaires with cover letters and instructions for distribution to the aforementioned constituency groups, and coordinated the return and organization of completed questionnaires. Each school was called at least three times: the initial contact, a follow-up call to confirm questionnaire receipt, and one to three times more to track the status of participants. All of this amounted to a tremendous amount of work, but yielded a very high response rate. Sixty-five percent of the schools contacted participated. Her contributions were highly valued and she is listed as a coauthor (Zeiger, Hobbs, Robinson, Ortiz, & Cox, 1999). I can't imagine having completed the article without her. I suspect other social work educators have similar stories of praise for their support staff.

Positive Time with Students Outside the Classroom

Traditional-age students, those who enter college at eighteen, nineteen, or twenty, often embark on a lifestyle radically different from any they have previously known. They may be living away from home for the first time in their lives. They may be struggling to establish independence from their immediate family. They may be struggling to make ends meet financially. They may be the first in their family to ever attend college. And they may be grappling to understand what it means to have a college education, deciding what courses to take, and determining which professors will best fulfill their learning needs.

Nontraditional-age students, some who are entering higher education after a prolonged break from high school (or after completing a high school graduate equivalency exam), have lifestyle adjustment needs as well. Perhaps they have been homemakers for the past twenty years. Perhaps they are desirous of a change to a career that will alleviate societal ills. Or perhaps they have personally benefited from the services of a professional social worker and wish to "give back" to individuals, groups, families, and their community.

Regardless of student motivation or background, social work educators find interaction with students outside the classroom to be rewarding. They really enjoy student advising; getting to know students and influencing their development is rewarding. One subject with nearly twenty years of experience offered the following insight:

> I learn so much from students when they're *not* in the classroom. I especially love meeting prospective students—the ones who are considering social work as a major. [I first ask them to] "Tell me about your interest in social work." This is often followed by: "Tell me what you know about social work." This opens up a world of stories from a world of backgrounds. I really get to know my students as people.

Often students will confide in their instructors outside the classroom. They are looking for guidance—beyond what courses to take. As one subject teaching in an urban setting explained:

> Students take advising seriously, not only in terms of what classes to take, but what they should do after graduation. Because they are [frequently] the first in their family to go to college, many feel alienated from their families—"You're better than me." Advising takes an incredible amount of time.

Advisors play a key role in the lives of students. It is an awesome responsibility. It is an honor to influence future social workers, even if it doesn't count toward tenure and promotion.

MEZZO AND MACRO BENEFITS

Observing a Program Grow and Develop

One of the advantages of longevity at the same institution is the opportunity to see one's department or school develop over time. Many programs have seen enrollments increase over the years. New faculty have been hired to accommodate the need for social work education programs. Programs that were launched twenty-five years ago with two or three faculty now have five, ten, and more. Departments have grown into schools. MSW programs have been added to BSW programs as social work programs respond to community needs for practitioners with advanced training. Off-campus and distance-delivered programs have evolved in response to the educational schedules of working students, and those living in rural communities. With a tone of pride, subjects spoke of how their programs have expanded during their tenure:

> Over the years, I've seen our program's credibility grow stronger on campus and in the practice community. Our graduates make a positive difference delivering high-quality social work services. Field agencies seek us out for interns. We have a good reputation. This didn't come overnight.

One subject with nearly thirty-five years of experience noted that he had been rewarded by seeing over thirteen hundred students graduate from his program. He stated:

> The university has given me autonomy; they've stayed out of my way. They've let us grow and be creative from BSW to BSW plus MSW and satellite campuses. We've received funding through Title XX [20] and IV-E—large amounts.

As a tuned-in interviewer, it was easy to detect pride in the facial expressions of subjects as they reviewed the longitudinal success of their programs' growth and development.

Positive Campus Connections

One of the unexpected pleasures of longevity cited by subjects was the positive campus-wide relationships they had developed. Subjects expressed satisfaction in collaborative efforts with members of departments other than social work. Interdisciplinary activities included research projects with two or more departments, participation in a faculty senate, and serving on a university-wide search committee for a new dean.

One subject was able to establish valuable connections with members of other departments by sharing social work outcome instruments during the time of a university accreditation self-study. Another subject, who became department chair, noted that his new role allowed him to become acquainted with chairs of other departments, and to expand his knowledge of how the university functions as a whole.

By venturing beyond one's department, faculty, whether they're serving on a tenure review committee or playing an integral role in the selection of a new college president, are able to take on new challenges and broaden their horizons. With the passage of time, social work educators are able to influence what happens on campus. They gain a seat at the decision table. In the words of one subject: "Being valued and respected in the academic community, I think the fact that I've been here so long [thirty-four years], I have a little extra pull in terms of [obtaining] resources."

While longevity does not guarantee the ability to acquire resources, the longevity of an academician who has earned the respect of her colleagues can go a long way. A veteran of over thirty-years' experience offered wide-ranging comments on her positive campus-wide affiliations:

> There are lots of opportunities to get involved campus-wide. Moving into athletics opened up so many doors I never would have expected. It made me a better teacher; it gave me inroads to places off campus where people don't go. Now I'm on the faculty senate—representing the coalition of intercollegiate athletics—working with the NCAA to build integrity in college athletes. I've served as an associate dean for two years. I was bored and came back to social work, but it opened up other opportunities. I understand [my institution] better.

Community and Political Impact

Positive impact on the local practice community and state legislation can be developed and nurtured through faculty longevity. Social work educators did not foresee these contributions. For example:

> One of the pleasant surprises for me was all the recognition by the state. The notion that at [a rural college in the Northeast] if you do good work it makes a difference. The community is manageable enough to influence governing boards. In politics, we make an impact; we advocate [successfully] for the poor. Students are involved in projects that shape the community. I have a sense of being able to *influence*; I really didn't know what it meant to be a college professor. I received a national community service award!

Subjects played major roles in the development of mutually beneficial working relationships between their social work education programs and local and state social service programs. One subject with twenty years of experience commented:

> I've been surprised by the willingness of people in the community to form partnerships, but it makes perfect sense. It closes the gap between academia and the "real world" of practice. It provides agencies with a labor force, and it gives our students the opportunity to apply their education, in a hands-on way, to real-life situations. When students complete their internships, they're well prepared for professional practice. They are ready to meet the needs of clients and the practice community.

Social work educators are sought to serve on councils on aging, boards of directors of youth detention centers, as consultants to state family and youth services divisions. Clearly, they make a difference outside of social work education programs.

Another unanticipated benefit of being a social work educator was the ability to exert political influence. Several subjects reported close ties with legislators. One such educator, with over thirty years' experience in the South, played an integral policy-shaping role by testifying before the Senate Committee on Juvenile Justice and Delinquency—which led to the passage of the Juvenile Justice and Delinquency Act. This in turn led to the deinstitutionalization of status offenders.

PERSONAL BENEFITS

Low Job Stress

Nature versus nurture. Do we experience stress at the workplace because of our nature? Or does the nature of our work cause us to experience stress? Optimally, a good job fit would result in a social work educator being productive, having a sense of accomplishment. Work-related stress would rarely rise to the level of having a negative impact on job performance or life outside the workplace.

Setting aside the debate on the origin of stress, it is telling that subjects described their experience of a career in social work education as being low stress. Granted, most subjects had already passed through the hoops of tenure and promotion (some more than twenty years ago), and many described those times as anxious ones. But overall, at the time of the interview, they reflected upon their careers as being minimally stressful. For many, teaching assignments were less than expected. They discovered ways to "buy out" courses affording time to conduct research, write, and publish. Administrative support and autonomy are part of the equation as well. As one subject noted: "I receive

strong support from the administration. I've come to realize I'm free; I'm politically free to speak my mind, to express myself. I can wear whatever I want
to work.

Work-Family Balance

Related to keeping stress at bay is the notion of maintaining a healthy balance between work responsibilities and family commitments.

A negative stereotype of workaholics suggests that they are so driven to
succeed at work that they neglect their commitments at home, and miss out on
fun times with their families. Their lives are said to be out of balance.

The consensus among subjects was that their social work programs expressed concern for their life outside of work. In the words of one veteran of
more than twenty-five years:

> I've been able to balance family and career. My college shows genuine con-
> cern for my life outside the profession. I didn't anticipate how much that
> would mean to me over the years, raising children. They really understand
> that if you're happy at home, you'll be productive [and happy] at work. It's
> in everybody's best interest.

Friendships

It's been said before: social relationships are important to social workers
and social work educators. Over time, friendships may evolve at work and at
annual conferences among colleagues who hold similar interests.

In chapter 8, subjects will give their reaction to a "dream" job offer: Under
what circumstances would they be willing to take a job at another location? And
if they did, what would they miss most about their current job?

And this is where friendships enter into the equation. Time and again, subjects commented that an unexpected benefit of their longevity at one institution has been the lasting and deep relationships they've formed with their colleagues. Even when offered a dream job, many said they would not want to
leave their collegial relationships (professional *and* friendship). For those who
did consider alternative employment, one of the most difficult parts of departure would be leaving friends behind.

Romance

Just as most social workers don't begin an academic career with a conscious design to form friendships, they likely don't enter academia with a plan
to find romance. While subjects were never asked about finding Ms. or Mr.

Right, two volunteered that an unexpected benefit of their job was meeting life partners at the same institution of higher learning (in other departments). I suspect the number is actually higher. After all, it's a personal matter, and not one subjects would necessarily freely divulge (regardless of the degree of subject-interviewer rapport). Nevertheless, romance did occur and was perceived as an unexpected plus.

Bumps in the Road

"Thinking over your career as a social work educator, what negative events or circumstances have occurred that you didn't expect or anticipate?"

Beginning a new academic position in social work (or any other discipline) with eyes wide open requires a careful assessment of positive and negative factors. This chapter, paired with chapter 4, will give the reader a balanced picture of what to expect from a long-term commitment to academia.

UNANTICIPATED CHALLENGES

Subjects did not foresee the following negative factors as they began their careers as social work educators:

Excessive workload demands;
Limited and unpredictable resources;
Low status of social work program(s) on campus;
Unprofessional behavior of colleagues;
High rate of faculty turnover;
Difficult administrators;
Inadequate pay/benefits;
Emphasis shifts from teaching to research;
Diversity issues; and
Disgruntled students.

Excessive Workload Demands

The following quotes typify concerns raised by subjects regarding excessive workload demands:

I haven't had a summer off as long as I've worked at the university. I went on a twelve-month contract five years ago. I work a heck of a lot harder than I thought I was going to have to work. I've had success with grants [but] only recently able to hire additional staff to manage projects. The hours have been much longer than I thought.

There's been an increase in the need for accountability: program reviews, annual reports, and post-tenure reviews—almost a lack of trust on the part of the university. Accreditation stuff is getting on my nerves. One reason I'm leaving is because we're going into another round [of reaffirmation of accreditation]. I had no idea about the amount of time that goes into accreditation. We're constantly trying to justify our existence to the university and CSWE.

Over the years I've seen a consistent increase in the amount of paperwork and reports that take away from teaching. There's not enough time to sit down and shoot the breeze with students. There's a cost to pay. As you get more involved in family activities [at home], you're less likely to come into work in the evening. Keeping a balance is difficult.

An excessive work requirement was the most commonly cited unanticipated negative aspect of a career in social work education. Huge amounts of time and energy are expended and invested in accreditation (and reaffirmation of accreditation) efforts. Consistently, subjects found the accreditation process to be challenging and draining—with an emotional and physical price to pay.

Inevitably, preparation and documentation take away from time "better spent" in class prep time, meeting with students outside the classroom, research projects, and production of scholarship. It's a lot of pressure and the stakes are high. So much hinges on the outcome: the viability of programs; faculty and staff livelihoods; credibility within the practice community; and, of course, the future of students and the clients they will later serve.

Another theme that emerged within the category of excessive workload was the notion of "missionary work." New tasks arise that are added to an already full schedule. With only so many hours in the day, something's got to give: life outside work; sleep; time with family; time to relax and catch one's breath.

Several subjects noted a new trend in social work education to market the profession in order to attract new students. Here, one subject expressed a strong opinion:

I'm overworked as it is. Now we're supposed to do marketing—in our spare time? Don't get me wrong; marketing our program and the profession is a good idea, but my plate is already overflowing. It takes away from the time

> with students we have *in* our program. I really value developing relation-
> ships with students; that's why we're here. If we're really serious about
> marketing, there needs to be course release time, or new hires—but I don't
> see that in the near future. Right now, it's "give, give, give."

The reader will recall that many subjects (thirty out of sixty-six) work in
small programs of two to six faculty. As representatives of these programs noted,
small social work departments must cope with unique demands. Often, faculty
wear two or more hats. Several subjects spoke of the challenges of not antici-
pating multiple demands, frequently without sufficient monetary and human
resources. They spoke of the pressures to maintain and justify the existence
of a small department on campus. Turnover within a department, due to a faculty member's failure to achieve tenure, accepting an offer at another program,
or retirement, was described as especially challenging for a small program.

The number of new MSW programs being added to existing BSW programs
has mushroomed over the past twenty-five years. When an MSW program is
added, even with the addition of new faculty, workloads increase dramatically
(Zeiger et al., 2005). In the words of one veteran of twenty years: "Adding the
MSW program has become an organizational nightmare. You have to put on your
long pants." Adding an additional program stretches resources, both human
and monetary. Sustaining the quality of a preexisting BSW program requires a
conscious effort as MSW accreditation requirements surface. One subject reflected upon six site visits alone in the first five years of her MSW program. A
fair distribution of workloads and the coordination of teaching schedules, staff
coverage, and committee meetings becomes more challenging. Organizational
structure is irrevocably altered as faculty numbers grow, in some cases to two
or three times their former size (Zeiger et al., 1999).

Limited and Unpredictable Resources

"You have to dance and sing to get the budget and resources you need, and
that can be tiring."

Many subjects bemoaned unpredictable resource allocations, pressure
to increase sources of revenue through external resources, and the struggle
to survive chronic threats (or in some cases—realities) of financial cutbacks.
Some spoke of living with a periodic or constant threat of having their program
eliminated altogether.

Some subjects reported frozen salaries (in one case, five consecutive years).
Others noted operating costs that had risen owing to inflation, without commensurate support from the college or university. Still others cited the pressure (or
dictate) to eliminate a faculty position following a retirement, and the reneging
on financial commitments to a social work program made by the administration.

Working environments may be less than desirable because of a lack of resources. One subject with nearly thirty years' experience at the same program gave the following example:

> Now there's a plan to put the department in a trailer for five years while they build a new building. What does that say to a site visitor? The administration doesn't respect faculty and student comfort. It took forever to get an air conditioner—and it needs to be duct-taped in the winter. Some faculty still don't have one.

Another subject spoke of the difficulties while serving as head of the department:

> I've learned of severe limitations, as a program director. I had little influence with the institution regarding resources needed to do a quality job. The games I had to play in that role were draining and too exhausting. I came to the realization that stand-alone BSW programs are so vulnerable. That came home to roost two years ago when the dean decided to eliminate social work.

But it's not just BSW or even small programs that fight for resources. One subject working in a large program (earlier defined as fifteen or more faculty) at a publicly funded Research I institution derided the state legislature for insufficient financial support, noting his state ranked near the bottom of per capita education spending. He also noted the per diem travel rate had been frozen since 1980 (not a misprint!): "It's tough to recruit people; you try to avoid talking about it until you sign the contract."

Implications are clear for questions that job seekers would be wise to ask. More will be said about these implications in chapter 10, "The Job Seeker's Primer."

Low Status of Social Work Program(s) on Campus

> Social work is viewed as a stepchild. The university does not value us. We are one of a few undergraduate professional programs in a major flagship institution. Social work does not enjoy high status like chemistry or physics. We are a small fish in a big pond.

> There is a lack of recognition. Social work is seen as just an academic program—not a professional program. Our place isn't quite carved out like other programs. There's a lack of understanding about the importance of field placements and the time required to establish and sustain them.

In public life, and even academia, the profession of social work is often misunderstood. Some would be hard-pressed to distinguish social work from sociology, psychology, or human services. In many quarters, social work lacks recognition as a bona fide profession. In fact, some members of society believe anyone with a good heart can do the work of social work on a voluntary basis— that no special training is required. It is viewed as a "soft" science rather than a "hard" science. It is an uphill battle to gain honor and respect. One subject described her program, existing within a multiprogram department, as being the "bastard child" of her institution.

As noted in the previous section, some social work programs face the threat, or the reality (as in the recent case of the social work program at the Rochester Institute of Technology), of being eliminated because they are viewed by administrators as lacking value or being a poor fit for the institution. Four different subjects expressed concern that their administrations lacked an understanding of CSWE accreditation requirements and the support needed to ensure a favorable outcome. Subjects spoke of some programs being favored over others on campus, in terms of respect, honor, and status. Here is one example of a "two-faced administration":

> There's a lack of support for our social work program on campus. Nursing dominates resources; we have to constantly fight for a piece of the pie, for acknowledgment that we even exist. That all changes when the site visitors come. [The administration] sings a whole different tune: "Oh, we think social work is wonderful; we're so committed to it." Is someone being played like a fiddle?

This section, and all sections within this chapter, is not meant to convey that all or even most social work programs are fraught with excessive workload demands, limited resources, and low status on campus. However, these problems are common and real, and worthy of consideration for those seeking a career in social work education. Their recognition is also valuable to those who aspire to improve academic life.

Unprofessional Behavior of Colleagues

"Incompetent colleagues hiding behind rhetoric"; prima donnas; difficult personalities; and disengaged faculty. They are not unique to social work education. Everyone knew at least one faculty member who "didn't fit in." Yet no one would describe himself or herself as being one.

In shear volume of interview time, subjects had more to say about this "bump in the road" than any other. One social work educator with over thirty years of experience had a lot to say on the topic of unprofessional colleagues:

I've seen posturing by a number of faculty—prima donna status—people not being honest, direct [there is a pause in the recorded portion of the interview as the subject goes into greater detail "off the record"]—incompetent faculty hiding behind rhetoric—some of it was very ugly. It stays in the culture for a long time. It feels like the culture's been poisoned—a toxic atmosphere undermining the program—especially with a small faculty. Social workers should know better, behave more maturely. Untenured faculty are afraid to come forward. We soft-step around this as professionals. We need to be courageous and take risks.

Several subjects spoke of living through stormy and hostile relationships with colleagues, and of faculty not speaking to each other in times of turmoil. They spoke of the idiosyncratic nature of some faculty members, and of varying levels of work investment. Some faculty, they stated, rarely showed up for meetings or chronically arrived late or left early. Others had "pet courses" based on individual wants instead of program needs and curriculum standards.

Another subject, with over thirty years of experience, mostly in social work education administrative roles, was quite articulate on the topic of "difficult people":

Personnel decisions are some of the most painful, troublesome, I've ever had to deal with. I'd rather deal with a grumpy student. I've had deans ask me: "Why do social workers have so much trouble getting along with each other? Aren't they supposed to know this stuff?" I've had faculty members who did not have much in the way of social skills—unethical in their behavior with one another, with students. If you go out of your way to hurt other people, you gotta expect that there's going to be consequences. Don't pee in your own sandbox. You can't think of yourself as an independent contractor without a sense of obligation to the rest of the group.

Optimally, one would look forward to coming into work each day. Yet it was common to hear from subjects that a negative unexpected surprise in their career had been disillusionment with coworkers—that "there *really* is treachery." One subject noted that "the anti-intellectualism in a goodly number of people in higher education has stunned me." Another subject noted that faculty can become consumed with matters of small consequence, stating:

It's hard to believe that adults can be so petty on things that don't matter. They only hurt themselves. Life is too short. We're privileged in these jobs—each and every one of us. We're in higher education. On top of that, we're in social work. That's the stuff that kills me. It's not budget; it's not administration.

One measure of professional faculty behavior is how well established faculty members integrate and welcome new faculty. One subject commented that she did not feel welcome by established faculty because she entered the program in a supervisory role, and was perceived as too young to be doing so. Another subject came into her position in her late forties and was greeted with hostility and a negative message: "You'll never get tenure." Both these subjects felt unwelcome upon entry. Other subjects remarked that they did not receive much in the way of mentoring, informal or formal. No one took them under their wing. They needed to learn to "swim" quickly, with little or no guidance.

Perhaps a valuable question to ask for job seekers is: "What kind of mentoring for new faculty do you offer?"

High Rate of Faculty Turnover

The following words from an Academic Nomad are revealing:

> There are so many things I wish I had known for all the different places I've been. I wish I had paid more attention to my instincts. The state of the college—I wish I had probed more, looked into the history of faculty attrition, *talked with people who had left.* I walked into a revolving-door institution.

What's the average shelf life of a social work educator in a given program? What steps do the program and the institution take to retain good people? These are legitimate questions to ask for job seekers, search committees, and administrators.

Faculty do not always transfer from one position to another with "plenty of advance notice." Likewise, they can depart at inconvenient times, such as in the middle of a semester, or immediately prior to an accreditation site visit. Some faculty are denied tenure and forced to leave.

Subjects noted that frequent turnover in a small faculty can be especially challenging—with workload readjustments to be made and new integration of working styles to be accomplished.

In part, the quality of the hiring process may impact faculty longevity. One subject, a department chair, noted that he had made "terrible hiring decisions" in the past, and didn't support people well enough to have them stay. Now, he is extraordinarily careful. Other subjects noted "pro forma searches," where administrators had predetermined decisions and faculty members (and unsuccessful candidates—who never had a chance) went through motions (and considerable time and effort) to make the process appear fair. As one subject noted: "You're playing deceptive games—messing with people's lives. It's not fair to other applicants. And it's not fair to the faculty and the integrity of the program."

Difficult Administrators

The reader may find it helpful to distinguish between different levels of administration. Depending upon program size and hierarchical configurations, there may be three or more levels of administration that impact a given social work education program: for example, program chair (e.g., head of a BSW program); department chair or director (e.g., head of a combined BSW/MSW program); dean of a college that includes more than one department or school (e.g., social work + nursing + criminal justice); dean of a school of social work (which may include a BSW, MSW, *and* PhD program); college or university provosts, vice presidents, presidents, and chancellors. What all these positions hold in common, more or less, is oversight of the affairs of social work education programs. In this section, unless otherwise stated, administration will refer to those who do *not* have daily contact with social work students and faculty (primarily deans, provosts, vice presidents, presidents, and chancellors).

Providing an atmosphere where subjects could speak freely about "difficult" administrators was a challenge. The topic arose midway through most interviews when unexpected occurrences were discussed. Confidence was assured, and, hopefully, the trust and rapport this researcher developed with subjects allowed them to speak openly and honestly. Subjects had a lot to say. For example:

> The personalities of some administrators (presidents, provosts) have made life difficult. One wanted all employees to validate *his* vision. "We'll put all ideas on the table." It was a lie [rhetoric]. Not all concerns could be voiced. Mine never made it to the list. Many promises were rescinded. For example: "You're next in line to be [department] chair."

One subject lamented that the administration was "not overly fond of faculty" and that the disdain was campus-wide. When I asked for specific instances she replied:

> A longtime faculty member died recently. At the memorial service, the president mispronounced her name, then walked off the stage and left the building. How disrespectful! We were all thinking: "You son of a bitch!" Former teachers become administrators and "go to the dark side." We always hope they will carry the torch for faculty. In all the years I've been teaching [about thirty], I've seen one who's done that [been supportive of faculty], and she moved back to faculty.

Subjects' negative comments regarding administrators were frequent, and to the ears of this researcher, genuine. Many described administrators who are manipulative and unethical, who impose their ideas and disrespect program needs, and who micromanage and are obsessed with power, control, and image. In the perspective of this researcher, this is more than venting or kvetching. Four dedicated social work educators who care about the future of social work made the following statements:

> The most difficult times I've had were dealing with the administration. They emphasized negatives—what the faculty *wasn't* doing, instead of positives.

> We had administrative problems: a bad vice chancellor, not friendly, [and] didn't understand social work. We had an administrator who stole resources from social work.

> We've had some God-awful deans. I served as an interim director, and that year we had the dean from hell, and she just didn't respect me. She was mean, nasty, and took money away from the department.

> The administration feels CSWE is too powerful and does not give us enough support for accreditation. The new dean of the college doesn't understand social work. Issues of confidentiality are not well maintained. Recently, the registrar sent out the database listing all students in the university who are on financial hold. I didn't need to know all that—just the social work students. The dean goes over my head without consultation—leaving me out of the loop.

Again, the message is clear for those seeking a position in social work education: know your administration and its history before you sign on the dotted line.

There are no guarantees here. Many subjects spoke of frequent administrative turnover, and outlasting several deans. In fact, one subject estimated the average "shelf life" of a dean to be only five years. Frequent adjustment to new administrators can be challenging. This begs another area of inquiry for prospective social work educators: What is the history of administrative leadership? How many leaders have there been over the last ten years?

The last two pages have not painted an attractive picture of administrators. And to be fair, there is another side to the story. Administrators frequently work with "difficult" faculty. Being an administrator is a demanding job with significant responsibilities. It can also be lonely. One subject, a program director who served as an interim dean, made the following observation:

> The hardest part of my job is personnel. I find it hard to discipline somebody, to terminate somebody, to confront unethical, poor behavior. Last

year I was ready to quit. The university process is so cumbersome—dealing with human resources, labor relationships, university council, and the dean. So much happens that must be kept in confidence, not shared with faculty. We had an out-of-control faculty member. It was hell. We lucked out. It could have gone on for five years. I've got to clean up the mess with limited tools. All this occurs in isolation, behind closed doors. A large part of [administrative] responsibility does not take place as part of a team. There's a dimension of loneliness; people have distorted perceptions of inactivity. A unionized shop creates an adversarial structure.

Inadequate Pay/Benefits

Repeatedly, subjects shared the value that salary was not a major source of satisfaction. Perhaps this is a popular sentiment shared by social workers and social work educators; they are not in it for the money. It did not occur to many subjects to negotiate a starting salary; they were happy to accept the "standard" offer. But after a while, reality sets in. Their financial responsibilities grow. The cost of living increases. They learn that salaries have been frozen, and that they lag behind comparable institutions in monetary compensation.

One subject entered academia knowing he would be earning less than he did as a social work practitioner. Thinking he'd only have to teach two days a week, he would have three days "off." Not so. In his words: "You always have less time." Many subjects discovered salaries had remained modest over time, with only periodic "teasers." "Unions have not been successful," lamented a veteran of twenty-eight years.

One subject coined the phrase "Skinner box raises," indicating raises would come at unpredictable times—not often enough to make employees feel secure, but often enough to keep them coming back in hope of something good being delivered.

Emphasis Shifts from Teaching to Research

I didn't foresee the college moving from an emphasis on teaching to [an emphasis] on research. We're falling into the inevitable position that we must [make this shift]—that research has gained the upper hand over teaching. There's a movement from ecumenical to evangelical, from liberal to conservative.

The shift in emphasis is not uncommon. However, several subjects decried the lack of support in terms of release time and travel funds to conduct research, give presentations at conferences, and work on publications. One subject noted the mixed communication of her institution touting the importance of globalization, while simultaneously cutting international travel funds: "There's a double message here."

As noted earlier, scholarly production requirements and support vary from one institution to another. Optimally, the support should be adequate enough to meet requirements for tenure, promotion, and professional growth.

Diversity Issues

Diversity issues that arose in interviews include gender bias, lack of diversity on campus, racial prejudice, and exploitation of ethnicity.

One subject was disappointed in the lack of racial diversity in the local population, the student body, and the faculty—noting about a 5 percent minority population for each.

When asked about unexpected negative experiences, another faculty member, teaching at an institution with students from over ninety countries, expressed feelings of being exploited. In speaking of her beginning years, she described:

> . . . being asked to join *so* many committees because of how they perceived my ethnicity. Now I pick and choose and say no. I don't consider myself to be a minority person. There is nothing "minor" about me. The term is very offensive.

Another subject spoke on the topic of racial discrimination, noting:

> There is a constant fight for identity. I've been asked to clean up a spill as if I was a janitor. There's still a good portion of my school that sees me as a "wetback," and they always will.

Yet another subject spoke of experiencing gender bias, especially in the early stage of her career:

> There was a gender bias I didn't expect. I'd challenge this today; I have more confidence. It's subsided. I don't experience it today. There was a department head that would pat women on the head—overtly—controlling—a put-down—not patting men on the head—or treating them at the same level.

It would appear that social workers and social work educators still have much to learn about diversity issues. New hires, "seasoned" educators, and administrators need to be sensitive to gender bias, racial prejudice, exploitation of persons of color, and the need to build diverse student bodies and faculty.

Disgruntled Students

Surprisingly, dealing with student complaints about such issues as teaching, grading, and course and degree requirements seldom arose during the interviews. Those subjects who did make mention seemed to take it in stride, as though student objections were a normal part of academic life.

> We do teach them to advocate for the best education they can get. We encourage their involvement in curriculum development. Sometimes they're not as tactful as they might be, but they are students and they are learning to speak their mind.

Still, subjects had stories to tell about "problem" students, who sometimes require enormous amounts of time, extensive documentation of facts, and consultation with legal counsel. Freeing up the time and resources spent on them would allow more time and energy for students who are hungry to attain professional social work knowledge and competencies.

A Note about Off-the-Record Comments

As a researcher, I consider the subject matter of this chapter to be sensitive. Talking about unprofessional collegial behavior is challenging. I have done my best to honor and respect my subjects. In some cases, subjects requested that I turn off the tape recorder so they could speak to me off the record. In my opinion, they really wanted to tell their stories. However, nothing said during these "off" times is presented here. I believe I have stayed true to statements that were made on the record.

I Wish I Had Known . . .

"Describe something you wish you had known before you accepted your current position."

This chapter provides the reader with an opportunity to learn from the experiences and wisdom of our seasoned subjects, social work educators with a combined 1,688 years of service. Analogous to chapters 4 and 5, this chapter gives those considering a career in social work education an opportunity to enter academia with eyes wide open, and with realistic employment expectations.

In part, responses to the topic of things they wish they had known serves to validate subjects' responses to the question: "What negative events or circumstances have occurred that you didn't expect or anticipate?" as covered in chapter 5. In fact, several items cited as "bumps in the road" were also things subjects wished they had been aware of prior to entering academia. These include excessive workload demands, non-collegial behavior, high faculty turnover, and the low status of social work education on campus.

TIPS FROM SEASONED SOCIAL WORK EDUCATORS

There are many things to consider when embarking on a career in social work education. Items new in this chapter include:

What to expect in academia;

Salary negotiation;

How to keep one's career in balance with life outside work;

How to teach/connect with students;

Understanding the process of accreditation;

Gatekeeping and legal issues;

Tenure, promotion, and academic competition;

Research and scholarship;

State support for higher education;

Campus politics;

How to be an effective administrator; and

More things I wish I had known.

What to Expect in Academia

Picture this: After applying for a social work faculty position, you have been invited to campus for a visit. The department has taken care of your transportation, lodging, and meals. You meet with students, faculty, staff, and the program director. Although no specific offer has been made, they all seem genuinely interested in having you join their social work education program. But you're not 100 percent sure this will be the best career move for you. You have one tentative offer in your pocket and are scheduled to interview at a third school next week. You are still recovering from jet lag, having arrived late last night from a different time zone. Now, after seven hours of what seems like nonstop meetings, you enter the provost's office. You sense that this is a key person in the decision-making process. You've little experience speaking to an "upper level" administrator. She invites you into her office. As you notice the rich-grained wood of her desk, her first question catches you off guard: "What questions do you have for me?"

What *is* important to know before you consider an offer? So much is at stake: your future, your family's future, and perhaps the future of your colleagues. A month from now, what might you regret not having asked? How about in a year, or a decade into the future? Should you ask about promotion and tenure? What about research support, or a vision of how social work fits into the university's mission?

In part, your questions will be a reflection of your personal needs, your view of social work education, and a compendium of what friends, colleagues, and fellow job seekers have encouraged you to ask. Your questions, even if answered with genuine responses, will not guarantee you a perfect fit in your new job. Further, academia is a complex enterprise, making it impossible to predetermine all relevant questions. In the words of one subject with well over thirty years of experience:

> You're not going to know everything before you get there. Wherever you go, there's going to be an item you didn't consider. There's likely to be some disillusionment. At [University X], I didn't know that Human Services was going to rip off the social work curriculum—including syllabi and textbooks. You can't know everything ahead of time. What do I wish I knew? That I'm not going to know everything. Be prepared to be surprised.

And from another point of reference:

> I was very naïve. I would like to have known how to negotiate salary, rank, and travel funds—and the extra things I see more astute faculty questioning. I would like to have known how to teach in a higher-education environment. What are the faculty development opportunities? Advancement, tenure, and promotion criteria—none of these were things I even thought about.

A common refrain heard among subjects who made a transition from graduate school to social work education was that their PhD program did not do a good job of socializing them to the academy, to academic trends, to scholarship expectations, grant information, salary negotiation, and accreditation. They didn't have a clear picture of what it would be like to be a faculty member, to survive and thrive in an academic world. One subject with twenty years' experience said he would have appreciated knowing the "survival rate" and the reasons former faculty had for leaving. For colleagues who did survive, he found some of them reluctant to share information because of the competitive nature of academia. In his words: it all boils down to who is number one and who is number ten.

Another subject, with more than twenty-five years at the same institution, offered her thoughts on how PhD programs might better prepare doctoral students for entry into professional social work education:

> I wish schools of social work would offer something more in mentoring teaching—perhaps by providing a sample curriculum. Why isn't there a class in PhD programs to examine classroom teaching, administration, etc.?* There's no embodiment of what it means to have an academic career.

Clearly, subjects supported a need for clearer expectations for those entering social work education. We now turn to specific items requiring increased awareness.

Salary Negotiation

"I was so thrilled to get a job, I didn't realize it was *possible* to negotiate a higher salary."

Many subjects spoke of their naïveté about accepting a salary. Today, with hindsight, they would be more assertive about their needs. No one had

---

* The author is aware of one such course currently offered in the social work PhD program at the University of Utah.

mentored them regarding salary negotiation. No one had encouraged them to research the history of institutional salary increases (or freezes, or cuts). No one had advised them to compare the salaries of peer institutions. And no one had suggested they consider benefits, such as travel funds, organizational membership fees, course load reductions, supplemental summer income, and professional development costs as *part of a negotiable package*. Moreover, they did not realize the significance of a starting salary being as high as possible because it establishes a baseline for future salary increases.

In general, new academicians are often so thankful to land a job, they underestimate their bargaining power. Especially in today's market, with more faculty positions available to be filled than qualified candidates to fill them, job seekers may have greater leverage than they realize. And while social work educators often downplay the need for a nice salary, years later, as their financial responsibilities grow, they may regret not having negotiated a better compensation package.

How to Keep One's Career in Balance with Life Outside Work

As we have established in the previous chapter, "Bumps in the Road," social work education, not unlike its cousin social work practice, can be a demanding career. How *does* one organize the multiple responsibilities of teaching, service, advising, research and scholarship, and a life outside of work? What is the secret to balancing a productive career and a meaningful life away from academia? With so many opportunities for professional development, service to the community, and unexpected fires to extinguish, how does one lead a balanced life? Where does the line between giving and burnout reside?

> This is something they didn't teach us in grad school. I'm not sure it *can* be taught. I think it's an art form to establish a research agenda, spend time with students outside of class—without shortchanging them—really master (and continue to update) the content of courses I teach, serve the needs of my department, *and* have some time to myself—so I can stay sane. I'm overwhelmed at times.

Sharing the load may help. As a graduate student with lots of energy, this author remembers concluding, early on, there would be no way I could keep up with course readings and assignments without working in groups to share the load. Clear and reasonable expectations, balanced allocations of responsibilities that tap into individual faculty member strengths, and a shared vision can make social work education a rewarding vocation.

How to Teach/Connect with Students

Most social work educators do not learn teaching (including class-management) skills in their MSW or PhD programs. For some, there was a dearth of practical knowledge: how to write a syllabus, order textbooks, grade fairly, understand different learning styles and needs, be creative in the class-room, prepare a lecture or PowerPoint presentation, or manage a classroom with obstreperous students.

Related to teaching effectiveness is knowledge of social work education curricula. Other than having attended an MSW program, a PhD program—which may or may not have been in social work or social welfare (CSWE requires doctoral faculty to have an advanced degree in social work or a "related field," which is open to interpretation)—or, in rare cases, having attended only a BSW program, many new faculty are not well versed in social work education requirements, especially at the baccalaureate level.

For the most part, new faculty develop teaching talents *after* they begin their academic careers. Learning how to teach occurs on the job. One social work educator with over thirty years' experience described his evolution in becoming a competent teacher:

> The first couple of years I thought I could just transmit knowledge from practice experience. I realized I needed to learn pedagogic skill. I acquired skills by observing other faculty and asking students what they wanted that they weren't already getting. I'd run my ideas by my peers and filter out the suggestions of self-serving faculty. I created my own bridge from practice to academia. I learned that doing is not enough. You have to break down the skills, values, and concepts of social work into a clear process. I had to learn to be organized.

It's akin to practicing tempo and scales before one can musically improvise.

Students can tell when a professor is new. "They know it, and they make you a mark." They may take advantage of your naïveté, your desire to please, and your vulnerability to manipulation. One subject recalled an experience early on in his career:

> I once had a student complain about a grade of B+ on a paper. She was emphatic. She had *never* received anything but straight As. Well, not quite. As I later learned, she had tried the same story with several other professors in different semesters.

New faculty need and deserve to come into academia with a pedagogical tool kit. But that is not enough. They will likely need mentoring and support throughout their academic careers in order to become competent transmitters of skills and knowledge.

Understanding the Process of Accreditation

In chapter 5, we established that accreditation, and reaffirmation of accreditation, is a time-consuming and labor-intensive endeavor. This section highlights subjects' lack of knowledge about the accreditation process at the time they began their social work education careers. Similar to teaching, most subjects reported learning about accreditation, including how to prepare for a site visit, *after* they entered academia.

As previously stated, many subjects were "in on the ground floor" for the establishment of their social work programs. As such, they often had to struggle, in many cases mightily and with little in-house support, to navigate the vicissitudes of putting together a self-study and complying with CSWE's accreditation standards. Repeatedly, subjects spoke of huge and often unanticipated time investments and steep learning curves ("It's been a challenge and an opportunity; it's also been a drain."). And as one subject noted: "CSWE says you need PhDs, yet PhD programs don't teach you how to teach, and they don't teach you how accreditation works."

A word of advice to those considering a career in social work education: learn where a program is in the accreditation cycle—then verify this information. Next, find out if the accreditation process will be a team effort. One subject, a veteran of twenty years' experience, reported:

> The social work program was not as close to being accredited as I was told. I was told the documents [for the self-study] were ready to send in; they weren't. This took away from time to conduct research and produce scholarship. Putting the self-study together detracted from promotion and tenure. I had heavy teaching loads and a lack of support from my colleagues.

Gatekeeping and Legal Issues

BSW, MSW, and PhD programs offer professional degrees. As such, especially at BSW and MSW levels, these academic programs prepare students to attain professional licensure for direct and indirect practice with clients. Their education is an awesome responsibility. Knowledgeable, competent, and well-trained practitioners can make a positive difference, changing the fabric of society.

One thing subjects discovered upon entering academia is that not all students enrolled in social work classes are appropriate for becoming professional social workers. A popular topic of conversation throughout the life (1994 to present) of the Listserv of the Association of Baccalaureate Social Work Program Directors (BPD) has been gatekeeping, that is, screening out students and potential students whose actions might be harmful to clients and damaging to the profession. The question of whether or not to admit students with criminal backgrounds to social work education programs has received a considerable amount of attention in recent years (Scott & Zeiger, 2000; Magen & Emerman, 2000).

As one subject with over thirty years of experience noted:

> Gatekeeping issues take time. There are students who desperately want to become social workers but can't survive academically. It's distasteful, but you have to be fair. It takes a long time [and a lot of work] to develop effective policies. Occasionally, students challenge academic decisions in court. Litigation may require a huge expenditure of time and energy in preparation of documents, meetings, and testimony. Inevitably, this competes with time otherwise spent on normal work activities. Prospective faculty may wish to investigate the social work program's policies related to "difficult" students (often found in a student handbook), and their history of litigation.

Tenure, Promotion, and Academic Competition

While criteria for tenure and promotion vary from one institution to another, most social work educators are familiar with the adage: "Publish or perish." However, information on what to publish, where to publish, and how often to publish remains a mystery to many social work educators, especially when they enter academia. The terms "tenure" and "promotion" often evoke anxiety (Henry, Caudle, & Sullenger, 1994). To complicate matters further, the term "publication" resides within the category of "scholarship," which is ambiguously defined at many institutions of higher learning. Adding more fuel to the fire, these definitions are mutable, so that the "rules of the game" may change several times from the way they were at the beginning of an academic appointment, as policies become altered, tenure and promotion committee member composition changes, and administrators come and go. The result is a moving target that changes shape. Tenure and promotion may have been "easier" to achieve five years ago, or the tasks a faculty member was told "counted" in the past no longer hold value.

The traditional three main areas upon which social work (and most other academic disciplines) are evaluated for tenure and promotion are teaching, scholarship, and service. A common refrain among subjects of this study was that these areas were not clearly defined when they began their academic appointments, and the weighting formula for each area was arcane. Further, they were not given clear examples for each category, nor were they informed of the track record for success and failure.

Regarding academic survival and the pressure to produce, one veteran of nearly thirty years made the following observation:

> I didn't realize I was getting into a research-intensive university. I became aware of the "tenure clock,"* and the need to protect time. No one's going to do that for you. The thing that counts is publication. Service doesn't count; teaching doesn't count. They say it does, but it really doesn't. It's really publication and bringing in grant dollars. There's not a lot of support for getting tenure. There's a high amount of turnover, and rules change for tenure and promotion.

What about service? Isn't that a source of pride for social workers and social work educators? As vital as it is, as much as it improves the quality of life for clients and community members, most subjects would agree that it remains undervalued, even superfluous, to the achievement of tenure and promotion.

How is the achievement of tenure and promotion influenced by academic competition? Inevitably, when faculty members "go up" for tenure or promotion, their achievements in teaching, scholarship, and service are compared to those who have gone before them, and to those who are "going up" at the same time. Official or not, an institution (or a department) may have a quota of how many promotions and tenures they award in a given year. Tenure-track faculty, who have yet to achieve tenure status, know they are being compared to one another, and, according to one subject: "Some people think they might lose their place on the ladder if they give out too much information. It's very divisive. In the academy, you can become very isolated."

The bottom line: new faculty deserve clear expectations and models for academic success. In the words of one subject: "Departments and institutions should make a clear statement that: 'By hiring you, we have confidence you will achieve tenure and promotion, and we will provide you with the support necessary to make it happen.'"

It would be wise to make a statement of this nature in job announcements.

Research and Scholarship

Related to achieving tenure and promotion is knowledge of how to conduct research and generate scholarly production. As discussed earlier, in the 1970s and 1980s, when many subjects in this study entered academia, a PhD was not as important a prerequisite as it has become over the last twenty years. Compared to BSW and MSW programs, research methodology is covered in far greater depth in social work and social welfare doctoral programs. Thus,

---

* Most programs allow faculty a limited amount of time to achieve tenure, typically five to seven years. If faculty fail to achieve tenure status, they lose their academic position.

at least in theory, a doctoral degree would give a new faculty member an edge in conducting research. Several subjects who received a PhD well into their academic careers, or not at all, said they wished they had acquired more knowledge of research methodologies before they entered academia.

Even among those with PhDs, many subjects admitted to being naïve and intimidated when it came to *how* to publish articles. They regretted not having learned more about how to produce scholarship that can make a significant contribution to the knowledge base of the profession and lead to the improvement of service delivery to clients and the community.

State Support for Higher Education

This item applies to institutions of higher learning that are publicly funded. Lean allocations for higher education as determined by state legislatures impact tuition costs and faculty salaries, and impede the maintenance, growth, and development of existing and new social work education programs. Faculty lines may be cut and research projects may be delayed, trimmed, or eliminated. The launching of new programs, such as Distance Delivery or a new graduate program may likewise be put on hold.

Subjects regretted not investigating the level of financial support for higher education in state-funded institutions. Admittedly, they said they "probably would have taken the job anyway," but it would have been nice to know the political climate up front.

One subject, a veteran of nearly thirty years, noted that the "potential for program growth is limited in [his state]. Higher education is not financially valued. Only 15 to 20 percent of funding comes from the state; it's tantamount to being a private college."

From this author's experience teaching at a publicly funded institution in Alaska, I can attest that *every time* the state legislature convened to discuss the budget, faculty, students, and administration awaited the result with considerable trepidation and anxiety. In my twelve years in Anchorage, departments were regularly asked to prepare budgets based on looming financial cuts. That was the norm.

Campus Politics

How do you cut through red tape? Who has influence? Who are the "right" people to talk with if you need resources? How are decisions made? A common unanticipated phenomenon voiced by subjects was the politicization of academia. For example:

> I didn't anticipate how political it would be. You have to kiss up to certain
> people. You have to know the right people, make sure you have the right

> people in your pocket. When I first arrived, I didn't know how to play the game.

> There are all these layers of bureaucracy—not just one supervisor. Like the tenure process—too many people have a say. Does everybody have a right to know how this person is performing? It's like having four or five bosses.

Faculty candidates would do well to explore the political culture of the institution *before* joining the department. What schemes for organizational change are on the horizon? Are there plans to consolidate or eliminate departments or programs? What is the reputation of social work within the institution—both current and historical? Concerning these matters, one subject offered the following advice:

> Ask straight out: How well do your department members get along? How are decisions made?—one person? Consensus? How are dissenting opinions treated? Ask outside the department. How does administration view the department? Know what you're walking into.

When I asked how one would assess the genuineness of answers to these questions, I was told that, while it was not easy, a faculty candidate could use social work listening skills. Pay close attention to body language. If you watch carefully, you can detect honesty and reveal challenges that lie ahead for the social work program.

How to Be an Effective Administrator

"They asked for volunteers, and I was the only one who didn't take a step backward."

Many subjects interviewed found themselves in leadership roles by default, rather than by design. Administration of social work education programs was *not* something covered in graduate school. As mentioned earlier, many subjects were pioneers, launching BSW programs in the 1970s and MSW programs in the 1980s and 1990s. Several wished they had more training, including learning the process of accreditation, before assuming administrative roles. This was especially true for subjects teaching in small programs. For example:

> I was starting a new program. Before we moved into the accreditation phase, I was a department of one. I was really starting from scratch. I had to search out people [outside the institution] who could help me. There was an extra layer of responsibility—figuring out how to put a program together.

Subjects spoke of needing a road map that didn't exist, and scrambling to find consultants. The learning curve was steep and the hours long. Grit, determination, and an enduring belief in the viability of, and need for, social work education sustained them.

More Things I Wish I Had Known

There are several miscellaneous "things I wish I had known" worthy of mention for those considering employment in social work education. Mostly negative, they range from subjects discovering that secretarial support was minimal to discovering the competitive nature of academia to realizing the pay was less than they had been receiving as social work practitioners. One subject wished she had known in advance how bad the weather would be, stating: "It's horrible in the summer. Lots of pollen, humidity—it's horrid."

Yet not all "I wish I had knowns" were negative. One subject displayed a broad smile as she commented:

> I didn't realize how wonderful a job could be—that I would fall in love with it. I didn't think it would happen. This is a place that brought so many parts of me together—that made me so comfortable. In a small way, I have an impact on so many students.

As I gazed into this subject's eyes, I believed every word.

In Search of Greener Pastures

No job is perfect. At some point in their careers, most social work educators wonder what a career in academia might be like at another institution of higher learning—perhaps in a different part of the country (Phillips, 2002; Richardson & McKenna, 2002; Childress, 2001; Tabachnick, 1992).

I asked my colleagues to reflect upon a time when they seriously considered leaving their longtime position as a social work educator. If they were offered a job elsewhere, had serious overtures, or otherwise considered an alternative place of employment, why did they ultimately choose as they did?

Given that forty-six of sixty-six subjects had spent the majority (60 percent or more) of their careers teaching in the same program, and thirty-seven had spent 90 percent or more of their time at the same program, surely they would have something to say regarding alternative pastures.

This chapter describes reasons for wanting to depart, and reasons for deciding to stay in place.

REASONS FOR GOING

Reasons for considering employment somewhere else fall into the following six categories:

Distaste for administrator(s) and/or administrative policies;

Departmental discord (with a subcategory on "the work of adulthood");

Program existence is threatened;

Desire for change;

Career advancement; and

Avoidance of impending accreditation.

Distaste for Administrator(s) and/or Administrative Policies

Lies, nonsense, exaggeration, and false promises—or in the eloquent words of one subject—"administrative bullshit." It's enough to bring a grown social work educator to tears. And it's enough to evoke a consideration of (if not departure to) an alternative place of employment. One subject described a nerve-wracking experience:

> I remember I was anxious about coming up for tenure. There was no clearly defined procedure. Our president said, "I'll close the school before I give anyone tenure." He finally capitulated. I applied for another job [in the interim], but then I got tenure. That took the onus off; it was a relief.

Does holding an administrative position foster the development of a personality obsessed with power and control? Or are people whose constitution includes a thirst for power and control more likely to seek administrative roles? What is clear is that subjects cited abuse of power and "difficult" personalities as major concerns. For example:

> We had a bad V.P.—a tough bird to work for. He was impulsive, with poor organizational skills and unpredictable behavior. He wouldn't show up for meetings *he* scheduled—but *I* would be expected to attend a meeting he called at the drop of a hat. I wondered: "What's the day going to bring?" He could be mean—say the nastiest things. He didn't think through what he said before he said it.

Fortunately, the above social work educator "outlasted" her administrator. But consider the energy she, and many subjects, expend in worry and anxiety that are by-products of working with mercurial and micromanaging administrators. Consider the loss of contentment and productivity. Administrators need to be cognizant of and sensitive to the impact they have upon social work educators' careers and job satisfaction.

Departmental Discord

Difficult personalities are not limited to administrators. One might reasonably expect that social work educators, in line with the NASW Code of Ethics, would respect the dignity and worth of their coworkers and behave in a trustworthy manner. Perhaps this notion is naïve.

> In the late '90s, our department was in turmoil—caused by difficult personalities more than anything. It was not a great place to work. Faculty

came and went on a regular basis [the turnover rate was high]. I applied elsewhere and was even willing to take a pay cut—but my husband wasn't able to find work there. It was a difficult time.

Subjects spoke of difficult faculty who were eventually fired, departed because they failed to achieve tenure, or took positions elsewhere. It seemed everyone could identify at least one "white whale"—in this case a nemesis, like the creature in *Moby Dick*, that had a toxic influence on collegial atmosphere in their social work education program. One veteran of more that twenty years contributed the following:

Prima donnas—I've seen my share. On the surface they've got the patter down—almost as if they've become the NASW Code of Ethics wired for sound. But what they say and how they behave are different. They are out for themselves, disengaged from other faculty, unwilling to share with others, and reluctant to learn from others. In short, they are poor colleagues.

Such "colleagues" are often unwilling to share in numerous departmental tasks such as admissions, preparation of self-study documents, and other miscellaneous and mundane but necessary work. They send the message: "I'm too good; I'm too busy" (M. I. Robinson, personal communication, December 15, 2007).

Related to departmental discord, subjects spoke of a desire to escape an overly competitive atmosphere. As one subject noted: "I was ready to leave after a year and a half because of fierce competition. Fortunately, I found support from a colleague and stayed."

The work of adulthood. Behavior and behavior patterns by colleagues that are problematic to social work educators are not the major focus of this book and merit further attention. It is significant that many respondents identified "difficult colleagues" or toxic relationships in academia as a factor that influenced the quality of their professional life. It is ironic that such relationships exist within social work faculties. Social workers, theoretically, are experts in relationship skills based on mutual respect, inclusion, reciprocity, conflict management, and cooperative problem solving. Teamwork, sharing of resources, collaboration, and common goals underpin effective social work practice. Yet, in the academic setting, hoarding of resources, competitiveness, and meeting personal over institutional goals were reported by several respondents.

Social work educators are not representative of the entire population. One can speculate that to have completed extensive undergraduate and graduate education requires some degree of competitiveness and goal orientation. Aspiration to increased economic, intellectual, and status goals is implied. We might further speculate based on the concept of the "wounded healer" (Lemire,

2007; Regher; Wilson Schaef, 1992; Maeder, 1989; Nouwen, 1979; Jung, 1954) that social workers and social work educators come to the profession with both genuine commitments to social change and some idiosyncratic universal needs for healing their own childhood wounds. All of these speculations are beyond the scope of this book and none precludes providing effective client-centered services and student-centered education. While difficult peer behaviors emerge in any setting, they seem especially problematic in departments of social work, which should model exemplary professional behaviors.

What happens between theory and practice that leads individuals to "act up" and "act out"? What happens (or doesn't happen) that produces difficult behaviors in bright, well-educated, committed colleagues? Like all professions, social work educators are vulnerable to active mental health and addictive disorders that can be identified and treated. However, in both subtle and overt ways, some adults remain unhappy, rigid, stubborn, oppositional, distant, narcissistic, passive-aggressive, controlling, or difficult. Occasionally, these behaviors reach the level of duplicity, subterfuge, and blatant intimidation and bullying. In the broader scope of development, how do adults become balanced, flexible, cooperative, and good colleagues?

A specific developmental process, identified as "the work of adulthood" (M. I. Robinson, personal communication, March 13, 2009), needs to occur. And it is, indeed, a process. The research and writing on individual development, family systems, and family of origin work is extensive and applicable (Capell, 1979; Munuchin, 1974; Satir, 1972; Satir, 1967). Parental alcoholism, abuse, or dysfunction, along with experiences related to authority and authority figures, power and control, and the many other influences on development shape "how we got to where we are." The work of adulthood includes recognizing these influences and addressing them through various options: self-awareness, therapy, self-help and support groups, personal-growth efforts, and spiritual development. Such efforts lead to a worldview that recognizes one's own fallibility, the limits of knowledge, the futility of control, and the paradoxical nature of the human experience. Inclusively, such work helps shape our worldview and results in recognizing the tentativeness of all knowledge; an openness to new and creative behaviors; and humility about our own place in the department, the university, the community, and the world.

Program Existence Is Threatened

Change or potential change in departmental status was also cited as a source of stress and a catalyst for the consideration of alternative employment. For one subject, thoughts of leaving were influenced by an administrator attempting to move the program from one city in a Midwestern state to another. During this time, she received several job offers and was tempted to relocate. In the end, she made the decision to remain in place owing to a sense of obligation to accreditation duties and family needs. The threat turned out to be hollow, but the anxiety she experienced during this time was real.

In a well-publicized case in the Northeast, one social work department was at first threatened, then phased out, and eventually terminated. As a subject noted: "It was a time of disillusionment. I ran up against bureaucratic nonsense. I interviewed elsewhere and was on the verge of moving but stayed for family reasons." The subject, whose talents were sought by many programs, eventually became employed at another social work program.

Desire for Change

Boredom. Curiosity. Adventure. The desire to try something new. Some subjects wanted to see if the grass was really greener on the other side of the fence. One veteran of nearly thirty years in social work education at the same program had a story to tell:

> I had a job offer. It was appealing in terms of a new setting. It made me rethink, and further appreciate, and realize that I could contribute more staying right where I am. In the end, I could not see further professional growth by moving. The value of considering another location was a way for me to reflect: "Am I really doing what I want to be doing?" There are parts of me I haven't yet explored, and I don't have to move to discover these.

Career Advancement

Stepping up by stepping out. One reason people consider changing jobs is because they believe they can advance professionally. Moving into a leadership position provides validation of competency, increased status, increased salary, a more substantial travel allowance, and perhaps a larger office. Consider the following quotation:

> There was a time when I believed the only way to advance was to leave. I interviewed for dean and director positions [in other states]. It was fueled by a bad administration here. In the end, I decided to remain [here] close to my parents.

Several subjects noted they had been locked into a salary structure that kept their paycheck relatively low compared to some of their more mobile colleagues. They were aware that the only way to receive a decent, more competitive salary was to move to a new setting. One subject had this to add:

> It's called salary compression. New assistant professors are offered salaries equal to what associates are making—some have been here ten years

or more. It doesn't seem fair, but it's a competitive market. I'm well aware that if I took a job somewhere else, I would boost my salary significantly. But there are other costs to pay by moving, and losses to consider, such as community contacts and family connections.

Avoidance of Impending Accreditation

Quick—how many social work educators love accreditation? That was a rhetorical question. While many subjects spoke of a sense of duty to see their programs through accreditation or reaffirmation cycles, others were quite candid in giving a less politically correct response. One veteran social work educator spoke freely:

> I know people who have timed their moves to other programs, or their retirements, to avoid getting mired in the process of accreditation. And I've seen a program's recent accreditation being highlighted as a recruitment tool. "Our program will not come up for reaffirmation for another seven years"—it's an attractive lure. I'm going to be honest here: I'm timing my retirement. I've fulfilled my obligations in the past. It's enough. I'm not going to stay on an extra two years. I have faith in my faculty. But beyond that, no program should depend upon the talents of one person to see them through a self-study.

Logical questions for a prospective candidate to ask while interviewing are: "Where is the program in the accreditation (or reaffirmation) cycle?" and "If I come on board, what will my role in the accreditation process be?"

REASONS FOR STAYING

Reasons for deciding to stay in place fall into five categories:

Security issues;
Deciding the grass isn't greener;
Life span issues;
Constitutional issues; and
Workplace issues.

Note that often these categories overlap. As will be revealed in subjects' responses, two or more categories frequently combine to influence subjects not to move.

Security Issues

Security issues include: financial security; family roots; health benefits; and attachment to community.

Financial security. When we think of security, financial security often rises to the top. Here, financial security is defined two ways: 1) having adequate sources of income to cover basic expenses (e.g., housing, food, health care, and utilities) plus a "reasonable" amount for leisure, entertainment, and savings; and 2) financial stability: having reliable, predictable sources of income now and in the future.

When considering a move, cost of living is a major financial concern. There is wide variance across our nation. It costs more to live in New York City, San Francisco, or Boston than it does in Nashville, Little Rock, or Indianapolis—considerably more. A "significant increase" in salary may seem tempting upon first blush, but after careful calculation, a move could actually result in a reduced standard of living. One subject told a story of why he decided not to move:

> I had two offers from New York, but the reality of uprooting a family and the comfort of being rooted put me off. The salaries were high, but so was the cost of living. In the end, it wasn't worth the move.

Another subject told a tale of "testing the waters" and the desire for validation. In the end, he decided he didn't want to risk financial instability.

> More than anything, I was looking for validation. I was trying to see if anybody thought I was worthy enough to come teach for him or her. And when I found out a couple of places thought I was, I thought, "Okay, that's what I needed to know; thanks for the interest." It made me feel better. Validation was nice. Becoming a [deparment] chair in '98—that's been enough of a challenge. In '90, I already had fifteen years into the state [retirement] system. Now I'm over thirty! I'm not into taking a financial risk.

Another component of moving from one location to another is the cost of relocation. In part, cost can be calculated in dollars and cents. But there are financial and emotional "hidden costs" in addition, such as hiring movers and time and energy spent planning and packing. As told by a veteran of twenty years:

> I've moved before and it's a royal pain. They gave me a moving allowance, which seemed generous at the time but it wasn't enough—about $3,000

short. And that doesn't tell the whole story—the time we spent packing, unpacking, organizing garage sales, deciding what to sell, what to keep, what to give away. It was a lot of time-consuming work. Then there was looking for a new place to live, figuring out a new community—the best schools, where to shop, etcetera, etcetera.

Family roots. Another security issue that influences mobility is the needs of both immediate and extended family. Historical roots in a given community, the desire not to uproot partners and children, and the desire to be close to aging relatives are primary considerations. The impact upon one's family is perhaps of greater concern in middle to late career stages, when social work educators are more likely to have children in school and be members of a "sandwich" generation. The following quotes speak to the decision to stay in place after considering other job offers:

I never seriously considered leaving. Family keeps you rooted. In the end, I decided to remain close to my parents. You don't have them all that long. I can wait to move.

It was wonderful to be considered, but I wanted to stay. My husband's practice is here; my family is here; we're established.

I ran up against bureaucratic nonsense; I was disillusioned. I interviewed elsewhere, and we were on the verge of moving to [another city]. I stayed because of family reasons; my wife's job was going well, and my son was doing well in school.

It appears that some subjects tolerated less than optimal working conditions—in a self-sacrificing manner—because the needs of their families came first. The following example reinforces this theme:

Over the last few years, this has not been a great place to work—faculty personalities more than anything. There were tempting offers in [two different states] but it didn't mesh with my desire to stay in the area. Family issues are paramount. My youngest child was about to graduate from college, and I was experiencing sandwich generation issues: the health of my parents, needing to work, needing to stay in the area for elder care and the children's school.

If the kids are doing well in school, your parents or in-laws need you, your spouse is happily employed (locally), what's a disgruntled social work educator to do? What if your partner and your kids don't want to move? It's a dilemma. Two subjects who wanted to move, but decided against it, said:

I thought: "Why am I doing this? I'm not having a good time. I'm spending most of my time [and energy] trying to figure out this controlling adminis- trator. I could go somewhere else." I did look around; people approached me [to take employment elsewhere], but I never applied. What kept me here was the realization that probably other places had people like that and there's no escape. In the end, I decided not to uproot my family.

There was a time I seriously considered leaving. There were major pro- grammatic changes—chaos in fact—changes in leadership—adding an MSW program. We brought in new faculty. There were environmental changes. I could have gone. I had several offers. But my daughter was in high school, I was finishing up my PhD, and I had two kids in college. I said [to myself], "I just have to ride it out."

Many wish for a life for our children that's better than the one we experi- enced. This may be at odds with personal ambition. The theme of compromise was common; family comes first. In the following example, a social work edu- cator with more than thirty years' experience at the same location tells her story:

There was a time when I was bored. I pursued many administrative posi- tions—but family comes first. My son had suffered losses. One [constant] thing in his life has been his home and his friends. As a child, I went to ten schools before middle school. I wouldn't do that to him. I wouldn't con- sider [moving] until he was out of college.

Moving has a ripple effect. More than one person's life changes. More than one person's environment, sources of support, and sources of comfort are im- pacted. It's an enormous decision with potentially long-lasting consequences. One final quote pertaining to family needs speaks to these notions:

I had an opportunity to become a dean in [a Midwestern state], but there were no domestic partnership benefits, and I didn't want to move our kids. The kids were elementary-school aged. We would be giving up more than we were getting. [When considering moving] you make a decision for lots of people when you have a family.

Health benefits. Prediction and control of physical and mental health ser- vices are important elements of security, perhaps more so as we enter the later stages of life. In part, security is derived from relationships, created and sus- tained over time, between health care providers and consumers. Close prox- imity to support systems increases in value as we journey further along our life span.

Most subjects are in the later stages of their careers. Issues of retirement and health care are more likely to be on the front burner. With respect for the privacy of my subjects, I offer no direct quotes under the category of health benefits. However, it is worthy of mention that no fewer than a half dozen subjects turned down job offers owing to serious personal medical conditions. They have "faced the devil." The desire to maintain relationships with trusted mental and physical health care providers, coupled by a reluctance to establish new relationships in a new setting, were viewed as a deterrent to relocation.

Attachment to community. Geography is important. Do you prefer urban or rural; mountains, plains, or rolling hills; the brutal cold of the Upper Midwest in January or the stifling humidity of the Deep South in July; big city or small town? And how about quality of life issues such as cultural diversity, "acceptable" amounts of smog and pollution, and the view of the landscape during the ride into work? How important is commute time?

Without betraying identities, many subjects, all of whom lived in different locations throughout the United States, claimed their geographic location was the best in the country, and would not consider relocation because nowhere else could be better. And perhaps they are all correct—on an individual basis.

Having lived in Alaska for twelve years, I know what it's like to see spectacular scenery every day. I also know what it's like to wait until past 10:00 a.m. for the sun to rise during six weeks of the year. There are tradeoffs everywhere. One person's paradise will court depression for another. Geographic areas offering attractions for some are annoyances for others. Some desire close proximity to arts and entertainment found in a large metropolitan area. Others prefer the peace and quiet of a life in the country.

Social work educators consider community service to be an essential component of their lifestyle, if not an important element of their job description. Whether by habit or design, subjects spoke of being rooted to community comfort and community obligations. They had developed ties. One subject commented:

> I've never seriously considered leaving because I knew we were locked in geographically. I've turned down offers because of professional commitments and community projects. And I'm tired of moving. Even though the children are grown, I want a home; it's that simple.

"It's that simple." Social work educators become involved in their communities. They have a sense of obligation and a desire to contribute. It feels good. It makes a difference. And for some, the longer the relationship, the more difficult it becomes to "start all over somewhere else."

Deciding the Grass Isn't Greener

After seriously considering alternatives, why did subjects decide to stay? How did they determine that the grass wasn't greener elsewhere? Some of the subjects expressed the following:

The status quo is just fine;

Difficult people are everywhere;

A new job isn't tempting;

It's all about goodness of fit;

Religious auspice;

Undesirable location; and

"Also ran" (close, but no cigar).

The status quo is just fine.

Yes, there have been many offers, but they just weren't attractive enough; they didn't offer anything different from what I had already done. If it's not going to expand my horizons, or offer me new challenges, there's no point in moving on. I'm at the tail end of my career; there really isn't much that would attract me. I'll probably just stay here until I retire.

There are other opportunities out there, but I like where I am [the area, the job] and want stability for my family. Job stability will help my family be stable. I don't want to start over proving myself [with tenure and promotion] for somebody. I get unsolicited offers frequently, but I've never even accepted an invitation to visit.

If it feels like home, if the environment allows you to be yourself—to optimize your potential, if you feel supported by the academic community, why look elsewhere? If there isn't a burning desire for a new adventure, why take the risk? Why expend the time and energy on a job search? As one subject reflected: "Sure, there are periods of disillusionment, but in general things are so good. I'm happy where I am. I've found the right place. It's a good feeling to find a place that fits."

For subjects who considered offers to return to practice (especially those in non-administrative roles), having summers off and a nice break in the spring and December/January, the choice to remain in academia was easy.

Difficult people are everywhere. As we have seen above under "Distaste for Administrators" and "Departmental Discord," there is no shortage of difficult people in the world. Of course, none of the participants in *this* study fall into this category, but they had encountered as least one such person in the

workplace. They are *everywhere*. The lesson? If you move from one job to another expecting an environment free of difficult people, you are in for a surprise.

Several subjects spoke of going on "fishing expeditions" (responding to a job announcement), looking for validation to see if they were marketable beyond their own institution. Often this was stimulated by a stressful relationship with a difficult colleague or controlling administrators. But even with offers, there came realizations. For example:

> What kept me here was the realization that other places had difficult people too. It may take a couple of years to get a lay of the land, but eventually you see who your potential allies are. Who are the people who look like allies [initially], then later stab you in the back? And who are the people who are genuinely helpful, who really care?

As one subject quipped: "There are no asshole-free zones." In that sense, there is no escape. Fortunately, there are decent social work educators throughout the country. They are the ones who truly live the values and ethics of our profession daily. They are the ones who believe in collaboration with their colleagues. They are genuine in their desire to unselfishly deliver the highest quality of social work education. And they, too, are everywhere. There is no escape.

A new job isn't tempting. One subject was offered an attractive position in a foreign country that initially seemed ideal; a beautiful location and a job description "that fit me to a T. The job didn't pan out (the position was cancelled), and it would have meant going from a full professor to an associate."

Other subjects turned down opportunities to move "up" to a dean position. One subject was thinking about retirement in the next five years and unwilling to move to a new geographic location. Perhaps the opportunity would have been more attractive at an earlier stage of professional (and life span) development.

Another subject rejected an offer because she wasn't interested in the duties of a dean. Here's her story:

> After tenure, around the time of my first sabbatical, I was approached to become a dean in [another location]. I was flattered, but I didn't pursue it. I've been asked to become a dean since then. I decided to stay because I had worked closely with the dean [here] and saw the pressures. I didn't want that for myself—all the fund-raising, the public relations, and personnel issues. There was nothing terribly wrong with what I was doing. The kids were doing well [and are] where we are. I'm happy not to be looking.

Another factor to consider, which will be explored more fully in the next chapter, "The Dream Offer," is the consideration of a significant pay increase that often accompanies a job with a higher status. Perhaps it would not be politically correct for a social work educator to voice a desire for a high salary. Nevertheless, subjects uniformly claim to value intrinsic rewards of their life's work well above monetary compensation. One subject, teaching in a small program, commented:

> There have been job offers at larger universities with higher salaries, literally three times higher at one place. It's never been a consideration because *context* has always been more important than salary. I would only change for challenges and opportunities that push me to a different level than I have experienced.

It's all about goodness of fit. Who doesn't want to be wanted? No matter how satisfied social work educators were with their current employment, they *all* acknowledged feeling flattered while being courted by another social work program. But as subjects were quick to observe, an offer is less attractive if it is not consistent with professional desires. One might hypothesize that the subjects of this study, with an average span of more than a quarter century of work experience, have attained a level of professional sophistication and emotional maturity (by-products of human growth and development) and are better able to select a position that fits their needs, more so than they were at the beginning of their careers. Simply put: they now have a better idea of what they want in life. They have developed discriminatory powers.

One subject was offered a position teaching in an MSW program, which would have been a departure from his career as a BSW educator. With BSW social work education programs outnumbering MSW programs by greater than two to one, 463 versus 191 (CSWE, 2007), surely such a transition would be a move to a higher level, like being brought up from the minor leagues to the majors, perhaps. Here's his story:

> A grad program approached me two years ago. They presented it as much more prestigious to teach graduate versus undergraduate. But I prefer undergraduate students, who are somewhat unsure of themselves, questioning their abilities, their deservedness. Seeing them develop, gain self-confidence, grow into professionals is amazing. Grad students come in with the confidence of having completed college, with more professional experience. But undergrad teaching is more rewarding; the changes are more dramatic.

Another change considered, but ultimately rejected, was moving from a small- (two to six faculty) or medium- (seven to fourteen faculty) size program to a large program housed at a Research I institution. One subject decided a campus with more than thirty thousand students, the accompanying bureau-cracy, and fourteen full professors in the social work program would be too radical a shift. Another subject also turned down offers from institutions that were too large for her taste. In the end, she disdained large cohorts of students, much preferring smaller classes. A third subject voiced a strong opinion about the downside of working at a research-intensive university. For her it was a mat-ter of living a saner life:

> Look at the quality of life at R-I institutions: multiple marriages, estrange-ment from children, poor social skills, no friendships because they're afraid to talk to each other in case someone will steal their ideas. I've had two different offers, but I'm going to live out my life here at . . .

One subject, an Academic Nomad, left a "high-powered" university, with over a thousand social work majors. He noted:

> It was not a "feel good" environment. I would never get full professor be-cause I didn't have the capacity or the interest to bring in million-dollar grants—and if you didn't, you were nobody. Since then, I've become sav-vier, more selective.

Religious auspice. Approximately one-third of all accredited social work education programs operate under religious auspices (Council on Social Work Education, 2007). The degree to which social work programs are influenced by religious doctrine—from faculty qualifications (screen at hiring) to curriculum content—varies from one program to another. For social work educators who were courted by a religion-affiliated institution, goodness of fit was an issue. A personal aside: My first academic appointment was at a small Catholic col-lege, St. Catherine in the city of St. Paul, Minnesota. The social work program at St. Catherine was a joint effort with the University of St. Thomas, just over a mile down the road. Upon hearing of my new appointment, a former classmate noted: "That's a lot of saints for a nice Jewish boy like you." She was right. I never acclimated to the crucifixes mounted on every classroom wall. While I was never asked my view on abortion during the hiring process, I heard from department members that they had been queried—presumably with their an-swer influencing the decision to be hired.

One subject, who turned down an offer from a religion-affiliated institution, raised the following concern:

> I didn't know about Southern Baptist Convention church policy and struc-ture; I could play innocent. I remember the requirement: "All faculty must be Christian." I remember saying to the president: "So if Jesus came you wouldn't hire him?" Last time I checked, he was a Jew.

Undesirable location. Location, location, location. We all have prefer-ences. Even if we work well beyond forty hours per week, we still spend a con-siderable amount of time in our non-work environments. Professional opportu-nities might be tempting, pay might be attractive, and notions of working with interesting colleagues might be alluring, but if the geographic location and qual-ity of life in a given community doesn't seem right, it's likely a red flag. For one person, being banished into a perpetual orbit around Pluto might be preferable to living in Dubuque, Iowa. Another person might *need* to live in a big city on the East Coast to feel alive. For some, living in close proximity to relatives (e.g., aging parents) may trump even the most lucrative job offer. Conversely, hav-ing a "buffer zone" from "difficult" relatives may be a reason not to live in close proximity. One subject told a tale of a community that did not fit his needs well:

> I wish I had known how parochial, how provincial the whole area was. It's uniquely out of sync with the rest of the country. If I'd known, I would never have taken the job. It's an isolated area of the country. It's an ingrown blue-collar community, anti-intellectual, steel and auto are huge—no college needed. It's a Balkanized society religiously and racially. There's a lack of culture—just drinking and eating. You can depend upon the same people to show up at the same bar every day.

"Also ran" (close, but no cigar). Today's job market for social work educa-tors is stacked in favor of job applicants; the demand far exceeds the supply. With program expansion, a wave of faculty retiring or approaching retirement, a steady increase in new BSW programs, and a dramatic increase in MSW pro-grams (Zeiger et al., 2005), the need for doctorate-trained faculty has never been greater. It's true now, and likely to be true for the next ten years or more.

But the subjects of this study have been around the block a few times and have memories of a more competitive job market in the 1970s and 1980s. Earlier in their careers, four subjects recalled how they seriously considered moving to another program in a new location. All had advanced to the "short list" and would have accepted the position had the offer materialized. Ultimately, they were not selected. Their reactions ranged from being happy they didn't make "the move" to mourning a lost opportunity.

Life Span Issues

A person's developmental stage has a major influence upon his or her de-sire to stay in place or relocate. Life span issues are divided into three parts:

Not wanting to physically move;
Not wanting to "start over" academically; and
Poor timing.

Not wanting to physically move. Perhaps the spirit for adventure wanes as we enter our forties, fifties, sixties, and beyond. Perhaps it is the physical labor, the disorientation of where "home" is, and the stress of decision making (e.g., What do I keep? What do I give away? What do I sell?). Sliced any way, moving is a major life event, perhaps more so as we progress through our life span. Mentally and physically, moving is a daunting task. One subject in the later stage of her career related the following tale:

> I'm done. It would take a major event to get me to relocate. I just don't see it. I've moved three times during my career and I have to say the thrill, the excitement is gone. It's no longer a matter of having the kids at home; they've been launched; they're out of the house. I just don't want to go through it again—the idea of all that packing! Having to sell the house, find a place to live, buy another one—it's more stress than I need. It's a ton of work, and I'm happy here.

Not wanting to "start over" academically. By and large, subjects tended to downplay any stress involved in the process of going up for tenure and promotion. But when asked to describe a time when they seriously considered leaving their job, and ultimately decided to stay in place, subjects said they had not wanted to relive the process of tenure and promotion. They were not eager to acclimate to a different academic milieu. The following quotes speak to this issue:

> There were other opportunities. I get unsolicited offers frequently—but I've never accepted an invitation to visit. I like where I am—the area, the job, and I want stability for my family. Job stability will help me be [personally] stable. I don't want to start over proving myself for somebody.

> It occurred to me when I was putting together my promotion and tenure materials: "This is a lot of stress"—not knowing the outcome—knowing that others had been turned down for petty reasons. I didn't seriously consider leaving. For one thing, my family keeps me rooted. But starting over, going through tenure and promotion again—no thanks!

It is important to reiterate that most subjects deciding whether to make a move were in the later stages of their careers. Especially for those who had spent the majority of their careers at one program, attachments would be difficult to sever. Considering a move was not on the menu for the following respondent, who had spent over thirty years at the same program:

> I don't think so. I'll be sixty next year. I'm positioning myself to take early retirement at age sixty-two. With everything it would take to dislodge, I

> really don't think it would be worth it. It means learning a whole new sys-
> tem. I would miss my colleagues. *A decade ago I might have had a different*
> *answer.* [Italics added.]

Poor timing. Speaking of life span development, timing is everything. For
example, a social work education program courted me shortly before I began a
sabbatical. I didn't want to sacrifice my sabbatical, plus I had a contractual obligation to stay another year *after* my one-year leave. Ah, dreams of what could
have been had the timing only been different.

An institution that wanted her to help create a new MSW program approached one subject. She interviewed, liked the program, but was knee-deep
working on her dissertation, and her dissertation was locally based. Moreover,
her husband and daughter didn't want to move. The timing was poor.

Another subject lived through what she described as "chaotic changes"
in departmental leadership, when an MSW program was added to her existing
BSW program. She had offers elsewhere, but family loyalty prevailed.

> I just had to ride it out. I was finishing up my PhD and had two kids in col-
> lege. I brought in new faculty; there were environmental changes; I could
> have gone. I had several offers, but I also had a daughter in high school.

Family needs and poor timing were major factors.

Constitutional Issues

Constitutional issues refer to a mind-set—one's worldview of work. Here,
the following three related elements are discussed:

loyalty;
accreditation obligations; and
determination to outlast a tyrant.

Loyalty.
> I have a sense of loyalty to the program.The [job] market is hot now, but
> I'm happy where I am. I've finally found the right place. It's a good feeling
> to find a place that fits.

Institutional and departmental loyalty sustain social work educators and
effectively deter them from seeking employment elsewhere. Further, especially
true for subjects who have spent the majority of their careers at one institution, their program may become an integral component of their identity. As one
subject poised for retirement after more than three decades at the same rural
program noted: "I have never given serious consideration to leaving because

people see me here." Another veteran of more than thirty years at the same social work program noted: "Leaving [this program] would be like wrenching a part of me. Loyalty to my academic family grows with each passing year."

Another dimension of loyalty is feeling a sense of obligation to students. One subject told a tale of tolerating a "difficult" administrator out of her concern for student learning needs:

> I've had some offers recently, but I chose not to abandon commitments to the students. The dean wanted to micromanage, control the budget, and go against CSWE standards. The dean decided to appoint someone to [a leadership position]. The decision was made, but I didn't find out until three months later. The students protested. I stay for the students.

Granted, there may be another side to the above story, but it illustrates faculty obligation and loyalty to students.

Workplace Issues

Accreditation obligations. As previously addressed, surviving CSWE accreditation and reaffirmation is an arduous task. Subjects spoke of not wanting to abandon their programs during their "hour of need." Their sense of obligation, and perhaps a consideration of courtesy and respect for their colleagues, influenced them *not* to leave during preparation of documents and/or a site visit. There is also a sense of pride and ownership that comes through. Here's a story from a seasoned veteran, who happens to be an experienced CSWE accreditation site visitor:

> There were several openings for deanships that occurred, and I was on short lists—but I felt an obligation to stay through [our] reaffirmation. I felt dedication to our program. The longer you're here, the more you know the university. I'm an integral part of decision making at different levels. You'd have to start from scratch at a different institution.

Determination to outlast a tyrant. As previously stated, "the average shelf life of a dean or director is about five years, and then they move on." If true, a social work educator might grin and bear a difficult administrator for about five years and hope for an improvement in the future. Such was the determination of one subject who vowed to "outlast a tyrant leader, and rebuild the BSW program." She was determined to rebuild what the administrator had "destroyed." The BSW program had had an outstanding reputation on campus and in the community. Eventually the "tyrant" left. Program integrity was restored, and the subject has remained—with no regrets.

Positive relationships with peers. It's been said before: social work is all about relationships. In social work education, collegial relationships are paramount. What's the most difficult aspect of leaving a job? Many would say it's the people—no longer being able to work with their colleagues, some of whom they have held close working relationship with for ten, twenty, even thirty years or more.

The Dream Offer

"Today, under what circumstances (if any), would you consider taking an academic appointment at another institution? If you were offered a 25 percent salary increase, your choice of the nicest geographic location, generous health care benefits, full professorship, tenure, and moving expenses—would you take it?"

How did well-seasoned social work educators respond to this idyllic scenario? For some, the notion of relocating posed too great a risk. One veteran of three decades at a private college took a long pause before responding. Her countenance conveyed serious contemplation. In the end, she replied: "That's a great question. I don't know. I find it very satisfying to do what I'm doing here. And maybe it's a risk I don't want to take. There are enough challenges here."

It may not be Utopia, but quantities are known. People become settled. Respondents became comfortable, accustomed to their communities, circle of friends, and sources of support. They became inured to their lifestyle and comfortable in their homes with the passage of time (Brown, 1967; Matier, 1985).

A common refrain among subjects was that they knew they had a good thing. Why choose to relocate? They knew the employment situations of their peers in other programs in other parts of the nation and were convinced, like the residents of Lake Wobegon, that they were "above average."

Most subjects were content to stay in place, and *nothing* could tempt them to move. Others were more adventurous. Some were ready to leave at the drop of a hat. Others required specific conditions to be met before they considered packing their bags. The importance of family, health care, geographic location, and finances were mentioned frequently. This chapter will be divided into the following five sections:

Reluctance to relocate;
Motivations to move;
Family first;
Money matters; and
Requisite requirements.

110

RELUCTANCE TO RELOCATE

No Interest

"Not even if the White House called."

There needs to be a damn good reason to pack one's belongings and leave community resources, friends, and colleagues behind. Compelling reasons must exist in order to abandon comforts and disrupt momentum. One subject, with three and a half decades' longevity at the same small (four-person faculty) social work department articulated his concern about sacrificing retirement benefits if he were to relocate:

> I wouldn't take it [the Dream Offer]. We're not at the top of the list for a whole lot of things, but we do have a good retirement program, so if you stick with it, you do pretty well retirement-wise. The longer I stay, the better my retirement will be. I don't want to mix and mingle different retirement systems. I'll be close to full salary at retirement. They reward you for your longevity. I'll be able to retire at sixty-one years of age.

Retirement is related to the welfare and financial security of self and family. Other concerns related to reluctance to relocate commonly voiced were less personal and related to collegial relationships. Indeed, positive collegiality appears to trump salary as an incentive to stay in place (Fogg, 2006; Harvard Graduate School of Education, 2006). Importantly, loyalty, commitment, and dedication to the success and vitality of one's social work program were commonly cited as reasons for remaining in the same institution of higher learning for an extended period. In fact, a sense of commitment was *so* strong, the thought of relocating had never occurred. When asked if she would be tempted by the Dream Offer, one veteran of over twenty years currently teaching at a newly launched social work program in a private college remarked:

> I don't want to relocate, but I didn't expect to make the moves I did. It would have to be a good offer, but I'm not interested now, at least until the program is up and running. It would take a lot to entice me away at this point.

Another subject with over twenty years' experience at a private college commented on why she wouldn't be tempted: "I like what I'm doing and I know it's not like that everywhere. I have a lot of friends [social work educators] in a lot of other places and they tell me what it's like."

Many subjects sincerely believed they had it better than their colleagues in other programs. Perhaps it's a form of rationalization, especially for those with longevity at one location. Or perhaps goodness of fit is unique to each subject. Paradise may be in the eye of the beholder.

Another common theme, especially among those subjects who had spent the majority of their careers in one location, was not wishing to "begin again." A veteran of over thirty years in a social work program located in the South noted:

> I'm a tenured full professor. I make a damn good salary. I'm in a great place. I can't even imagine . . . The thought of beginning a new job where I'd have to learn all the politics and ins and outs is absolutely overwhelming to me. I can't answer [the Dream Offer question] rationally. You'd have to *double* my salary, give me a teaching load of one course per semester, and put me up in nice digs. I have absolutely no desire to leave.

Or as another subject with over a quarter century of experience stated: "I know when I've got it good and I've got it good. It's not easy starting over." It all boils down to "Is it worth it?" It may not be worth the time and energy to physically move, and mentally shift gears. Some subjects were reluctant to move because they truly believed they were currently *in* a dream job. Some believed the losses suffered from a move would be too great. In the words of one subject with over thirty-five years of experience:

> It would have to be something really exceptional—like Hawaii. I'd have to *give up* [italics added for emphasis] all my professional involvements, my political connections. I'd have to become a super-bureaucrat [move into higher administration]. I don't think that's going to happen. I'm content to stay where I am; it's a great life."

Life Span Issues

It became clear over the course of listening to my subjects' stories that answers to the Dream Offer question were greatly influenced by respondents' life stage. Here are some examples of thoughts voiced by my colleagues who were nearing retirement. First, from a veteran of thirty years:

> At this point in time, we [my husband and I] feel so grateful for the positions we have, and the opportunities we have to do wonderful things. To have a wonderful community is food for us; it's a good fit. I've never been motivated by money and academic rank. I appreciate this interview because it forces me into a reflective mode. I appreciate things more.

Another subject, with nearly thirty years of experience and nearing retirement, commented:

I wouldn't move. I'm building up a significant pension. It wouldn't be worth it. I'm happy where I am. My health's not so good; I don't have the energy to move. Ten years ago, yes, as long as it would have been in the same geographic region. I would have switched in a millisecond ten years ago.

Ah, ten years ago . . .

Answers to the Dream Offer question appeared to be influenced by life stage. And so, about a third of the way through conducting these interviews, I added the probing question: "Ten years ago, how would you have responded?"

For one subject, now an endowed chair and a dean, ten years ago the answer to the Dream Offer question would have been an unqualified yes. Now, with a sizable bonus if he remains another two years, he can't imagine a better offer and has "no desire to launch another career."

After a thoughtful pause, weighing the pros and cons, another seasoned veteran, with three and a half decades of experience, made the following remark:

A decade ago, I might have had a different answer. But *at this stage of my life* [italics added for emphasis] I don't think so. I'll be sixty in February. I'm positioning myself to take early retirement at age sixty-two. With everything it would take to dislodge, I really don't think it would be worth it. It would mean learning a whole new system. I would miss my colleagues.

Friends, colleagues, and family: they are familiar refrains in the concert of life. For many, their importance grows stronger as individuals progress through their life spans. Friends, colleagues, and family are the glue that holds people together. Family needs trump personal ambition. The following dialogue places an exclamation point on the importance of family:

"A move would mean I, my partner, and our parents would all have to move. It's a nice fit here. I would lose my 'buds'; you can't put a price on that."

"Does that become more of an issue as you progress through your life span?"

"Yes. People inevitably leave, but there's still a connection and grounding. Any move would have to be with tenure and full professorship. Even then, it would be difficult."

An Academic Nomad with well over thirty years' experience commented on being *tired* of moving: "It is highly unlikely I would go anywhere else. I'm three years from retirement. I just bought a cabin. I don't expect to go anywhere. I'm done."

Perhaps, even for those with a track record of four, five, or six diverse locations, respondents have come to a point in life where they just want to settle down. With a good retirement plan, established relationships with trusted health care providers, nearness of family and friends, and a special community and home, many believed they were already living the dream.

A final thought on the reluctance to move comes from a veteran of over thirty years: "Ten years ago, yes, but now I'm living in a 'feet-first house'; they'll have to carry me out. I've got a great environment."

MOTIVATIONS TO MOVE

Not everyone responded to the Dream Offer with reluctance. Many eyes widened in response to this question. Motivations to move are divided into three categories: intolerable working conditions; attraction to the Dream Offer; and the opportunity to become a dean or director.

Intolerable Working Conditions

The importance of collegial relationships has been highlighted in chapters 3, 4, and 8. It is safe to say that the quality of relationships with one's workmates has a major influence upon job satisfaction. One subject from a small social work department noted that if office dynamics became oppressive, he would give serious consideration to moving elsewhere.

On a different level, administrative *mishagas* ["craziness"] can lead to thoughts of relocation. One subject at a private college reflected upon a time when fundamentalist religion had a heavy influence over the college, noting: "It was a good time to retire; the changes were difficult to tolerate." Another subject, with over twenty years of experience, noted that if her administration ever became oppressive, like so many she had heard about [the ones *below* average], she would seriously consider moving on.

"With the Dream Offer Package, I Wouldn't Have to Think Twice."

Seemingly ready to leave at the drop of a hat, an Academic Nomad pondered the question, then remarked: "I've been living my life this way [frequent moves] so long, I'd be afraid not to go. I wouldn't have to understand why."

The reader may be thinking: "I'll bet those who were tempted by the Dream Offer are likely to have *less* years of social work education experience." Not so. Here, for illustrative purposes, I will utilize quantitative data. The average number of years taught by the eight subjects who voiced a strong interest in the Dream Offer was 24.2, about the same as the average of all sixty-six subjects (see statistics on page 3).

Faces beamed in response to the pretend offer. Typical responses included: "Sure, are you kidding?"; "I'd *definitely* be tempted"; and "How long would it take me to pack and call the moving company?"

Coincidentally, one Academic Nomad had recently accepted an offer that included all the incentives listed in the Dream Offer, noting: "My new job has it all, everything you mentioned. I can't complain."

If Offered a Position as Dean

A few subjects reported they would be seriously tempted if they were offered a postion as dean. But for one subject, this was little more than a hypothetical construct. He noted: "It's [the Dream Offer] not going to happen. A dean position on the water would do it, but I would never be selected; I have too big a mouth."

FAMILY FIRST

Many subjects commented that moving was a family decision. Obviously, when a professor moves from one program to another, many lives are affected. Aside from the impact on colleagues and students, a spouse or partner must also move and change jobs. School-age children often leave their friends and familiar surroundings. Weekly dinners with friends or relatives may occur only once or twice a year.

Subjects spoke of the need for securing employment opportunities for their mates and consideration of their children's needs as a requirement for a *family* move. The following quotation illustrates this point:

> The only way I'd take a job is if there was a good job in the area for my wife. We tried a one-year commuter relationship with my wife in [another state]; it was very tough. Now, I would not consider a move until my youngest daughter finishes high school, and that's three years from now.

It is important to note that sometimes social work educators relocate not because of a need to further or change their own career path, but rather to accommodate the needs of other family members. One subject noted, "If my wife needed to move to [another state] to take care of her mom, I'd go along." Another subject commented that she would be willing to relocate ". . . if my husband was miserable at his job and needed to move." When considering a move, family often comes first.

MONEY MATTERS

If asked to create a hierarchy of needs for job satisfaction, where would social workers in this study place a highly competitive salary? Would their response be influenced by political correctness (i.e., "I'm influenced more by helping others than by having money in the bank.")? Perhaps. Whenever the subject of money arose, subjects uniformly responded that an increase in pay was relatively unimportant. Salary was not the main force of attraction. A quote from a subject in a southern university reads as follows:

> I'd be real tempted [by the Dream Offer], but for me it's always been about more than the money. More important is: Where can I make the biggest difference? Where can I make an impact? Life would feel boring—real boring if I couldn't do that—no matter how much I was being paid.

The need to be challenged, to be able to spread one's creative wings, to make a valuable contribution to the profession of social work education, and to be in an environment that fosters professional growth—these were stronger factors than salary and fringe benefits. In fact, one subject with more than a quarter century of social work education experience noted that she would consider relocation if the job were stimulating, even if it resulted in a drop in income:

> Yes, I could be tempted by something that is beyond where I am now professionally. I would take a *de*crease in salary if it led me to something new—something more challenging. My family has moved on, and I now have the freedom to think this way.

Apparently, a 25 percent increase in salary was not enough to tempt some subjects. When I designed the interview question, I reasoned a leap from $60,000 to $75,000 (or $80,000 to $100,000) would be enough to lure some folks. Not necessarily. A "huge" increase? Maybe. How much would be enough? Subjects were not specific. But clearly, more than a 25 percent increase would be required. And the timing would have to be right. One subject with twenty-eight years' experience commented:

> I'd still consider doing something else—but not for 25 percent more. Timing is not right for movement right now. I have a child: he's happy in junior high. Five years from now it's a possibility, but it must be a good fit, a significant role: the school *really* wanting me and me really wanting the school. Twenty-five percent would be a bare minimum.

Even if a new employer picks up the cost of relocation, there are potential hidden costs of making a geographic move (Peterson, 2006; Wilson, 2000), some with, some without a dollar amount. As one subject with over twenty years of experience noted:

> There's more than the check you cut to the movers. There's the stress of packing, deciding what to keep, what to give away, and an anxious assessment of material possessions. What do I really need? Why have I kept these clothes so long? And when I arrive, in addition to new job acculturation, there's adapting to a new community—finding resources, setting up utilities, learning where to shop, changing my wardrobe, learning new traffic patterns, the best restaurants, and where to have fun. All the while, you're living out of boxes for weeks or months. It's not my idea of a good time. It all gives me pause when I consider a move.

REQUISITE REQUIREMENTS

Some subjects were willing to accept the Dream Offer, but only if one or more critical conditions were satisfied: geographic location and goodness of fit.

Geography

There was an impressive range of geographic preferences expressed. One subject was open to the possibility of moving to picturesque parts of North Carolina or New England—a sharp contrast to her current "ugly" place of residence in the South. For another subject, a warm climate was a must. Other preferences included Memphis, Tennessee; Washington, D.C.; California, "close to the ocean"; and "somewhere in the mountains."

One respondent with seventeen years of social work education experience gave an immediate and strong response: "Location? It would have to be New York City. I've never been satisfied with a small town." I probed a little further, asking: "What is it about New York City that provides such a strong attraction?" She responded:

> The energy in New York City—you can plug into the intensity 24/7. It's the humanity—riding the subway with thousands of people. It's an emotional thing; I never feel alone.

For others, New York City would feel claustrophobic and intimidating. Utopia has multiple locations.

Geographic preference involves more than a desire to live close to the mountains or the water, or a fondness for a particular region of the country. Geographic preference is strongly influenced by a desire to be near family members. For some, being "within a day's drive of my parents" was a must. For one subject, being "within an hour's drive" of her grandchildren was a non-negotiable requirement.

Finally, an issue that becomes stronger as we progress through the life span, a requirement mentioned by several subjects was the need to be in close proximity to high-quality health care, either for themselves or their loved ones.

Goodness of Fit

As stated in chapters 3 and 4, the best fit occurs when social work educators are in an academic environment that allows for opportunities to blossom professionally. True goodness of fit is mutually beneficial because positive professional development enhances the quality of social work education programs. The positive chain of events continues: quality programs are more likely to produce high-quality social work practitioners.

For many, goodness of fit was the trump card:

> A good salary is nice. A good health care plan would certainly help. And a nice location, like you said. But none of those would be enough if there weren't a mutual admiration society. You know, I'd really want to be there if their desire to have me was equally strong. It's my ego, I guess; I need to feel I'm needed.

Goodness of fit was also articulated as the need to be challenged professionally. As one subject with nearly twenty years of experience remarked:

> I wouldn't want to continue doing the same old things. I'd have to know I could make a real difference. A new job would have to stimulate my creative juices, to allow me to contribute in new and different ways—ways I never knew possible. I'd love to take a program in a new and exciting direction. I see life—true living—as an adventure—sailing into uncharted waters. That would be exciting!

What Have You Done for Me Lately? The Quest for Professional Resources

Social work educators who participated in this study were asked to describe what tools and supports their social work programs provide to ensure their professional success. Respondents were also asked what more their programs could provide to assist them in their professional development. Responses cover a wide range of topics, from health care benefits to grant-writing support, and from "start-up" funds to guaranteed sabbatical leave. Before exploring these items, however, a discussion of the relative nature of institutional resources is in order.

Depending upon an institution's financial health, history, and cultural norms, the identical level of resources (structural and financial) for professional development may appear generous by one person's standards, and parsimonious by another's. For example, moving expenses for new faculty at a state-funded college on the East Coast are currently (a non-negotiable) $1,500, which is seen by the institution as a significant improvement over the previous allowance of $0. Contrast this with another public institution on the West Coast, where a recently transplanted faculty member was able to negotiate "basically unlimited" moving expenses. In fact: "They basically paid for everything—even the packing and the unpacking! They really wanted me and I guess they saw it as the cost of doing business. I was able to negotiate a sweet deal."

Standards vary. Some study participants expressed deep appreciation for the "little" they received, while others expressed a sense of entitlement for perks others would deem "very generous."

Geographic proximity to conference locations may impact travel expenses for professional meetings. For example, social work educators from Alaska, Hawaii, or Guam are more likely to pay a premium for transportation to the contiguous U.S. states. In contrast, social work educators residing in the eastern half of the United States are less likely to incur high transportation costs, and are more likely to have alternative means of transportation, such as trains or autos, available to them.

Recently matriculated PhDs may not realize salaries, benefits, and resources for professional development are negotiable items. As one subject stated:

> After years in graduate school—living off graduate assistantships and student loans—I was thrilled to be offered a real salary with retirement benefits. It was all too good to be true. "You mean you're going to *pay* me to do what I love?" It never *occurred* to me that I could negotiate a better deal. I was worried that if I asked for more, I'd lose the job. Today things are different. I have a little more savvy. I understand the job market. I hold the advantage. I know there are plenty of options and they need me just as much as I need them—maybe even more.

Many new faculty must learn how to access resources. One subject spoke of a "steep learning curve" in obtaining financial support:

> I admit I was naïve at first. I began to see that some people had "inside information." Where did they get it? It was a mystery for a long time. I had to develop savvy in obtaining funds. It was a maze. It seemed like not all my colleagues were willing to share information—after all, I would become their competitor. So much for social work collaboration! Slowly, I learned that there's money available—but you needed to know who to approach, how to communicate effectively, and, in short, how to work the system. Let's face it; some people know how to shake the money tree better than others.

One might expect institutional size to be correlated with the amount of money available for professional development. To an extent, this is true. For example, social work colleagues from research-intensive institutions were more likely to speak of "start-up packages" as a perk for new faculty. However, some subjects from smaller programs reported doing quite well in terms of opportunities and support for professional development. The following quote comes from a member of a two-person social work department, within an institution of about a thousand students:

> For a school and a program our size, we do extremely well. An endowment [fund] gives every faculty $600 per year for travel and/or professional membership. They also pay for NASW and BPD dues and attendance at BPD conferences. They are generous with time off to attend professional meetings. They funded my doctoral work; I was gone for a year and received three-quarters salary. We have a good library budget for social work holdings. We have money for accreditation and CSWE membership. More money is always good to have, but we feel like we are pretty lucky compared to other schools.

RELATIVE RESOURCES

Six topics, which may be viewed on a continuum, will be discussed briefly:

Autonomy (good vs. poor);
Travel funds (generous vs. inadequate);
Physical space (nice offices and classrooms vs. inadequate ones);
Scholarship support (good vs. poor);
Professional development support (adequate vs. inadequate); and
Quality and number of support staff (adequate vs. inadequate).

Autonomy

Mostly, subjects spoke positively about their level of autonomy as academicians. They described autonomy and "academic freedom" as built-in features of teaching in an institution of higher learning. One subject, a social work administrator with a résumé of nearly thirty years in social work education, noted:

We have "responsibility-centered management." I have my own budget. The money we make we keep. We have lots of decision-making power. [We are] in charge of our own destiny, or own autonomy. I didn't know how important it would be. I love the autonomy. It makes it easier for the administration, too.

Another subject, with nearly twenty years' experience at one public institution, also praised her level of autonomy:

We have shared-governance heaven. The administration comes to the faculty *before* decisions are made. I have a full-time assistant and a tech person for the doctoral program. We have a great deal of autonomy. The dean leaves us alone 99 percent of the time.

Subjects also lauded their ability to craft their own syllabi, and to infuse their areas of expertise and experiences into course content with little or no micromanagement from administration.

All comments regarding autonomy were not positive. Subjects spoke of two "autonomy deficits" worthy of mention. The first item mentioned was lack of budget control, often accompanied by unpredictable monetary cuts, chronic threat of cuts, and "fear-producing" exercises. One subject noted: "There's this game they play: show us what you would do with 15 percent less. It's never happened, but it's not fun." The second item mentioned was referred to as "the inability to penetrate the insulation of problematic faculty." It was noted: "Union protection and tenure make it extremely difficult to get rid of deadwood. I wish there was a way we could have more control."

Travel Funds

The ability to attend workshops; to exchange information with colleagues face-to-face; to stimulate new ideas about teaching, research, and service; to present research findings in a public forum; and to build camaraderie and create a shared sense of purpose are some of the positive by-products of attending conferences. Attending social work conferences, be they regional, national, or international venues, is a key element in the professional development of social work educators.

However, within the profession of social work education, the playing field is far from level in terms of being able to attend conferences. Some institutions "expect" faculty to cover at least some of the expense. And, as one subject from a relatively small institution noted: "Lord help us if we want to go to more than one conference per year."

Social work education conferences often compete for attendance—not necessarily by meeting at the same time of the year—but by forcing professionals to choose between attending one conference or another (or *another*) because they can only afford to attend one per year. An alternative for some is to tap into their own financial resources ("It seems like my salary gets lowered a thousand bucks or more every year."). Rising transportation, food, and registration fees only exacerbate this dilemma.

Imagine attending a conference on a yearly travel allowance of $600.* One subject considered this "reasonable" compared to other colleagues receiving *no* travel funds. Consider the cost of attending just one national conference. The registration fee for the 2008 annual BPD conference was $295, and the 2008 CSWE annual conference fee was $335. When one adds the cost of lodging for three or four nights (even sharing with roommates), meals, air and ground transportation, and out-of-pocket expenses, travel allowances are easily exceeded. As a member of a small program noted: "There's a mind-set here: you have to make do with what they give you. I'm always digging into my own pocket."

Another seasoned professional, with a quarter century of social work education experience, noted: "We could always use more funds for professional development and travel. It's not fair to ask faculty to be scholars and not provide them with resources they need to succeed."

But while some subjects "got by" on three-figure amounts, others reported

---

* While subjects were not asked to state a specific travel fund amount, many reported receiving allowances in the $600–$800 range.

more generous financial support. One subject with close to thirty years' experience—and also from a relatively small college—noted:

> I've done really well. I've *never* been denied [funds for] going to a professional meeting. I've heard of people who have to find roommates in order to attend. Don't spread this around, but I've never had to do that. I've never paid for anything out of my own pocket.

In another example, a subject with nearly thirty years of experience spoke highly of his professional travel opportunities: "Faculty receive funds for two conferences per year, plus another $1,000 for professional travel. I'll be funded to go to London to give a presentation."

One lesson to be learned from this discussion on travel funds: job seekers and those seeking to hire new faculty members should consider travel funds as part of a hiring package. From the job seeker's perspective, travel funds could be a negotiable item.

Physical Space

Work environment is important and may have a positive or negative impact on one's mood, comfort, and level of productivity. When considering office space, conference rooms, and classrooms, the following questions arise: Is the climate control decent (adequate heating in the winter, adequate cooling in the summer)? Is the air quality healthy (adequate ventilation, freedom from toxins)? Is lighting adequate (from windows and/or artificial sources)? Is the physical space appealing to the eye (do you have a view of cinder blocks, or do you look out of a window and see a grassy meadow?)? Is the amount of space adequate for educational needs (are classrooms crowded, are meeting rooms large enough, or do you feel cramped in your office?)? And, is the location of classrooms, conference rooms, and offices on campus convenient for faculty, staff, and students (e.g., are faculty offices next to one another in the same building, or are they in separate locations?)?

Subjects who spoke highly of their physical space ("state-of-the-art buildings, 'smart' classrooms [with integrated LCD projectors and Internet connectivity], and a wireless campus") tended to represent larger, more financially solvent institutions. One subject, a veteran of more than a quarter century at the same large university, commented:

> They nurture people to want to stay. There is genuine concern for faculty welfare here. We have windows that open and shut the way they're supposed to, plenty of space for group meetings, small and large, and we're even close to parking and the cafeteria. It's as though they want us to be happy, to have creature comforts, and to make this our home.

Other subjects held a different view, some literally. They came from small, medium, and large programs, housed within institutions ranging from small to medium. One subject, a veteran of three decades as a social work educator, expressed clear negative feelings regarding his physical environment (from which he recently departed):

> The space was abominable. We were crammed into rooms, compared to other programs. This should have been a clue that social work was undervalued compared to other academic programs.

Another twenty-five-year veteran spoke of a never-ending competitive battle with other programs on campus for adequate space for social work faculty, staff, and students:

> There's always a struggle for resources as a small program, for example, having enough secretarial support and adequate office space. There's a mind-set problem: "I have to make do." There's been a recent change in office space and it's nicer now, but it's been a long time coming.

Some programs have less available office space than faculty, who are sometimes accommodated in adjacent offices or even in a different building. This is especially true for programs that have undergone recent expansion, such as with the current trend of launching MSW programs (Zeiger et al., 2005). Subjects spoke of problems being apart. For example:

> The office space and the classrooms are fine, but faculty are not all together in one location. We live in two different buildings, about a ten-minute walk apart. And in one of those buildings, our offices aren't next to each other. It makes it hard to have those in-the-hall informal chats. Ever since we expanded, I miss that. I wish we had one common space. It would build a sense of unity. The administration keeps sayin' . . . But the budget is tight—who knows when it will happen?

Scholarship Support

Even among colleges and universities self-identified as primarily "teaching institutions," a national trend exists, with its concomitant expectations for faculty, toward increased scholarly productivity. For many faculty, especially those who have been at a teaching institution for twenty years or more, the relatively new movement to increase scholarship is coupled with a need to develop resources and carve out time to submit grant applications, conduct literature reviews, analyze data, write articles, and present the fruit of one's labors at public forums.

Nationally, there is wide variation among programs in terms of teaching load. I recall as a doctoral student, that some professors had most, if not all, of their teaching assignments "bought out" by grants and research endeavors. At research-intensive institutions this is not unusual. "Normal" course loads tend to be smaller: one or two courses per semester. In contrast, teaching-intensive institutions may have a "normal" course load of three to four courses per semester.*

Adequate release time was a "hot topic" among subjects. The level of support afforded them for scholarly production varied. On one end of the continuum, these was strong support:

> We have a two-plus-two teaching load [two courses for fall semester plus two courses for spring semester], but the average is two courses per year due to buyouts. In addition, there's internal money for start-up projects for new faculty.

A subject at a smaller program also voiced satisfaction for scholarship, even with a large course load:

> Our workload is four-four, and that's hefty with the newer scholarship expectations. Teaching is still primary. Individual programs define scholarship. The administration is good at providing course release time to write the [accreditation] self-study. And resources are good to succeed professionally, but that's only recent. Now it *is* possible to get a workload reduction to work on scholarship.

Generosity is relative. On the other side of the coin, a subject in a small department noted:

> We're on a four-four load and faculty hate it. There's a double message. With a push for increased scholarship, it's difficult to find the time to do it. Course reduction for research is possible, but there are lots of hoops. I feel fortunate to teach here, but there are morale problems.

One subject, a veteran of more than thirty years, noted: "There's not much time other than sabbaticals and unpaid leave. There are no buyouts." A common sentiment voiced, especially among subjects from small- and medium-size programs, was the lack of time needed to produce scholarship. For one subject the launching of an MSW program exacerbated this:

* There is more to the story. If a faculty member plays an important role in accreditation or reaffirmation efforts and is not compensated with a course reduction, the workload may balloon, resulting in less time for scholarly production (not to mention stress and exhaustion).

> What I need is more time to write. Developing an MSW program, preparing accreditation documents has sucked away time. While the school is incredibly grateful about the development of an MSW program, they don't cut you any slack about not publishing. My workload has doubled.

Another issue that arose among subjects was the ambiguity of what constitutes scholarship. Just what does constitute a "worthy" scholarly product? One veteran of nearly twenty years neatly captured this dilemma:

> I guess that's the $64,000 question: What constitutes scholarship? I've been on several tenure review committees and everyone seems to have a different perspective. To complicate matters, the "standard" at the point of hire may change five years down the road. It's confusing to pursue a moving target. I've seen one-page "articles" count the same as a twenty-pager. I've seen some journals declared more prestigious than others, without rhyme or reason other than a reviewer's bias—and no advance guidance to the candidate—*don't* publish here, *do* publish there. It's an inhumane process, and the worst part is, we do it to ourselves. As social workers, we should know better.

Professional Development Support

Social work education is a noble profession. We want to make a difference, one that will alter the fabric of society. We want no less than to impart knowledge and build competencies among the social workers of tomorrow, which will in turn empower clients to realize their potential, and shape policies that will create a more just society. It's a tall order and a humbling responsibility.

Just as a social worker's education should continue beyond the point of receiving a diploma (consider the double entendre "we learn for life"), as social work educators, we have a solemn obligation (and hopefully a thirst) to pursue professional development throughout our careers. To the extent that an institution is able to support the professional growth and development of its faculty, social work educators, students, local communities, and society as a whole will benefit.

Granted, the notion of "adequate" professional resources is relative. As one subject noted: "I'm not a high-maintenance person." Also, consider some faculty and administrators are more adept when it comes to what one subject describes as "mining the system." Notwithstanding these caveats, most subjects reported that their social work programs and their host institution provided them with adequate resources to succeed professionally. What follows is a representative sampling of their contentment. One subject commented:

> There's great support for professional development. [I] came in at the beginning of the semester; there was a new computer on my desk. Everything from the old computer had been downloaded onto the new one. We get new computers every three years. Our building has been renovated. My office has a window wall and total privacy. I received a $4,000 professional development grant without having to apply. There's not much else I'd want. We have a small department, but they treat us well.

Another added:

> They've done very well. I've never been denied going to a professional meeting. Even though this is a teaching university, I've never paid for anything out of my own pocket. I've heard of people who've had to find roommates to make ends meet in order to attend a conference. I haven't had to do that. I have everything I need to grow professionally.

Still another respondent noted:

> The college has enabled me to make important contributions. I serve on the board for the Center for Research and Teaching. We create policies to reward faculty with funds for faculty excellence. I've become more aware of trends and developments campus-wide. On a professional level, I've been able to develop new curricula areas. For example, I teach a course on the Holocaust. I've been able to institute a service-learning component in our Intro [Introduction to Social Work] class.

And, finally:

> They provide me with just about any resource I ask for: research assistants, computer equipment, and software. They give me money to attend conferences, and they pay my dues for social work organizations. There's not much more they could do that would make my life easier. I'm in a good position.

Another side to these glowing descriptions of support for faculty development emerged. Some faculty do find it necessary to share rooms, pay for their meals, and pick up the tab for professional memberships. And times are changing at many institutions of higher learning. The U.S. economy is not strong and many education budgets have been trimmed, or have not kept pace with inflation. Rising transportation costs have exacerbated financial woes.

Several colleagues spoke of the challenge of adding new projects with a level or diminishing budget. As one veteran of more than twenty-five years at a small program noted:

> The department has always done well. I've always gotten money for con-
> ferences and workload releases for writing and research. But times have
> gotten tighter. The curriculum is so complex. We try to do such a good job
> that we overload ourselves, like a runaway train. We've got lots of projects
> to be supported and sometimes *make our jobs harder than they should be*
> [italics added for emphasis]. We are prisoners of our own device.

Social work educators are eager to please. They will extend themselves to deliver a quality program, sometimes at the risk of compensating for requisite resources with their desire and dedication.

Quality and Number of Support Staff

The final topic viewed on a continuum is the quality and number of staff that are supportive to faculty. This includes secretarial support (e.g., coordinating a luncheon for field supervisors, monitoring office supplies, ordering textbooks, coordinating faculty appointments with students, prompting faculty with important due dates, assembling grant applications, and guiding students and department visitors to sources that will best meet their educational needs). It's often been said that if one *really* wants to understand the daily functions of a social work program, just ask the support staff. They are excellent purveyors of knowledge (Zeiger et al., 1999).

A support staff person who has worked at a social work program for an extended period of time (five, ten years or more), is likely better equipped to navigate her (for it is usually a female) way through the maze of academic bureaucracy far more efficiently than the average faculty member, and perhaps most administrators.

In addition to reliance upon dependable support staff, many faculty are, with the aid of graduate and teaching assistants, able to pursue scholarship projects with greater ease. While student workers filling these positions are more transient (usually in place for no more than a semester or two), they do provide valuable contributions. With assistance in literature reviews, data entry, and data analysis, faculty are afforded more time to formulate ideas, write, and publish.

The number and quality of support staff and graduate and teaching assistants may be viewed on a continuum, ranging from inadequate to adequate. One subject had strong words of praise for her support staff:

> I can't imagine what life would be like without Roberta and Marcy [names
> are fictitious]. They are the glue that holds the department together. They
> are our ambassadors; they are the first point of contact for students and
> visitors. They are deeply invested in the success of our students and

faculty. They know how to cut through red tape. I like to say that nobody is irreplaceable, but the loss of our support staff's accumulated knowledge would be devastating.

Do you type your own syllabi? Do you analyze your own data? Do you even collect your own data? Do you have time to keep current with literature in your area(s) of expertise? The answers depend in part on your resources (and, likely, time-management skills). These may be useful questions to ask and have answered when considering a job offer.

OTHER BENEFITS, AND SOME DEFICITS TOO

In addition to the "relative resources" viewed on a continuum (autonomy, travel funds, physical space, scholarship support, professional development support, and support staff), many additional resources were lauded, while some aspects of working in social work education were left wanting. These are presented below as benefits and deficits.

Benefits

Educational leave is available at some institutions for faculty to pursue doctoral education. A workload reduction is available in some programs that afford time for faculty (especially new faculty) to work on their dissertations.

One subject from a research-intensive university noted that all social work faculty receive a one-semester course release to fulfill a research agenda, *every year* until the achievement of tenure. Faculty also have the option of "banking these releases to create a 'mini-sabbatical.'"

Another benefit, noted with pride by one subject, was a guaranteed (without competition or application) one-semester sabbatical every seven years. While this may not seem generous by some people's standards, some faculty mentioned that they had *never* been afforded the opportunity for a sabbatical. Others noted that the process was highly competitive, sometimes within their own programs (imagine the ramifications of two full-time faculty from the same department of four or five, taking sabbatical leave during the same year).

Summer support was also touted as a benefit. One subject with almost twenty years' experience, noted:

I've always had a nine-month contract, but I've had maybe one summer off. It's been my call. It's not an expectation, but there's a tacit policy: if you want to teach in the summer, you can. It's an extra source of income that I have come to depend on.

Several subjects mentioned grant-writing support as a benefit. Institutions of higher learning realize that when faculty receive grants, the institution, the program, and the faculty achieve greater status. Subjects cited on-campus resources available to them to assist in obtaining internal and external funding and understanding standards and procedures such as calculating benefits and institutional overhead.

Teaching-improvement opportunities were also cited as a benefit. Sometimes occurring on campus, sometimes off, faculty were supported in attending workshops to hone their pedagogical skills. Attendance was considered to be part of their "paid time."

Strong technological support was the pride and joy of many subjects. State-of-the-art hardware and software, ongoing information-technology training, new equipment every three to four years, and for many a "wireless" campus were stated as pluses. One subject spoke for many when he stated: "Technology tools are excellent."

Bringing students to conferences, while expensive (depending upon geographic proximity) and relatively rare, was cited by a few subjects as beneficial. In the same way faculty are able to grow professionally by attending conferences, student attendance enhances educational development.

Tuition waivers available to immediate family members were cited as an important benefit. For those subjects with college-age children (past, present, or future), this can translate into thousands of dollars in savings. One subject noted an extraordinary benefit: her university's willingness to pay for faculty children's education at any private college or university in the country!

Health care benefits may be viewed in terms of three dimensions: cost, quality, and the non-contractual benefit of emotional support. Although difficult to measure in dollars and cents, emotional support should not be taken lightly. Perhaps it is due to a strong sense of caring for others that social work educators are very willing to pitch in for a faculty member who is physically ill or must take a leave of absence due to an emotional loss.

The need for emotional support is not limited to times of loss or illness. The road to tenure and promotion is often rough, with bumps and potholes. Even post tenure and promotion, social work educators continue to crave support, respect, and validation as professionals. Subjects spoke of the significance of their dean or chancellor demonstrating genuine support for the value of social work education.

Finally, clear, realistic expectations were cited as an important benefit. When new faculty are brought on board, what are the chances of professional success? How is success defined? Will the definitions change between the time of entry and the time of tenure and/or promotion? Does the institution give clear guidelines and models for success? Or is it left to the whims of tenure review committee members who may have an axe to grind? Subjects who had an accurate view of what to expect in their academic careers were the most satisfied. Others had a different reaction.

Deficits

A sink-or-swim mentality exists in some programs. Perhaps this is more the case at larger, research-intensive institutions where "publish or perish" is a modern-day reality. One subject, who recently departed from a large school of social work, commented on the competitive nature and challenges for minority faculty: "People openly acknowledge it's sink or swim. Minority [faculty] have been casualties. They've had different ways of knowing and didn't fit into the system." Certainly there are "casualties" in every profession. But how many of these were "setups"? How many lives have been disrupted by arcane expectations and inadequate systems of support?

Another deficit, already mentioned, is the double message in academia: do more without additional resources. As previously noted: "It's not fair to *ask* faculty to be scholars and not provide them with the resources they need to *become* scholars." To encourage faculty to increase their scholarly productivity and maintain a four-four teaching load is tantamount to promoting anxiety and burnout. There exists wide variation among social work programs across the nation with regard to course load, class size, and scholarship support. A prospective faculty member would be wise to compare the benefits and deficits of more than one program.

Low pay was cited as a deficit. The notion of low pay is, of course, a relative concept, mediated by the cost of living. For example, it is far more expensive to live in Boston or New York than it is in Pittsburgh or Phoenix. Low pay may be viewed on two levels: pay relative to one's colleagues at a comparable institution, and pay relative to other academic programs at the same institution (business and engineering were frequently cited as programs commanding higher salaries). Also, the reader is reminded that the average length of service for subjects of this study is over twenty-five years. Many bemoaned the fact that they were "locked in" to a lower salary structure than their newly arrived colleagues. Despite a significant difference in years of service, some new faculty were actually receiving salaries close to those with twenty or more years of experience.

More faculty lines are needed. One subject noted that there were three hundred social work students and only eight full-time faculty in his program. His research class had an enrollment of forty-one. Other subjects spoke of too much reliance on adjunct faculty. Still others expressed displeasure that teaching overloads (e.g., five-four instead of four-four) had become institutionalized: "Once in a while they're nice, and I can use the extra cash, but it's at a point where it's become expected. And they lay this guilt trip: 'If not you . . .'" If faculty consent to overloads, the administration may be less likely to support additional faculty lines.

More help with accreditation is needed. As previously noted, accreditation and reaffirmation of accreditation are daunting tasks, requiring exorbitant amounts of time on top of a "normal" academic workload. The task becomes all consuming. Ask anyone who has ever made a significant contribution to a self-study document. It's difficult to make scholarly contributions and simultaneously attend to accreditation needs.

With extra support during the accreditation process, for example course releases and additional secretarial services, perhaps social work educators would not have to sacrifice their level of productivity in scholarship, teaching, and service.

THE NEED FOR LEADERSHIP TRAINING

There is a need for training faculty for leadership positions. People are being placed in leadership roles without training or preparation [for administrative roles]. They end up in these positions owing to political connections and happenstance rather than a solid track record. There are too many decisions based on political whim.

Relatively few subjects had aspired to become social work educators. Likewise, few social work educators aspire to become social work administrators (or intend to be, as one subject quipped, "going over to the dark side"). As a wave of social work education administrators retire, it behooves our profession to promote and support faculty moving into administrative roles.

The next chapter will serve as a guide for prospective academicians. Based upon the wisdom of seasoned social work educators—nearly 1,700 years of collective experience—what considerations should job seekers have when selecting a venue for their career in social work education?

The Job Seeker's Primer

There's so much to consider when looking for an academic home. As an active job seeker, you'll want to stay attuned to many factors, some obvious, others less so, that may have a significant impact on the quality of your life and the lives of those you touch.

What factors should a future social work educator consider before committing time, energy, and (frequently) geographic relocation to launch a new career? How can you prepare for this significant transition with eyes wide open? To answer these questions, experienced social work educators were asked, based upon almost 1,700 years of collective experience, to give advice to prospective faculty, new to the job market, seeking an academic appointment. What should candidates consider, good and bad?

Chapter 10 is divided into five parts: establishing a mind-set for a smart search; factors to consider *before* visiting a campus; what to know *before* and what to learn *during* the visit; factors to consider during the visit; and post-visit reflections.

ESTABLISHING A MIND-SET FOR A SMART SEARCH

It's a major decision—one that will impact family, friends, colleagues, students, and the quality of social work education. And it will likely affect your personal happiness. Choose carefully. Choose wisely. Here's the good news, as noted by a veteran of thirty-five years in social work education: "This is a wonderful time, and probably will be for the next fifteen years, for finding a job in the field of social work education. *Look around,* there are more jobs than people to fill them."

He's right. As noted in the introduction, with large numbers of professors retiring, the number and size of social work programs increasing (BSW and especially MSW), and the number of doctoral students remaining relatively flat, it's a great time to be looking for a career in social work education. Job seekers can afford to be selective. You need not leap at the first offer that appears on your plate.

Let's explore the scenario of you being invited to the campus of a potential employer. You need a job; they need an addition to their faculty. Likely, your prospective employer has invested resources in bringing you onto campus, feeding you, and providing lodging. You have made it to the short list. You may assume they are serious in bringing you aboard.

Let's assume that your decision to visit the campus is not a desperate measure. Let us further assume that you are genuinely interested in a job at Glorious University. The visit will likely include meeting students, community members, librarians, presenting a colloquium, and participating in interviews with faculty members and administrators. The interviews should be a two-way procedure: you are being interviewed to see if you would complement the program, and *you are interviewing* your potential colleagues to see if the position will fit your professional needs. Consider the following advice of a three-decade social work educator:

> Take a social work perspective. You are not just filling an academic slot. Take the stance that you are seeking a position within the context of a department, an institution, and a community. You're not just getting a job; you're making a commitment to the institution and the community. Give serious thought to the challenges that may lie ahead. You are about to make a huge decision with lasting impact. How flexible are you willing to be? What can you tolerate? Where will you draw the line? What about climate? If living in cold weather would be a serious issue for you and your family, don't apologize. Pay attention to the strength of your reaction if you're invited to visit a campus in Duluth or Buffalo. If living in muggy weather drives you crazy, think twice about moving to the Deep South.

Also consider the words of two other veterans of thirty years:

> Don't come if you're looking for money alone. [This may be tempting after many "lean" years of graduate school.] Be committed to the students, the community, and to social work education. Balance your desires. Don't ask about "me"—ask about the practice community, the program, and the students.

> Look for a place that genuinely wants to help you grow, and is willing to support you. But have a humble mind-set. Don't just ask: "What can you do for me?" Also ask "How can I help you best?" Work together. Talk about a plan for the next five or six years that will make you the best faculty member you can be. Ask "What can we do for each other."

Remember you are entering a buyer's market. A social work educator and administrator with thirty-five years of experience likened the search process to a shopping excursion:

> See it as if you're going into the shopping mall and you're going into the Gap looking for clothing. Explore the merchandise; try it on. Go down to Banana Republic and do the same. Stop at Brooks Brothers. Go across the street to Nordstrom. Keep feeling, keep trying things on, keep inquiring. Circle around again to see where the best fit is. Talk to other people about the best places to shop, but use [and trust] your assessment skills to make the decision. Be up-front in your questions; the job market is not a game. Feel free to ask questions of those *you* are interviewing. Be as natural and genuine as you can. Learn more about the people who are interviewing you. Ultimately, you have to trust your gut; and when you do, it will be right.

In other words, like Luke in *Star Wars*, you must "trust the force." Look for a place where you can grow and flourish. This sounds like straightforward advice, but in the heat of the moment, with so much on the line (and factoring in jet lag), such advice may be hard to remember and follow. I asked the following question to the subject who made the above statement: "What are common mistakes people make when going on a job search?" His reply: "They're looking for the money, the 'package.' When that happens, I think they miss looking for the nature of the people they're going to be working with, the relationships that faculty will have with each other." Further discussion on the importance of collegiality will appear later in this chapter.

"The bottom line" has become a hackneyed expression. When it comes to developing a mind-set for the best social work education position, the "top line" and the bottom line are one and the same. "It's really about fit more than anything else." In the words of a respected social work educator with more than twenty years' experience:

> Know what you do well. Sing boldly what you do well. Seek out an institution that will honor your strengths—but don't be a hero. If you are being asked to save the day, run, run, and run! Find a fit for you rather than you conforming to the institution. Look for an institution that appreciates your gifts, challenges you, and supports you in your growth.

Effective social work education is dependent upon healthy working relationships between colleagues. An impressive curriculum vitae may be little more than window dressing, masking a colleague who is a prima donna or who has otherwise failed to complete the work of adulthood (see pages 93–94). A major component of goodness of fit is considering how you will be treated as a human being and a professional. Consider the words of an Academic Nomad:

> Are there faculty who would really like to work with me? People could be "outstanding," even famous, but not give you the time of day or the support you'll need to succeed professionally. Having publications up the wazoo doesn't do it. Looking good on paper is easy.

FACTORS TO CONSIDER *BEFORE* VISITING A CAMPUS

Perhaps you have signed up with CSWE's teaching registry. Perhaps you have responded to an advertisement posted in the *Chronicle of Higher Education*. As a doctoral student who has successfully defended a dissertation, faculty have recommended you to colleagues in other social work education programs.

You are about to enter the job market. The odds are in your favor. The phone is beginning to ring. Your e-mail in-box is filling up with solicitations. Social work programs are offering to fly you in for an interview. Here are six factors* to consider prior to your visit:

Program and institutional history and mission;
Institutional auspice;
Institutional emphasis (teaching or research);
How to articulate what you have to offer;
How to articulate your goals; and
How to negotiate.

Program and Institutional History and Mission

"Do your homework. Investigate the program. Find out enough to ask intelligent questions about the program and the institution. Go online. Look at the catalog." The above sage advice is offered by a veteran of more than twenty-five years as a social work educator and one who is currently an administrator.

Carefully reading program and institutional Web pages and fact sheets will give you a favorable edge when you visit. It will enable you to make intelligent choices. Be critical. Read between the lines. Programs won't advertise their flaws. Be skeptical. Look beyond the written word. Has the institution or the program ever been on academic probation?

---

* The weight and relevance of each of these factors will vary according to one's needs, personality, and individual taste both during and after a visit. Job seekers may find it useful to create a matrix and assign point values to categories. A matrix may be especially useful to those comparing two or more job offers.

The statement "Do your homework" was a common refrain. An Academic Nomad with more than twenty-five years' experience offered the following advice: "Go to the Web site. Who are the faculty? What are their research interests? How do they fit with yours? How could you supplement or complement their program? Understand their mission."

For all the options you explore, your aim should be to find the best fit between your needs and institutional and program goals. Subjects noted that becoming aware of departmental and institutional structures could augment this fit. Job seekers must have a clear notion of the mission and vision for social work education. As one subject noted, you must:

> "Look at the culture of the school and the department. That's got to fit. What do they value? How do they work? What are the priorities? What are the goals? Do the mission of the university and the social work program align with *your* professional philosophy?

Institutional Auspice

Social work programs come in different sizes, have different numbers of students and faculty, and exist within different auspices: public and private (which may or may not be religiously affiliated). Chances are, if you hold a PhD in social work (or a related field), you received your education from a relatively large institution that operates under public auspice.* It does *not* mean you are destined to teach in the same size institution or under the same auspice. In fact, if the subject sample for this book is representative, today's job seeker will likely *not* teach in an institution offering a PhD in social work (see page 4).

Whether an institution is public or private may not hold value for all job seekers, but many subjects asserted it could make a difference in terms of student access to higher education. Some noted the large difference in tuition cost, which can run three to four times higher at a private institution (student loans can ease the financial burden temporarily, but will have to be repaid with larger monthly payments and for a long period of time).

Many subjects stated a strong preference for teaching in a public institution. For example:

> Education is expensive and I don't see a way around that. But I believe in *public* education. The state *should* make an investment in society's future. Private schools are out of reach for too many—a poor match for social work values. We can shape society by providing entry to students who

---

* Massachusetts is an interesting exception to the generalization that most states' doctoral social work programs are found at public institutions. As of 2008, there were five private (Boston College, Boston University, Brandeis, Simmons, and Smith) and no publicly funded PhD social work programs in that state.

would otherwise not have the means. Higher education should not be an exclusive club. I like teaching students who are the first in their family to attend college—something you're more likely to find at a publicly funded college.

Religious affiliation may be an issue for some. Job seekers may prefer to work within a particular denominational orientation such as a Lutheran- or Seventh Day Adventist–sponsored institution. Others may feel out of place or restricted in an institution aligned with a specific religion. My first teaching position was at a Catholic college. In five years, I never acclimated to the crucifixes hanging behind me on the classroom walls.

One subject noted that "what you teach may be restricted at a religiously affiliated school." Does the school take a stand on issues such as reproductive rights or sexual orientation? Will your academic freedom be limited by the standards of a private institution? Or might it be enhanced?

Institutional Emphasis

As previously addressed, there is a national trend within institutions of higher learning to increase research activity and scholarly productivity. This is particularly evident at institutions offering doctoral degrees. Nevertheless, there is a range of expectations among social work programs across the United States. For some, teaching at an R-I institution holds more prestige. Fair questions to ask are: How important is prestige? Is an R-I school the best fit for your professional goals? And what sacrifices are you willing to make? If you love teaching *and* you love research, unless you want to give up sleep and a life outside of work, you may have to clone yourself to excel in both arenas. R-I institutions tend to have lighter loads to allow time for scholarly production. Another word of advice: "It is nearly impossible to teach a four-four load and publish ten articles every five years. I don't know anyone who can pull it off and remain human."

Again it's a matter of taste. One subject with thirty-five years of teaching experience described an early part of his career at a research-intensive institution: "I was deeply unhappy at [Big Name University]. I didn't get tenured, but it helped to have worked there because of the reputation and the contacts." Another subject suggested that job seekers "avoid R-Is. Look at smaller schools and communities. It's satisfying to be a big fish in a small pond."

How to Articulate What You Have to Offer

Even though it's a buyer's market, you will have to present more than a well-crafted curriculum vitae and a smile. Again, this will require homework, because in order to articulate what you would bring to a program, you must study the program first. Be someplace where you can be yourself. Be forthright about what you value (without aggrandizement). Addressing this concern may require forethought and rehearsal. In the words of one subject with twenty years of experience:

> I've interviewed at many schools, and I've served on numerous search committees. Lots of people can look good on paper, but when you meet, it can be a completely different person. I want to work with people who are *excited* about coming here. I want to work with people who can not only complement but also *ignite* our program. Candidates need to be knowledgeable, articulate, and enthusiastic. In the end, I'm going to ask myself, is this someone I'd really like to work with? Will he or she add spice to the program?

How to Articulate Your Goals

Let's be honest; social work is not a purely altruistic profession. Ambition is real. In addition to articulating what you have to offer, it is fair and reasonable to express to your future employer and colleagues what you hope to achieve professionally. What are your goals for the next five years and beyond? "Think about what you want to accomplish in your career. Keep your eyes on the prize." If you are comfortable as you articulate your desires on a campus visit, it's a good sign. You will project confidence, and you feel at ease expressing yourself to potential colleagues.

As one subject noted, if you have a research agenda, a certain amount of passion and commitment needs to show through. And it doesn't hurt if you can align your desires and career goals with the mission of the program and the institution.

Another perspective related to professional achievement expressed by a subject relates to pace, realism, and humility. She noted:

> Set realistic goals for what you want to accomplish in the first year. For example, don't try to write a book and teach four classes per semester. Start slow. You'll be learning a whole new environment. This is a whole new world. Learn how to play the academic game.

In other words, don't promise what you can't deliver. Chances are, your prospective colleagues will appreciate your honesty. If they don't, that should be a warning sign.

Finally, in the words of a veteran of five different social work programs: "Ask the search committee: 'What do you think *I'm* going to need to be successful, and what do you have to offer me?' It's really about fit more than anything else." How the committee responds to your inquiries may speak volumes about your future colleagues, and your future as well.

How to Negotiate

Negotiating a livable salary is important. Know what you're worth. Know what comparable institutions are paying a new assistant professor. Information is often a matter of public record and may be found in publications such as *Academe*. But be warned, the local cost of living may effectively cut into your salary. The rent in New York City is a tad higher than in Salt Lake City.

You *are* entitled to decent compensation. Do not sell yourself short. One subject lamented: "Some people don't have the sophistication and knowledge, feel shy, or feel lucky just to have a job offer. Too many doctoral programs don't train their students in how to negotiate a fair salary."

On a personal note, when I was hired for my second faculty appointment, I was offered an effective $5,000 yearly raise. Granted, I had been receiving a relatively low salary compared to my national peers, but I was still in heaven. I thought I'd be bold and timidly asked if I could receive another $100 per month. It was a scary moment. Not only was I afraid of having my request denied, I worried that I would be told to look elsewhere. My request for the additional $100 was met with a "Sure, okay." It was too easy. I kicked myself for not asking for more. To this day, I am convinced I could have done better. I had gone into the supermarket on an empty stomach. I was naïve.

Negotiating a salary shouldn't feel like buying a car, where the dealer holds all the aces. A starting salary is critical. As another veteran of more than three decades advised: "Negotiate the very best salary and working conditions you can get. Because you may be locked in." What does it mean to be locked in? It could mean yearly "increases" that are less than cost-of-living increases; or worse, it could mean having your salary frozen.

While salary is important, many candidates don't realize there are other items that may be negotiated. As previously mentioned, at some programs (R-Is in particular), a "start-up" package for new faculty is not uncommon. A start-up package may include computer equipment, guaranteed funds for travel and professional development, and research support. Other possibilities include course reductions (to allow time for curriculum development, scholarship, assessment, or accreditation efforts), supplemental compensation (above "normal" contractual obligations) for summer teaching and "special assignments," and relocation expenses (which could amount to $5,000, $10,000, or more!).

WHAT TO KNOW *BEFORE* AND WHAT TO LEARN *DURING* THE VISIT

Two items are important to consider: knowing as much as you can in advance about your potential colleagues, and assessing the integrity and personality of the director or department chair (who will likely have a role in your future evaluations).

Your Potential Colleagues

Learning about your colleagues will be a key component of your visit. It is also possible to learn about your potential workmates *before* you set foot on campus. You may be able to arrange a meeting at national or regional conferences. At the same conferences, you may be able to observe them delivering a workshop (getting to "know" them before you meet in person). You may also log on to a faculty Web site, or Google your potential future colleagues to learn of their backgrounds, accomplishments, and scholarly interests. As a grounding framework, according to an Academic Nomad, you can ask yourself:

> How well will you fit? Will you be nurtured? Will you grow? Do your homework [sound familiar?]. Go to the Web site. Who are the faculty? What are their research interests? How do they fit with yours? How could you supplement or complement [them]? Examine and absorb the program's materials. Figure out how you can meet their needs, and how they might fulfill yours.

Leadership Assessment

You may come into contact with a dean or director before a campus visit. This person will likely play a key role in future evaluations of your performance. The personality and integrity of a department leader is an important factor to consider before you come on board.

Subjects raised the following questions worthy of consideration: "Is the program director warm? Supportive? Aloof? Autocratic? Sensitive to faculty needs?" "Will you have to 'boot lick' in order to succeed?" "How strong is the departmental leadership? Is leadership turnover frequent?"

As a seasoned social work educator and administrator advised: "Look at the dean [or director] closely.* A leader can help or hinder a career."

One subject, with more than a decade in social work education, suggested asking the dean for references, noting: "The dean's reaction to your request might be telling." She also suggested holding conversations with recent hires, asking: "Has the dean been honest? Do you feel supported?"

FACTORS TO CONSIDER DURING THE VISIT

There is so much to know, and so little time. Picture this scenario: You've done your homework. Your ticket is in hand. Tomorrow afternoon you will

---

* The "shelf life" of a dean or director may be limited. One cannot assume the leader who hires you will later evaluate your tenure and promotion file.

be arriving in Somewhere, U.S.A., perhaps jet-lagged, with one or two days to gather information that will inform a life-altering decision. Whom should you be sure to meet? What should you be sure to notice? What questions should you be sure to ask? Here are thirteen factors to consider while you are visiting a campus:

Collegial atmosphere;

Faculty morale;

Mentorship;

Professional development opportunities;

Assessing the work environment;

Workload expectations;

How is the social work program perceived on campus?;

Fiscal health of the department and the institution;

Program development and stability;

Town–gown relationship;

Current and former students;

Teaching assignments; and

Pay attention to epiphanies.

Because of the large number of factors, descriptions of each will be limited.

Collegial Atmosphere

Although interview data for this book were never quantified, when subjects were asked what advice they would impart to prospective faculty, new to the job market, the interview invariably turned to the topic of collegiality. How do faculty behave? How well do they work together? Do they support one another? Is their interest in you genuine? A social work educator and administrator with more than a quarter century of experience offered the following words of wisdom:

> Get to know the social work faculty. Do they impress you as selfish or generous? Junior faculty depend on the quality and generosity of senior faculty. How are you *treated* on the visit? Do they meet you at the airport and escort you to your lodging and campus? Is your visit overly structured with no time to wander around? Is there too little structure—as if they didn't put much energy into your visiting experience?

For some, the notion of vying for tenure, promotion, and sabbaticals may conjure visions of a competitive atmosphere (a competitive atmosphere is a non-collegial one). A social work educator with seventeen years' experience articulated this concept:

> Do you see yourself working with these people as colleagues, competitors, or both? People coming up for tenure are measuring themselves against others. This can lead to stress, anxiety. It can drive them *away* from working with each other because they are in competition. Look at power dynamics [when you visit]. Look for signs of pathology among the faculty.

Subjects repeatedly spoke of the need to explore workplace climate, and to gauge how well faculty work together. What is the culture of the department? Do faculty seem overly serious or stressed? How common is genuine laughter? For better or worse, you may be experiencing your future "home." As a veteran with more than thirty years' experience suggested: "You will live there every day. Will you be able to get the support you need, not just to survive, but thrive? Is mentorship available? Are there people in the department with whom you can be vulnerable?"

The need for camaraderie, and the need for a "family" were voiced frequently. More advice from a veteran of thirty-two years:

> Be very, very aware of colleagues; it's an applicant's market. Get a sense of whether your potential colleagues are more than "people you can live with." They should be people you can enjoy, engage in intellectual discussions with, [who can] aid you in your scholarship, and help you in the growth of your pedagogical skills. *Can you have fun with these people?*

Find positive collegiality—supportive colleagues, who do not engage in infighting. Look for a supportive environment where people won't see you as competition—"withholding information that would help you become a better educator." One subject noted that institutionalized merit increases set up a system of losers and winners, and in the end, are divisive.

Here's a challenge: In your jet-lagged state, with so much at stake, how do you accurately assess collegiality in a new environment? I posed this question to my interviewees. Many paused for thought, and many offered valuable advice.

Sample approaches include carefully reading job announcements, literally ("we have a great collegial atmosphere"), and in between the lines ("this seems like a place where I could grow professionally"). When you meet with faculty members in a group setting, be a careful observer of body language. Here is advice from a veteran of three decades:

> How do you measure collegiality? No one's going to say, "Ever since I've become less engaged, I wouldn't go to an extra meeting if my life depended

on it" or "I hope you don't mind working with a prima donna, because I
have to come first." Do ask: "What would other colleagues say about you?
What would colleagues outside the department say about the department?
Could I talk with them? If I make a commitment to the department, what
kind of commitment are you going to make to me?"

Subjects emphasized the importance of solid social work assessment skills.
Use listening skills. Look for nonverbal language. Notice how faculty interact
with *each other.* You can tell just sitting around the table if there's humor, if the
interaction is genuine, or if people are *trying to act nice.* Here are some specific
suggestions:

Notice if people are working in pods. Are people's doors shut? How do
people act at your colloquium? Are they hypercritical, pretentious? Is
there competitive horseshit? Are they focused on what to say *to* you versus
learning *from* you? Are they tuned in? Have your radar on: Are you going
to be entering a world of conflict?* You want to avoid toxic environments
where people are at each other's throats.

How do you measure collegiality during a visit? As subjects repeatedly
noted, you can't fake civility. "Observe . . . do people joke around? Do they
laugh?"

Faculty Morale

Subjects emphasized the importance of faculty morale. How satisfied are
faculty with their jobs? How happy are the workers? "If faculty are miserable,
you'll be miserable too." Do faculty feel weary or tired? In the words of a veteran of nearly three decades: "Do people feel good about themselves, their
work, and the institution? [If so] that's the place you want to be. Otherwise, it's
no fun."

"Internal problems are not good. You need to have good assessment skills."
Absorb. Intuit.

One indicator of faculty satisfaction is turnover rate. What is the average
"life span" of a faculty member? Why do they leave? Why do they stay? Investigate. Find out who has moved on and arrange a candid conversation. Did the
person leave for professional advancement or because he or she was treated
poorly (or maybe some of each)? All programs will have interpersonal conflicts,
some more than others. Look at the length of time people stay in the program.
How frequent is the occurrence of searches to replace existing faculty? Ask

* Conflict does not necessarily lead to a toxic environment. A certain amount of conflict is normal and
potentially healthy in any social work program. How people *deal* with conflict is critical.

how many have come and gone in the last five years. Ask yourself: "Am I going to be able to stay around?" Or is there a revolving door?

Mentorship

Related to collegiality is the availability of mentorship for new faculty. Mentorship can range from informal (nonscheduled visits by a department chair or other faculty members) to formal (regular, scheduled appointments with an assigned mentor). A mentor-mentee relationship may involve meetings with a mentor who is a member of the social work faculty, or with a faculty member who teaches in a different program.

What are the benefits of a mentorship program? A mentor-mentee relationship is a statement of investment and commitment toward the professional success of newly hired faculty. One subject, teaching in a large metropolitan area, noted how a mentor could assist in the challenge of switching from the role of practitioner to that of professor:

> New faculty need support to make the transition from the world of social service to academia; it's not an easy transition to make. It's seductive because you think it will be much easier. It's not. A mentor would be helpful.

As previously noted, good colleagues don't withhold information that would enable fellow faculty to succeed professionally. A mentor can assist new faculty in navigating the waters of tenure, promotion, building a research agenda, and effective interaction with students, faculty, and administration. Mentors might help new faculty connect with key players in the practice community, make introductions, read drafts of articles, or review abstracts before they are submitted to conferences. Further, a mentor can be a confidant, someone with whom newcomers can be vulnerable.

There was a strong consensus among subjects that during a visit to a prospective place of employment, job seekers should explore mentoring options. A strong mentoring program validates the professional worth of new faculty.

Professional Development Opportunities

Professional development is at once an opportunity and an obligation for the growth of individual faculty *and* social work programs. Effective professional development requires structures, resources, and sustained institutional commitment.

As previously discussed (see chapter 3), high-quality social work education requires a commitment by faculty to "learn for life." Teaching effectiveness and research skills are not mastered by virtue of completing a graduate degree.

Neither are they perfected in the first five or ten years of teaching—if ever. There is always room to grow.

Fair questions to ask, in the words of a thirty-two-year veteran, are: "What will your new place of employment do to aid you in your scholarship and development of pedagogical skills? Can you get the support you need?"

Subjects spoke of the need for new faculty to be consciously nurtured—not thrown into the deep end of the pool to sink or swim—but to have *all* faculty members share responsibility for the development of new faculty. In the words of an eighteen-year veteran:

> The department *should* help with professional development, help newcomers balance research, teaching, and service for tenure and promotion. Faculty must feel valued. Expectations for "demands on time" must be reasonable. How supportive of your research agenda will the department be? *Get specific examples* of the tools and resources faculty have been given to grow professionally. What types of grants have faculty brought in? Is grant-writing assistance and training available? Ask about the history of professional-development funds. Have they ever been frozen, reduced, or increased?

One way for new faculty to develop professionally is to initially include them in existing research projects. A reasonable question for a job seeker to ask is: "Are faculty willing to share their scholarly efforts and/or collaborate with incoming faculty."*

Further, a workload reduction in the first year of employment to support a neophyte in developing a research agenda and acclimatizing to academia is reasonable. In the words of an administrator and social work educator of nearly three decades: "Look for a place that *wants* to help you grow, and is willing to *support* your achievement." Another educator, with three and a half decades of experience, added: "Find out in advance if you will be supported with faculty development funds. What do they provide to improve and update the quality of teaching? Will there be support to attend professional conferences?"

Subjects advised job seekers to inquire about technology and equipment. How often are computers replaced? Is software, complete with updates on a regular basis, an entitlement? What is the quality of technical support?

Assessing the Work Environment

Your place of employment may be your home away from home. If you feel cramped, if the lighting is insufficient, if the air quality is toxic, or if the temperature is uncomfortable you are likely to be less content and less productive. Subjects

---

* Collaboration in scholarly efforts might serve to lay a solid foundation for the subsequent establishment of an independent research agenda.

advised job seekers to consider asking the following questions: Is it important for you to have a window with a nice view in your office? Are offices, classrooms, and meeting spaces adequate? What about space for storage? Is paint peeling from the walls? What's the track record for maintenance? Are faculty offices in close proximity to one another, or are social work faculty located on two or more floors, or in two or more buildings? One subject, who had "been around the block" for two decades, made the following suggestions for things to notice outside the department:

> When you visit, take a good look around the entire campus. Ask yourself: "Does the library have a comfortable feel? Are the grounds and the architecture pleasing to the eye? If you like old buildings and ivy-covered walls, look for them. If it's a sunny day with a temperature that pleases you [low 70s, low humidity?] and flowers in bloom, try to envision what it would be like with inclement weather."

Workload Expectations

Workload expectations *do* vary from program to program. For example: "normal" course loads may range anywhere from three to eight courses per academic year (or as high as ten with "institutionalized" overloads—see below). And because social work educators care deeply about building knowledge and competency for the next generation of social workers, and because they are dedicated professionals, they may easily be persuaded, and feel obliged to operate at overload capacity. In the words of a twenty-year veteran:

> The notion of overload may be institutionalized. That is, faculty regularly teach an extra class (or two) each semester and receive extra pay. It's "voluntary" but the expectation is there. They may feel guilty ("we can't find anybody else"). Overload may be informal too; people are asked to perform unanticipated or unexpected tasks. Again, this taps into a sense of obligation "for the good of the department." Untenured faculty are especially vulnerable. Morally bankrupt administrators may take advantage.

A professor's work contract may not accurately reflect workload expectations. For example, a typical contract for many faculty is nine months per year (e.g., September 1 to June 1). With a nine-month contract, faculty are not expected to work (or be paid) during the summer, unless they teach an extra course or have a supplemental contract. Does this mean they are free to go fishing or wiggle their toes in the sand somewhere for three months? Maybe. Maybe not. Prospective faculty would be wise to ask future colleagues how they typically spend their summers. Is there a (unwritten) cultural and professional expectation that faculty will need to attend meetings, trainings, or orientations when they are "off contract"? During the normal academic year, does a culture exist where faculty are expected to read and respond to e-mail messages at night or on weekends?

One subject with eighteen years of experience in a BSW program noted the reality of "hidden" work hours catering to student needs:

> When considering a new academic appointment, think about workload requirements. Students have extensive needs. Some students have self-esteem issues. They need to professionalize their comportment [how they present themselves]. When it comes to meeting student needs, there's more involved than class time and regular office hours.

Nurturing students may require extensive time and energy. If students expect you to be available by e-mail or phone during nights or weekends there will be less time for scholarship and curriculum development. Explore cultural norms before you sign on the dotted line. Minimize surprises.

A common suggestion for job seekers was to have clear expectations for teaching, service, and research related to the attainment of tenure and promotion. The amount of "protection" in terms of course release, or other workload reduction, especially in the first year, was commonly viewed as a reasonable request at the beginning of one's career. As noted by a thirty-three-year veteran: "If the university is trying to load you up with four courses the first semester [you teach], they obviously don't value your research." Another subject with nearly thirty years of experience cautioned job seekers to "clarify expectations for tenure and promotion so you don't get blindsided." And a final quote in this section elaborates the point:

> I've seen it happen: faculty chasing a moving target. New administrators come in and the landscape changes. The requirement for the number of articles to be published *increases*. It's enough to drive you mad. My advice? Get the requirements in writing when you sign on. And learn the track record for tenure and promotion. How often do people get turned down? *Why* do they get turned down? Just how reasonable *are* the expectations? Do faculty truly receive the support they need?

How Is the Social Work Program Perceived on Campus?

Like individuals, social work educational programs need validation. How does the host institution view the social work program(s)? What steps has the administration taken to demonstrate its commitment to accreditation, reaffirmation of accreditation, faculty development, and program innovation? Interviewees encouraged job seekers to ask for specific examples of administrative support for social work education. Don't be shy; ask for evidence of support. Pay attention to vocal tones; listen for pride.

Subjects also encouraged job seekers to explore the reputation of social work among professors teaching in *other* departments. One social work educator with more than a decade of experience suggested that future social work educators would be wise to:

> Find out how other departments within the institution perceive social work. Is there positive regard? I love being involved in interdisciplinary projects. I'd suffocate if I never left my own department. We have a good reputation across campus and I believe it's *because* we serve on campus-wide committees (and do well) and collaborate with our peers in other departments.

Fiscal Health of the Department and the Institution

As mentioned earlier, when I interviewed at the University of Alaska in 1995, I learned that my annual starting salary would be $5,000 greater than my previous academic appointment. I was thrilled. *It never occurred to me* to inquire about the history of salary increases. Only after I began my employment did I learn that salaries had been frozen (pun intended) for the previous four years.

Do your homework. In reading job announcements, be sure to notice caveats such as "position availability contingent upon funding." Peruse a ten-year-old university catalog and compare it to a current edition. Do the same programs exist? Have departments been eliminated or added over time? Has the number of faculty increased or decreased? Answers to these questions may tell you if the institution is solvent, or in trouble. A subject with nearly twenty years' experience as a social work educator offered the following suggestion:

> Ask faculty and administrators blunt questions. Have there been recent cutbacks? Which programs are on the chopping block or threatened with elimination? What about student enrollment? Going up? Going down? Is student recruitment a necessity for program survival? Are class sections being added, consolidated, or eliminated?

For many institutions, salaries are a matter of public record. A little research might reveal the history of increases, decreases, and freezes. If the information is not readily accessible, ask administrators directly. You have a right to know about the institution's fiscal health. You have a right to know what you can reasonably expect in the future.

Program Development and Stability

Where is the program in its accreditation cycle? How stable is the program in terms of faculty turnover and leadership consistency? In chapter 5, we discussed how the accreditation process can consume vast amounts of time and energy for faculty and staff. Once a program has established complete initial accreditation, an eight-year cycle begins, culminating in reaffirmation of accreditation in the eighth year. The sixth, seventh, and eighth years can be particularly work-intensive in terms of preparation and writing a self-study document. As one subject with nearly twenty years of experience noted:

> Look at job descriptions carefully. Some will say: "Our program has successfully been accredited and will come up for reaffirmation in [six, seven, or eight years]." *That's a point of attraction.* But not everyone will tell you up front where they are in the cycle. You may have to dig. And if you discover that the next self-study must be completed within the next year or two, be prepared for a heavy workload, and potential stress.

Program stability is juxtaposed with accreditation because frequent faculty turnover (including leadership turnover) may complicate the accreditation process. Existing faculty may pin responsibilities on the infusion of fresh blood to shore up (perhaps shaky) accreditation efforts. If turnover is frequent, self-study continuity may become compromised. A veteran of more than twenty years offered the following suggestion:

> It may be worth your time to uncover the history of faculty searches over the past five or ten years. If you find that searches are a "normal" yearly activity, or if department chairs come and go frequently, it should tell you something about program stability. You may be entering a world of trouble, especially if a self-study is due soon.

Town–Gown Relationship

Just as individuals exist within social environments, social work programs exist within communities. And because an integral part of social work education requires students to perform hundreds of hours in internships in local and regional social service agencies, the relationship between a social work program (and its host institution) with the community is critical. For better or worse, as social work programs place students in field placements, and as they launch graduates into the profession, a program's reputation is built. Credibility and program value are established. It does not come overnight.

A dynamic community advisory board fosters a successful town–gown relationship, between a social work program and the social work practice community. Board members often include current and former students and faculty, local practitioners (practicing or retired), agency administrators, and governmental officials. Advisory boards provide a vital link between the world of academia and the community. Advisory boards are a vehicle that fosters social work education that is relevant to present and future needs of social service consumers and practitioners. Consider the words of a social work educator with nearly two decades' experience:

> Find out if a community advisory board exists. Who's on it? How often do they meet? How active are they? Ask for specific examples of how they have been able to work with faculty to shape curriculum now and for the future. It should be more than an effort to make CSWE happy. Community members are key stakeholders.

Social work has a solemn responsibility to improve the local environment. A social work education program must establish a positive reputation on campus and among local social service agencies. As subjects were quick to point out, it is important to inquire (perhaps anonymously) about a program's reputation. Do agencies eagerly seek students for field placements? Are program graduates snapped up as employees when they near or complete graduation? A veteran of three decades in social work education suggested a series of questions to consider:

> If you are looking for a job, check out the track record of graduates. Are they successful in finding jobs? Are they making a difference in the community? Are they in leadership roles? What about [BSW graduates] getting into MSW programs? What's the integrity of the institution? Do faculty and staff garner respect?

When I inquired how one could find answers to these questions, the subject responded: "Talk with field instructors, talk with faculty *outside* the department, and talk to grad schools that accept [the program's] BSW graduates."

Current and Former Students

They are primary consumers of social work education. How would you describe current students and program graduates? What are the characteristics of students the program is hoping to attract in the future? A subject with over thirty years of experience suggested the following: "Take a close look at the students. How diverse is the student body? What is their intellectual capacity? *Could you have an impact?*" [Italics added for emphasis.]

The remainder of this section is a compendium of ideas, suggested by subjects, for learning about social work students. Attend a class or two. Notice the level of student engagement. Are they hungry for knowledge? Are they open to different ways of learning and knowing? Do students with social work practice experience appear bored, passing the time while they wait for a diploma?

Do students feel a sense of entitlement or privilege? How common are first-generation college students? Is there a wide range of socioeconomic status among students that will be representative of the clients they will later serve? If lack of diversity among the student body is a concern, learn about efforts to recruit a more heterogeneous population, such as increasing the number of students of color.

Discover where program graduates are today. What is their impact on the practice community? Ask prospective colleagues to give you specific examples of how former students are improving the lives of clients and shaping public policies.

Teaching Assignments

The first faculty meeting I ever attended, as a newly minted academic, was devoted to determining who would teach classes in the curriculum for the upcoming year. There was little room for negotiation. On a huge whiteboard, there was a large blank matrix inscribed with time slots for the rows, and course numbers and names for the columns. Per established protocol, the faculty member with the most program seniority chose her six classes; the faculty member with the next most years of service in the department chose another six; and so on. After everyone had made their selections, vacant slots were assigned to new hires and adjunct professors. It may not have been the best use of employee strength or desire, but it was an unambiguous process.

Reasonable questions to ask when you visit a campus include: How are courses assigned? Is there room for the development of new courses? If so, can you give specific examples of recent courses that have been integrated into the curriculum? What are the expected days and times faculty are expected to be available to teach (and attend meetings)? Do faculty *fairly* share teaching responsibilities, or, as one subject with nearly fifteen years' experience lamented:

> Do faculty have too much freedom in determining days and times they want to teach? It's like pulling teeth around here to get faculty to teach on a Friday. In the real world, people work on Fridays. People are spoiled.

Whether some faculty "don't do Fridays" or not, a new employee has a right to have accurate expectations regarding course assignments, and a right to know if teaching assignments are fairly distributed. Moreover, it would behoove job seekers to use their best assessment skills to determine the existence of a healthy match between faculty desires and program needs.

Pay Attention to Epiphanies

"Find a place that appeals to your heart, not just your pocketbook or your ego."

The year was 1995. I interviewed at three programs within a short period of time. In the end, I had three offers on my plate at once (four, if you count the option of staying in place). How did I reach a decision? I trusted "the force"—an overwhelming power. The minute I landed at the airport, I *knew* I was in the right place. The faculty, the students, the community members, and the physical environment—everything clicked.

Collegiality, scholarship support, workload expectations, salary and benefits—I considered all these factors. But when the decision needed to be made, I went with my heart. It's not a scientific process, and it's not right for everyone. But the "wow factor" is worthy of consideration. It's a gut-level response. Choose wisely and take your time if you are able.

POST-VISIT REFLECTIONS

You've completed your visits. You've written thank-you notes, perhaps confirming a sustained interest. You may even have an offer or two "in your pocket." You've had time to process your visits with those you love and whose judgment you trust. What's next? Suggestions for post-visit reflections are divided into the following categories:

collegial assessment;
infatuations;
future considerations;
an honest community assessment; and
goodness of fit.

Collegial Assessment

Much has been written in this chapter regarding the assessment of one's future colleagues, before and during a campus visit. Collegial assessment bears mention as a post-visit reflection because of its critical value. Whom you work with; how they behave; and their level of maturity (emotional and professional) will likely be correlated with your future job satisfaction. Collegiality is often equal to or even more powerful a valence than specific work activities.

In any social work education program one may expect bumps in the road in dealing with the most professional of colleagues; no one has been able to cultivate a thorn-free rosebush. However, as subjects repeatedly noted, collegial quality varies from one program to another. The range runs the gamut from pathological to nurturing. As previously stated, relationships play a key role in the success of social work and social work education. In the words of a well-seasoned social work educator:

> In considering the strength of factors to [take into account] before select-
> ing a job—a job that may turn into a commitment for twenty or thirty
> years or more, I'd place collegiality at, or certainly near, the top of the list.
> Choose wisely; your happiness may be at stake. Ask yourself: Will you be
> able to trust your future colleagues? Can you have a good laugh with these
> people? Are they human?

Infatuations

Two types of infatuation will be mentioned here. First: the program's attraction to *you*. It is tempting to accept a job where you are truly wanted, where
you are told: "With your strengths, you would be a perfect fit for our program."
It is easy for a candidate, fresh out of graduate school, to be swayed by flattery.
But it may be dangerous and eventually regrettable to take the first offer that
surfaces. It's risky. Will it be the only offer? How long should you wait to see if
other offers emerge? Most programs will allow you a "reasonable" amount of
time to make a decision. If you do have multiple offers, they may not appear "on
your plate" at the same time. It then becomes a high-stakes game—not recommended for the faint of heart. It may be a challenge to trust "the force."

Another type of infatuation may be your professional attraction to one or
more specific faculty members (who may or may not be previously known to
you). You may be thinking: "Wouldn't it be great to work with Professor X?" But
listen to the advice of a veteran who has been teaching a quarter century at
a large public university: "Don't glom onto any individual. Things do change.
People do leave. Look for a program that will give you support for the rest of
your life." Faculty *do* leave, either for more challenging (or less oppressive)
employment, or to retire. Collegial relationships are important, but often eva-
nescent. The faculty you found so appealing at your visit may be gone by the
time you arrive, or shortly thereafter.

Future Considerations

After you accept an academic appointment, if you decide later in your career to relocate, how will your résumé look? This may be the last thing on your
mind as you make your decision (and a moot point if you spend your career at
one location), but it is an important consideration. Contemplate the words of a
thirty-five-year veteran:

> Go to a place with the best reputation. Be *able* to move place to place so
> you can do well in the academic marketplace. I was deeply unhappy at
> Gunzhet Macher* University, and I didn't get tenure. But it helped me to

---

* *Gunzhet macher* means "big shot" in Yiddish.

have worked there because of the reputation and the contacts. It's hard to know [in advance] how long you will stay, be able to say you worked at a place that people respect.

Perhaps the above quote smacks of elitism, but it is worthy of consideration in the eyes of at least some academicians. Where you have worked may rival the value of what you have accomplished.

An Honest Community Assessment

During a one- or two-day visit, with so much to consider, it's challenging to assess the livability of a community—not only for yourself but also for family and loved ones who will be moving with you. Accepting a job in a new geographic location may mark a major life transition in terms of physical terrain, climate, health care facilities, culture, population density, ethnic diversity, recreation, transportation, and language accents. Proximity to friends and relatives deserves serious consideration (a blessing or a curse). Would you be bored in a small town? A rural location may seem romantic on the surface, but would you miss urban amenities? Are you willing to move from a cosmopolitan environment to one that is more provincial? Would a "normal" commute time of ninety minutes (each way) significantly lower your quality of life? If you are accustomed to living closer to work or school, are you really willing to become a commuter? What if you have to live an hour's drive away because the cost of housing is too dear as you approach campus? Or perhaps you would relish commuting for daily "decompression time."

What about the needs of your family? If you have school-age children, you'll likely want to be confident that the quality of local education is good. If your spouse or partner will be relocating with you, employment options may be a deal-breaker. If you are considering relocating to a relatively distant location (e.g., from the East Coast to the West Coast), it may be important to live near a major airport or rail station so you may easily connect with business associates or relatives.

Conduct a careful environmental scan before you accept a position that may have lasting impact on so many. It's a key element in the goodness of fit (see the following section). Day-to-day work activities may be satisfying but, as a subject with more than thirty years of experience (all at the same program) noted: "You may be in the middle of an oasis in a barren desert, and that could suck out all of your lifeblood." As social workers, we should appreciate the importance of a person and a family *within* a community.

How easily might you adjust to a new environment? Will you kick yourself in January, when you're spending an hour shoveling your driveway because there's three feet of snow on the ground? Will you spend the summers hugging an air conditioner to offset the humidity, wondering what possessed you to move to the Deep South? These are critical components to consider.

Goodness of Fit

In the end, you will need to decide if you can make a positive impact. Do you have something to offer that will be a complement to the program you are seeking to join? Can the program provide you with the tools and support to develop and grow professionally? It is much like a marriage. If the values, passions, and goals for each party are alike, the chances for long-term success will be good.* And like a good marriage, it helps to enjoy each other's company, to have stimulating discussions, and to have fun together.

How do you evaluate goodness of fit? My decision to teach in Alaska (yes, it is part of the United States) for twelve years defied many suggestions put forth in this chapter. In 1995, while living in Minneapolis, I was interviewed over the phone by seven search committee members from Anchorage. I recall having my *Social Work Dictionary* opened to an entry for "Generalist Practice" in case they asked me for a definition (they did). A week later, I found myself on a six-hour direct flight to Alaska—never having visited this Land of the Midnight Sun, not knowing a soul, and with minimal expectations. The minute I disembarked from the Jetway, I knew I was in the right place. Everything I encountered during my visit: the faculty and administrators; the students; the scenery; the fresh halibut and salmon; and especially the live moose that stood a mere ten feet from me—all added up to an overwhelming sensation: "I belong here." Indeed, I remained twelve years.

Alaska would not be a good fit for many. Long winter nights and geographic isolation are not everyone's cup of tea; and it is probably not reasonable to expect a powerful epiphany to occur. But I believe chance favors the prepared mind. I believe I completed my homework, and decision making took its "natural" course. Was it a good fit? Definitely! Was I lucky? Perhaps. Do I suffer from delusions at times? Don't we all?

As subjects repeatedly advised, it is wise to aim for a balance between intellectual and emotional assessment skills. As an educator with more than twenty years of experience recommended:

> Go for a good fit between the institution's goals and your needs. If you like to spend lots of time with your family, an R-I school may not allow you the quality of life you seek. Look into smaller, more teaching-oriented programs. Look for a supportive environment where people won't see you as competition.

* This assumes you have a reasonably clear vision of your values, passions, and goals.

An Academic Nomad made the following simple, yet elegant suggestion:

> Ask the search committee: "What do you think I'm going to need to be successful? What do you have to offer me?" Their response, in content and tone, may tell you everything you need to know. It's really about fit more than anything else.

Another professional social work educator, with nearly thirty years' experience, offered the following thoughts regarding measurement of goodness of fit from a collegial perspective:

> How well will you fit in with the faculty? That's concern number one. Will you be nurtured? Will you grow? Do your homework *in advance* to really know your future workmates. Office space and resources are nice, but if people are miserable, you'll be miserable too.

Time and again, subjects emphasized the importance of person-in-environment. As an educator with three decades of experience in the same (relatively remote) location advised:

> Take a *social work* perspective. You are not just filling an academic slot. You are acquiring a position within the context of a program within an institution within the context of a community. It's not just getting a job; it's making a *commitment to the institution and the community.*

Finally, a social work educator with three and a half decades of experience presents a good summary statement regarding goodness of fit. He offers a relaxed, thoughtful perspective:

> This is a wonderful time for finding a job in the field of social work education, and probably will be for the next fifteen years; there are more jobs than there are people to fill them. Make sure it's a good fit. Make sure the faculty share your academic and personal interests. Would you feel comfortable working with these people? If you love to teach, go to a place that reinforces that. You don't have to replicate the program [where you received your PhD]. I've seen some really bad fits [such as] someone who wants to be a researcher and goes to a BSW program to teach four classes per semester with no time or support to conduct research.

Chapter 10 has addressed many factors to consider. Select the ones that resonate best with your career goals and take them to heart. Beginning a new academic position *is* like entering a marriage. Your expectations are positive, but sometimes, perhaps after the honeymoon is over, things are not so smooth.

Evaluate the rough spots. Variables change. We cannot predict the future. And as careful as we may be, there's still risk. The successful job seeker is challenged to decide which factors are most compelling and relevant to his or her unique needs. Such is the nature of an imperfect world. But if you are fortunate, chance will favor those who have foresight.

Next, chapter 11 examines a successful search from an alternative perspective—that of a faculty search committee. The seeds may have just been planted in chapter 10.

Faculty Search Committee 101

If academic job seekers are the buyers, then faculty search committee members are the sellers. Ideally, the search process will result in an outcome that satisfies both parties. A reality today, in 2010, and one that is likely to continue for at least the next ten years, is that there are far more faculty lines to be filled in social work education than there are job seekers. With new BSW programs, and the sharp increase in MSW programs (Zeiger et al., 2005), new academicians are needed more than ever. A quick glance at the Listservs of BPD and NADD reveals a tidal wave of job announcements targeted at future social work educators. With a growing number of retirements on the horizon (many social work educators—baby boomers—are currently in their fifties and sixties), the number of PhD graduates remaining flat, and estimates that only 50 percent of all social work PhDs will enter academia, we have a growing crisis. Demand has surpassed supply.

Sixty-six subjects, virtually all of whom have served on numerous faculty search committees, were asked the following questions:

> In a highly competitive job market, what can a faculty search committee do to attract and retain highly suitable faculty?
>
> What advice would you offer to faculty search committee members beyond the "usual stuff?"*

Regardless of the balance of supply and demand, the challenge of bringing competent candidates into the academy will have a major impact on the success of social work education, the future of our profession, and the quality of life for society.

Adding new members to one's family will have lasting consequences. An intelligent search requires conscious planning in order to yield long-term dividends. Consequently, chapter 11 is divided into five main sections:

---

* "The usual stuff" includes quantifiable items such as academic preparation, teaching and practice experience, and scholarly productivity.

establishing a mind-set for the search; preparation for candidates' campus visits; job announcement suggestions; considerations during the visit; and post-visit analysis.

ESTABLISHING A MIND-SET FOR THE SEARCH

Establishing a mind-set for a successful search is defined as the adoption of a conceptual framework that will strengthen the odds of attracting candidates who will meet program needs, and that will also foster the professional growth and development of new faculty. Four elements, as noted by social work educators, are worthy of consideration: developing a robust pool of candidates; marketing skills; honesty; and humane treatment of candidates.

Developing a Robust Pool of Candidates

When adding additional faculty lines, filling a vacancy created by retiring faculty, or replacing a faculty member who has taken a position at another program or departed for personal reasons, it is important to beware of replicating existing faculty. In the words of a social work educator with thirty-five years' experience:

> Don't look for people who are like you and represent your interests. *Develop a robust pool*—diverse in terms of accomplishments and potential. Get on the phone; talk to people about the positions. Expand your horizons.

The message from subjects was clear: to sustain social work and social work education as dynamic professions, a periodic infusion of "new blood" is essential. Search committees should not limit themselves to more of the same. "Don't look for clones!" To truly grow and develop, a social work program must make a conscious effort to recruit faculty who will challenge existing curriculum and academic policies, who will speak in a different voice, while at the same time embrace commonly held values and ethics of social work and social work education.

Further, subjects suggested the importance of attracting multiple candidates whenever possible. A social work educator with twenty years' experience offered the following advice:

> First, and you may want to get this in writing, make sure you have academic support to bring more than one person on campus—*and not* assume those candidates will a) remain desirable to the search committee after a face-to-face meeting, and b) will still want the position after the visit; candidates

may take another offer or decide your program didn't measure up to *their* standards. If possible, gain assurance from the administration that you will be able to bring to campus additional candidates if needed. Whatever you do, don't settle for a candidate due to pressure from the administration or from fear of a "failed search." Don't rush to judgment. Cast your net wide. Field a diverse pool.

And finally, in the words of a social work educator with fifteen years' experience: "Be patient. Wait for the right person. Wait for the person who will be the best fit. It's worthwhile."

Marketing Skills

The job market for social work educators *is* highly competitive. Further, competition will increase as the number of social work programs continues to grow. Although most social work educators don't hold a college degree in business administration, it is in the best interest of search committee members to develop marketing skill savvy. To create a good match, you must know (and believe in) your product, and know your audience well (Brown, Rice, Angell, & Kurz, 2000; Nelson, 1997). Further, you must consciously establish a competitive edge. Do not rely on salary or institutional history to attract suitable candidates. Other elements contribute to a successful hire. In the words of a social work educator with more than three decades of experience:

> You must offer more than money. Sell resources. Sell *less quantifiable* resources. Articulate how the candidate would be a complement to the program. Sell the students. Sell diversity, a positive town–gown relationship, opportunities in the practice community, and a chance to impact local boards, provide training for the community. Sell grant opportunities, and opportunities to conduct research in the community.

The above list of attributes must be fact, not fabrication. The "sales pitch" should reflect reality and genuine pride. You must believe in and project the value of your program. Pride doesn't occur overnight. In the words of a social work educator with nearly three decades of experience:

> You must have a good product to sell, promote, and attract the best candidate. Be able to *demonstrate* that people are happy, that there is a high level of morale, vision, and excitement about the future, and that there are enough resources to support faculty. Have something that's special, not universally available. You can't fake it. You have to build a foundation. You need an attractive product *before* a search is launched. You can't sell it if it doesn't exist.

Honesty

In a research project, the purpose of a cover letter is to inform potential subjects what they might reasonably expect to experience during their participation. Likewise, potential hires have a right to know what they may reasonably expect after the point of hire. Accentuate the positive, yes, but do not blow positives out of proportion. Be aware of flaws, take ownership of shortcomings, and don't sweep them under the carpet. Be truthful about what is possible. Don't offer what you can't deliver. Be prepared to provide evidence (a track record) of what faculty may and do achieve (e.g., grants, scholarship, curriculum development). Do your homework. Be able to justify and articulate your pride. In your eagerness to hire, you may distort (consciously or not) information or gloss over important facts. *It is better to be respectful.* Honesty can pay long-term dividends, such as a good night's sleep. An experienced social work educator with three decades of experience nicely articulated the connection between honesty and respect:

> Be honest. Be transparent. Say: "This is what we do well; this is where we suck. This is where we want to grow. We think there's a potential fit here." *If you can't state this honestly, there should not be a campus visit.* Ask the candidate: "What do you think? What can we do to help you get the information you need to make a decision about your life?—because your growth is really important to us." Are the program mission and the candidate compatible? We don't deserve them if we can't be good to them.

Subjects stressed the importance of being honest when describing a "typical" day at work. They highlighted the need for clear workload expectations, including cultural norms (e.g., "We are all expected to work in the summer even though we don't get paid."). They emphasized the significance in revealing strengths and flaws of the program and the institution, and issues relevant to promotion and tenure (including "case studies" of those who have succeeded and failed).

Finally, the words of a social work educator with three and a half decades of experience places an exclamation point on the need for honesty:

> Colleges bill themselves as being people friendly; they aren't necessarily. Treat candidates honestly—there's a real tendency to "spin" positions, paint rosy pictures. That will come back to bite you. Give candidates a fair orientation to the campus as a whole. Give them a tour of community resources—more than just driving through neighborhoods. Prepare [accurate] information about housing, cost of living, and schools.

The Humane Treatment of Candidates

> I doubted, in fact, that we ever *were* attracted to them [the prospective faculty members we interviewed]. They represented what was left after we'd winnowed out the applications that were personally threatening. To hire someone distinguished would be to invite comparison with ourselves, who were undistinguished. Rather, we reminded each other how difficult it was to retain candidates with excellent qualifications. To make matters worse, we were suspicious of any good candidate who expressed interest in us. We suspected that he (or she!) might be involved in salary negotiations that currently employed him (or her!) and trying to attract other offers to be used as leverage with their own deans (Russo, 1997, p. 18).

Richard Russo's fictional (?), albeit cynical, account of the academic hiring process should give us pause as we consider the addition of new members of the "family." Ideally, search committee members will be secure enough not to feel threatened by a stellar candidate. And candidates will not be suspected of having ulterior motives that belie a sincere interest in being hired.

While this section on the humane treatment of faculty candidates has not been endorsed by the Society for the Prevention of Cruelty to Animals, candidate comfort is paramount. Candidates may be apprehensive before, during, and after a campus visit. Factors of travel fatigue, jet lag, a potentially life-altering decision to make combine to create a mixture of excitement and anxiety. A candidate needs an extra dose of dignity and respect. Candidates deserve to feel valued. If you are a member of the search committee, don't skim over the candidate's curriculum vitae twenty minutes before the person's arrival. According to an Academic Nomad, with well over thirty years' experience:

> Do your best to make candidates feel comfortable and wanted versus "prove to us that you are good enough to come to our university." That will put people off. Convey your interest in the candidate; make them feel wanted. Hook them up with faculty who have similar interests, like people of color with people of color.

Thoughtful touches are a plus. A conscious investment of time and energy into candidate comfort will not only pay dividends, it is humane. In the words of a social work educator with a quarter century of experience:

> Facilitate. Make it happen. Communicate: "We really want you." Out of half a dozen interviews when I was searching, only one search committee said that to me. Provide the opportunity for candidates to have lunch with

faculty who have recently joined the program. Make them feel welcome. Give the opportunity to visit with future colleagues. Set up a structure to make it happen. Send interview questions in advance so candidates may prepare. Understand it's a life change for candidates and their families. Be respectful. Be nice. Don't treat candidates as inferior. Don't intimidate.

I recall interviewing at the Annual Program Meeting of the Council on Social Work Education in Reno, Nevada, in 1990—thirteen interviews in the space of two days. I was young; I needed the work. I faced a wide range of opportunities, but one interview stood out. It was with an R-I institution and I was *grilled* by five professors who, to be diplomatic, seemed greatly impressed with themselves, and displayed schadenfreudistic tendencies. I felt used and abused (I think I regurgitated my lunch shortly following the inquisition). Faculty candidates (and any human being—for that matter) deserve dignity and respect. Social work educators should know better.

Returning to the campus visit, subjects agreed that it is helpful to conceptualize the search process as an investment in future program success. As a veteran of eighteen years noted:

> You must have a genuine commitment to potential faculty, confidence in their ability to succeed, to grow professionally, and to achieve tenure. If you can convey these desires, their visit will be a more pleasurable experience.

Finally, a social work educator with more than thirty-five years' experience offered a useful idea for the structure and length of time of a candidate's on-campus visit:

> Give candidates plenty of time to interact with faculty and students—more than a day if possible. Allow them time to experience the community, field agencies, and client populations. Remember it's a daunting task for jet-lagged candidates who may have just come from, or are about to go on, another campus visit [or two!].

A final note on respect: Fifteen years ago I was flown to a campus to visit and be interviewed. My prospects looked promising. The chair of the search committee gave me a campus tour. I recall asking if I could visit the library (how strange, I thought, that a library visit was not on the itinerary). His response was "I don't know why you'd want to see the library." The faux pas reverberated in my ears. It was a deal-breaker. In the end, I took a job at another university with a dynamic library staff.

PREPARATIONS FOR CANDIDATES' CAMPUS VISITS

After establishing a mind-set, which includes commitment to developing a robust pool of candidates; honing marketing skills; honesty; and humane treatment of prospective faculty, candidates come to campus.

Pre-visit considerations as described by experienced social work educators are categorized as follows: review hiring mistakes; professional networking to identify viable candidates; a conscious effort to search early; challenges for smaller and rural programs; a conscious effort to attract (and later sustain) candidates of color; cultivating relationships with promising doctoral students; and other pre-visit ideas.

An important recruitment tool is a well-crafted job announcement/description, which may be disseminated online, posted at conferences, or mailed to social work educational programs throughout the country (and beyond!). A sample job description will appear later in this chapter.

Review of Hiring Mistakes

Goodness of fit does not happen just because the stars are properly aligned. Most subjects could recall a hiring mistake, some preventable, others not. Here are two examples and remedies as articulated by eighteen- and thirty-six-year veterans, respectively:

> We've had mentally ill people, one man who committed assault and battery, and plagiarism. Some faculty use their positions as a stepping-stone. [In a buyer's market, the temptation is greater.] Faculty have had affairs with students, ruined lives, drinking during the day. Networking in advance might help [avoid] these mistakes.

> To be honest, in the last five years, we've made a choice that wasn't a good fit. What could we have done? I still don't know the answer. I don't know what we would have done differently. Be realistic in the job announcement; have pre-visit phone interviews; give the candidate a realistic view of the program, university, and community. Encourage candidates to be open with their needs. Give them lots of time for informal dialogue.

As faculty composition changes or increases, there will always be a certain amount of risk, accommodation, and compromise. Mistakes are to be expected. Hiring well—with thoughtful suggestions offered in this chapter, may minimize faculty turnover. Frequent hires, especially "replacement hires," require time, energy, and expense. With less resources spent on searching, more capital is available for curricular and professional growth and development.

Professional Networking

The importance of professional networking to identify viable faculty candidates cannot be overestimated. Have you ever known a graduate student whom you could envision becoming a social work educator? Many subjects could recall being taken under the wing of a trusted and inspirational professor, and were encouraged to pursue a PhD and enter the academy. We cannot depend upon job announcements, listservs, and advertisements in the *Chronicle of Higher Education* to attract the best candidates. Informal networking can fill the gap.

Aside from contacting colleagues by phone, local, regional, and national conferences are great venues for networking. Know what you have to offer, sharpen your marketing skills, and spread the word.

It may be tempting to rely on letters of recommendation, but as a social work educator with more than four decades of experience noted:

> Most letters of recommendation aren't worth the paper they're written on. Pick up the phone and call people, develop national connections. Gather off-the-record information [this may violate Equal Employment Opportunity Commission guidelines]. Call people in PhD programs. Get to know people who lead PhD programs. Don't be overly committed to credentials; look past them. A candidate's judgment doesn't show up on a vitae.

Go After Candidates Early

Faculty searches are not always predictable: A "reliable" faculty member announces her resignation in June—she has taken a position elsewhere that will begin in September; another faculty member tragically dies in an auto accident the week before class begins in January; administrative funding unexpectedly comes through in July.* Ideally, a search receives administrative approval a year or more in advance of a start date.

Let's assume you have approval to hire two tenure-track positions for the 2011–2012 academic year. It's now spring 2010. Is it too early to begin recruitment? No! The first step is to identify program needs. Perhaps you are looking to build a concentration in aging, or children's mental health. Or perhaps you are in the planning stages of developing an MSW or PhD program. Identify your needs *first* and allow a job description to logically flow. Next, in the words of a twenty-five-year veteran: "Get the jump on your competition. Have your job announcement approved and distributed before you go to the APM in the fall [for a position that will begin one year later]."

---

* An earlier job posting stating "contingent upon funding" will be less attractive to job seekers.

Once upon a time, the Annual Program Meeting (APM) of the Council on Social Work Education (aka "The Meat Market") was held in February or early March. It was *the* venue for job seekers and hiring committees to meet and woo each other with their assets. Matches were made, and contracts began in the following autumn. Recently (beginning in the fall of 2007), the APM was moved to the fall, in order to gain an advantage over the SSWR (the Society for Social Work Research), which had begun holding annual conferences in January and scooping up job seekers, especially those with burgeoning research agendas. In the words of an educator with two decades' experience:

> It's a reflection of market conditions. Everyone's trying to create a competitive edge. There're simply not enough applicants to fill the vacancies— and I don't see any relief in sight. Competition is fierce—especially among small and rural programs.

Challenges for Smaller and Rural Programs

Small and rural programs tend to be geographically isolated from major population centers (and airports). If you were born and raised in an urban setting, where your family and friends continue to reside, what might motivate you to relocate to a rural setting? Search committees would be wise to set their sights on candidates who are committed to staying in the community (Phillips, 2002). A social work educator with eighteen years of experience in a rural setting offered the following observation:

> People are not inclined to come to [Small Town University] unless there's a geographic tie or they have relatives. We need to advocate for higher salaries to offset this. We have to give a balanced picture; be honest about limitations, but link candidates to resources and unique features of the area. Let's face it: the "wonderful ones" aren't going to come unless Auntie Hooha lives nearby.

Living and working in Alaska for twelve years, I saw many faculty come and go. Many people I've met have a romantic, if somewhat distorted, vision of life in Alaska. Living through a winter or two, where the sun doesn't rise before 10:00 a.m. six weeks a year (11:00 a.m. in Fairbanks) can be a sobering experience (or influence one's level of alcohol consumption).

I was fortunate to fall in love—a twelve-year-long romance with the scenery and wildlife. And there was the guaranteed conversation starter: "I'm from Alaska." But lack of relatives, distance from close friends, and geographic isolation (Seattle, a three-and-a-half-hour plane ride away, is the nearest major city), eventually took its toll. In the end, the "fit" no longer seemed appropriate.

Attracting Candidates of Color

In attracting the best possible candidates to a career in social work education, another challenge for programs, large and small, is to attract and sustain a diverse faculty that includes people of color (Frankl, 2003). A conscious effort is required. One subject, with a quarter century of experience teaching in the southern United States, offered the following perspective:

> It's a challenge to recruit African Americans. You can network at conferences. You can purchase directories of HBCUs [Historically Black Colleges and Universities], make phone calls, visit campuses, and work with the social work community. Once we get people here, they love us. You have to reach out, sell yourself, and sell your school. We've had some success at HBCUs.

Another strategy suggested by subjects may best be described as a "grow your own" approach, where minorities* are encouraged and supported in pursuit of a PhD. One subject, with three decades' experience at the same college, suggested a long-term approach to hiring persons of color.

> Help minority students get a PhD, and have them return to teach. There's an advantage to having home-grown applicants with community roots. Considering what we spend on searches, it seems a worthwhile investment.

Subjects repeatedly mentioned the importance of adding a genuine personal touch. Candidates must feel valued and wanted before and during a campus visit. In recruiting faculty of color, one subject suggested arranging "lunches with minority faculty for minority candidates, to see what it's like to be a minority here." In a competitive market, thoughtful touches, if not contrived, may make all the difference in the world.

Cultivating Relationships with Doctoral Students

Cultivating relationships with doctoral students may be viewed as a long-term strategy. As a veteran of nearly twenty-five years (including numerous stints on search committees) suggested:

> Don't wait until candidates are about to graduate. Get to know them *sooner*. Invite them to your campus to give a guest lecture, to get a taste of life on your campus. If your budget allows, bring potential candidates in from out of town. This extra effort may yield future rewards.

---

* Subjects often used the terms "people of color" and "minorities" interchangeably. The term "minority" did not sit well with one subject, who noted: "There's nothing minor about me." She makes a good point.

Making the transition from doctoral student to tenure-track professor will never be seamless. But "community outreach" may make the move less scary, and even build excitement. Inviting doctoral students onto campus to give a guest lecture, or perhaps to serve as an adjunct professor for a semester-long course, may acculturate potential professors to the academy. Prior experience makes for a smoother transition.

Other Pre-Visit Ideas

Establishing a competitive edge often means going the extra mile, being creative, and impressing candidates with a refreshing, honest approach. Honesty may include acknowledging flaws as well as assets. Remember that a visiting candidate may be entering a strange new world. Sending a color brochure or a video in advance may build positive anticipation, and provide pre-visit familiarity and comfort.

Another thoughtful consideration is to provide interview questions in advance. In the words of a twenty-two-year veteran of social work education:

> I don't think most programs think to send questions in advance. Maybe they would rather test applicants—place them on a hot seat, so to speak—see if they can think on their feet. But why make them suffer? It just adds to the anxiety. The candidates to whom we give interview questions in advance are *so* appreciative. They say it gives them time to seriously think about the questions, and to understand what is important to us. And their answers tend to be thoughtful. The search committee still gets the information it needs to make an informed decision, and makes a positive statement to candidates: respect versus torture.

JOB ANNOUNCEMENT CONTENT

Job announcements for social work educators tend to be alike, and not particularly eye-catching or creative. Most programs will require approval from a department of human resources, which may require specific language and content including rank, minimal qualifications, a statement encouraging women and minorities to apply, and the ubiquitous "salary commensurate with experience." Uninspiring, to say the least.

Subjects suggested the following items that can be included in and enliven job announcements, while illustrating a program's unique features: competitive salaries; low-turnover rates; investment in new faculty; articulation of vision and accomplishments; a humane environment; a formal mentoring program; and highlighting attributes of your program that place it "far from the madding crowd" (see pages 173–174).

Competitive Salaries and Other Forms of Compensation

In a buyer's market, salaries, benefits, and other forms of remuneration must be competitive. Faculty should not feel pressured to take on additional work to earn a fair wage. Remember, cost of living (housing, food, transportation, goods and services, utilities, taxes, etc.) varies widely across the nation. Seventy-five thousand dollars in Laramie, Wyoming, or Lawrence, Kansas, will buy a lot more than $75,000 in Boston or New York City. In the words of an Academic Nomad:

> It's a competitive world and the economy is not stable. If you live in a part of the country where the cost of living is high, be prepared to offer a higher salary. If candidates have done their homework, they'll know that the value of a dollar in Town A is different than Town B, so don't try to make misleading comparisons. And don't offer extra work—like course overloads—as a way to supplement income. Overloads have a way of becoming institutionalized. Faculty feel obliged to teach extra courses "for the good of the department." In the end they take a toll; people burn out.

The initial salary incoming faculty receive is an important part of compensation, and may have a lasting impact if future increases are minimal or frozen. However, there are other forms of compensation that will enable faculty to save money and succeed professionally (Wilson, 2000). In addition to offering a truly competitive salary, one in line with the local cost of living, a job announcement might offer a reduced course load for the first semester, to allow new faculty to become acclimated. Other ideas offered by subjects to be mentioned in job announcements include assurance of course releases for curriculum development and course releases for accreditation work. Additionally, funds to attend conferences and funding for professional development can be guaranteed. Also, consider offering a "signing bonus"; even $500 or $1,000 could separate your job announcement from scores of other, routine ones.

A final form of compensation is coverage of moving expenses. Earlier in my career, I made three professional moves to new academic settings. For the first two, my new employers covered moving expenses in full. For the third move, I was "offered" a standard sum of $1,500. There was no negotiation. I pleaded that it didn't make sense for a new employee to go into debt to begin a new job, but my request fell on deaf ears. This wasn't a "deal-breaker," but for other candidates, noncompetitive moving expenses could be a decisive factor.

In a competitive market, logic suggests that a statement be made in the job announcement that moving expenses will be covered, or that a moving allowance of X dollars will be provided. It should not have to be a point of negotiation.

Low Turnover Rates

A certain amount of faculty turnover is to be expected (Lewington, 1999). People do retire. People move on to other professional opportunities. They move because of important family needs. And a position may suddenly become available owing to illness or death.

If you work in a department where faculty searches are all too frequent, where new hires are part of a normal routine, it's likely more than a coincidence, and may be an indicator of program instability. If such is the case, this section is not for you. However, if searches *don't* occur on a yearly basis, and faculty turnover is a relatively rare event, then you have reason to be proud. You have an empirical indicator of job satisfaction. You also have valuable information to include in your job announcement. You might even include a statement in your job announcement such as: "Because faculty searches are a rare event, and because they consume time, energy, and resources, we are able to channel the savings into the professional development of our faculty."

Investment in New (and Continuing) Faculty

A high-quality job announcement should articulate how the program and institution will invest time, energy, and resources for new faculty and for *all* faculty throughout the span of their academic careers. A job announcement should convey the message: "We will help you to succeed professionally." Express confidence in new hires to achieve tenure and promotion. Such a statement must be genuine. Point to a track record of faculty achieving tenure and promotion if you have evidence to support your claim. In the words of a veteran of twenty-two years:

> Be specific about job expectations and promotion and tenure requirements. Make sure to mention you will support your "investment"—that you don't have a sink-or-swim attitude. Be honest about challenges and limitations, but also say you will protect non-tenured faculty from time-consuming tasks.

Pledges of technological support, and time to prepare tenure and promotion material, can be placed in a job announcement (and later supported with action). If prospective faculty directly hear confirmation of support from faculty who have achieved tenure and promotion, they are likely to be impressed.

If your program has the ability to provide development opportunities for faculty, especially when they are new, you have a selling point. Give examples of grant opportunities that have made a positive impact upon the community. A subject with twenty-five years' experience offered one such example:

Funded by the Administration of Children and Families, and in partnership with the Office of Children's Services (OCS), the School of Social Work conducted an extensive study of children aging out of foster care. Based upon a detailed report, the OCS has developed and implemented an independent living program successfully employed throughout the state.

Articulation of Accomplishments and a Vision for the Future

In a competitive world, you must sell your product. If you have something to talk about, by all means speak. Has your program recently achieved accreditation or reaffirmation? Tell the world about it! Do your graduates go on to become leaders in the local practice community? Advertise it with illustrations. Have you recently launched a distance education program that is attracting students from far and wide in droves? Don't be shy! Do you have exciting concentrations in health care, juvenile justice, or aging? Shout it from the rooftops. Convey your pride and enthusiasm. Consider the advice of a social work educator with three and a half decades of experience:

Define your uniqueness; define your strengths, cultural amenities, your ability to effect change in the community. Show candidates how easy it is to get involved. Be honest; let them know if the university is growing or if you have to battle to save what you have. Point out hi-tech amenities, positive features of the physical environment, and plans for the future.

As subjects noted, successful hires benefit from the articulation of a well-defined mission. Prospective candidates have a right to know your program's vision for the future.

A Humane Environment

A program that demonstrates—in both words and behavior—respect, courtesy, and support for a healthy, balanced life favorably impresses most candidates.

Consider a candidate's delivery of a colloquium. In the words of a social work educator with more than thirty years' experience: "Make a good impression. Come on time. Turn off your cell phone. Don't grade papers." If faculty are attending because they feel an obligation rather than a genuine sense of interest, it will send a negative message to the candidate.

Here's a personal anecdote relating to courtesy. I was flown in for an interview and campus visit. The nearest airport was seventy-five miles away. The head of the search committee suggested that I rent a car and drive from the airport to the campus. I doubt it occurred to her to meet me at the airport and welcome me. I was not favorably impressed.

Live a balanced life. We've all heard the adage about all work and no play. Leading a one-dimensional life is a predictor for burnout and coronary disease. Nurturing faculty involves a conscious effort to respect and support a balanced life. In the words of a veteran of twenty years, this means:

> Not taking advantage of a faculty member's desire to please, not taking advantage of someone's fear of achieving tenure or promotion, and not playing "guilt games." I've seen enough abuse to know that academic pressures erode the quality of life. You might think social workers would know better. The message "we support living a balanced life" needs to be delivered *before* candidates are hired. Faculty need and deserve time away from work. We all need periodic restoration. If I were a candidate, I'd want to know: "What does the program do to ensure that faculty get regular downtime?"

Formal Mentoring

As previously mentioned, navigating the waters of academia may be a daunting endeavor. Institutional policies and cultural norms may seem foreign, even nonsensical. In the words of a social work educator with fifteen years' experience: "Senior faculty should 'bring along' junior faculty. If schools are going to sustain themselves, then senior faculty are going to have to give mentoring, and be accessible."

Mentoring includes offering emotional and practical support. Formal mentoring requires an assigned relationship between a junior and a senior faculty member. Being a mentor is a work assignment. It denotes a sense of obligation and commitment to acculturate new faculty to social work education and the institution. Ideally, the mentor becomes a trusted confidant and disseminator of practical and honest information that fosters new-faculty professional success. Meeting frequency between mentor and mentee can be negotiated to meet individual needs, and may decrease over time. The availability of a formal mentoring program, announced *before* the point of hire, is a statement to prospective faculty that the program values their professional success.

Far from the Maddening Crowd

An effective job announcement entices the reader with a mixture of program excellence and a wonderful environment. Consider inclusion of the following issues while crafting your statement:

A positive reputation both on campus and in the community

A low turnover rate among faculty and staff

Faculty and our graduates making a positive impact on the local community

A genuine commitment to new-faculty success
A wide range of faculty-development opportunities
Treating our colleagues with respect
Supporting a healthy balance between work and family life
Living in a community rich in cultural diversity
Geographic advantages
Accreditation status

Consider the preceding list a guideline. The above elements are not intended to be exhaustive, and not all will apply to every program. Additionally, elements may be customized to accentuate unique features of individual programs.

CONSIDERATIONS DURING THE VISIT

Your invited guests are about to arrive. Letters of interest, curricula vitae, e-mail messages, and even phone conversations are no match for the in vivo experience of a face-to-face visit.

Considerations during the visit are divided into seven factors: honesty; sharing dreams; the personal touch; respect; a formal interview; campus orientation; and community resources.

Honesty (Revisited)

Honesty has been mentioned under "Establishing a Mind-set for the Search," but it bears reiterating here. Accentuating strengths, while minimizing (or failing to mention) areas in need of serious repair is an exercise in deception with negative long-term effects. If problems exist, acknowledge them, and articulate a plan for addressing them. Distortion of reality is a lose-lose scenario. If new faculty will be asked to play a key role in the preparation of accreditation documents, *let them know before the point of hire.* If teaching overload is a "normal' way of life and an expectation, don't withhold this critical information. The analogy of informed consent applies here. In order to make an informed decision that will have a lasting impact, a candidate needs a clear conception of what to expect in a career in social work education at Nirvana University *before* he or she signs on the dotted line. In the words of a veteran of eighteen years in social work education:

> There must be honesty in describing the job, the institution, issues related to tenure and promotion, clear expectations; and a message of clear commitment to new faculty and *genuine* confidence in their success, ability to

grow professionally, and achieve tenure. After all, we're making an investment in their future.

A reasonable foundation for treating candidates with honesty requires an honest examination of your social work program. In the words of a social work educator with thirty years of experience:

> Search committees should assess themselves first. Most faculties are not honest with themselves. Strengths, areas to improve, track records all need to be examined with a microscope. How do they handle student needs? What about class meeting times? Do they serve the needs of faculty or students? Are they structured to minimize faculty time on campus? If they can't be honest with themselves, how can they be honest with prospective faculty?

Sharing Dreams

Social work educators and administrators are architects and builders of the future of social work practice. Their responsibility is to build a curriculum that will empower students to become knowledgeable and competent professional social workers. Effective social work education must do no less than inspire students to alter the fabric of society.

In order to act as an agent for positive societal change, social work education programs must openly share their hopes, dreams, strengths, and limitations. It's an extension of honesty. It's also a golden opportunity to express pride and enthusiasm in your program, and voice excitement about the future. If it comes from the heart, if your passion is genuine, candidates will be favorably impressed. If candidates are intrigued and inspired by what you have to offer, you may have a good fit. Consider the words of a social work educator with more than three decades' experience:

> Expect high performance from your candidates in their presentations and interviewing. *Let them know that in advance.* At the same time, be open and candid about problems so there will be no surprises later. Be honest. Share struggles, hopes, and dreams.

A final note to this section: avoid pomposity. No program has determined *the* best way to deliver social work education. It's fine to show excitement and pride, but big egos can be a deal-breaker.

The Personal Touch

Offering candidates a genuine personal touch is a courteous gesture that will convey respect and make visitors feel valued and welcome. A greeting at the airport, a bouquet of flowers, or a special dinner in their honor at the dean's house sends a positive message of goodwill. Since so much is at stake (e.g., relocation of a family, the reconstitution of a "family" of colleagues, the quality of a social work education program), it is important to humanize the situation. It is likely *all* parties will be a little nervous. There may be some tension in the air as everyone wants to make the "right" impression.

Candidate comfort is paramount. One personal touch can come a day or two before the visit. As suggested by a veteran of more than thirty-five years in social work education, get on the phone and confirm plane reservations and airport pickup arrangements. Using informal language, convey your enthusiasm for the candidate's impending visit. No script is needed here. You should genuinely be looking forward to the visit. Candidates appreciate the reassurance.

While structured time during a visit is necessary (e.g., meeting with a group of students for lunch; meeting with the provost for afternoon tea; a formal interview), it is important to also allow for unstructured time. Allow time for candidates to meet with individual faculty, or with a small group of recently hired faculty to get the informal scoop from a newcomer's perspective. Encourage candidates to ask blunt questions should they so desire, such as "What's the faculty-turnover rate like?" and "How is social work viewed by the rest of the campus community?" Above all, in manner and words, communicate to candidates that it is an honor to have them visit and consider a career at your program. Regardless of the search outcome, we all want to be wanted. Don't be coy. If you are really interested in having a candidate join your team, say so with an open heart.

Respect

Really listen to candidates' needs and interests, and really respond to their inquiries. A campus visit is a golden opportunity. Look for intangibles that don't show up on a curriculum vitae and cannot be measured by a given number of publications. It's okay to ask tough questions such as "What's the most frustrating situation you've faced in a classroom and how did you handle it?" But don't bait candidates; don't attempt to ensnare them. In fact, a respectful gesture would be to send candidates interview questions in advance.

A respectful mind-set goes beyond meeting program needs. A respectful approach must include a genuine appreciation of the professional needs of a faculty candidate. Be honest about the amount of support you are able to supply. If you aren't sure, admit it. An Academic Nomad, who is now a social work administrator, offered the following opinion:

> [Say to] a candidate: "Tell me what you need to succeed." You might not get it, *but I need to know.* If we can't do it, or get it, you deserve to know. We may be able to reach a compromise, or you may need to look somewhere else.

Asking a candidate to present a colloquium is a wonderful opportunity to measure goodness of fit for the search committee *and* the candidate. A colloquium affords a candidate the opportunity to demonstrate his or her expertise. The search committee should work to publicize the event, let all faculty know they are expected to attend, and perhaps require students to be there. Faculty and students will have an opportunity to learn something new. They will see a candidate "in action." Does the candidate communicate effectively? Does the candidate add a dimension that will complement the program? It is often an accurate barometer.

Faculty and student behavior during a colloquium is critical. Consider the words of a social work educator with more than thirty years' experience: "Make a good impression. Come on time. Turn off your cell. Don't grade papers." If faculty are attending because they feel an obligation rather than a genuine sense of interest, it will send a negative image to the candidate. Keep in mind the candidate will be observing the faculty and students "in action." Are they truly interested? Do they ask interesting questions? Do they respect what you have to say? Could you see yourself working with these people? Is this a good fit?

A Formal Interview

During a campus visit, formal interviews with faculty and administration may take place. The fact that a candidate has made it to the short list, has been invited onto campus, should convey a message to all parties of a commitment to serious consideration. Consistent with an attitude of respect, candidates should not be placed on a "hot seat" and "grilled." This does not mean you should avoid challenging questions. It *is* important to ask questions that will afford candidates the opportunity to demonstrate their knowledge, competency, creativity, and commitment. But as previously mentioned, when possible, send candidates interview questions in advance. Give them time to formulate their responses. Honor their presence. Their future is at stake. So, too, is the future of your program and social work education. Consider a formal interview a two-way process, an opportunity for all parties to explore the goodness of fit, and to truly learn from each other.

Campus Orientation

University and college campuses are unique working environments. They comprise far more than classrooms and offices. Many professors see them as a home away from home. Unlike most work settings, a campus may encompass many acres and feature lakes, gardens, physical fitness centers, libraries, student unions, athletic stadiums, performing arts centers, and historic buildings. The physical appearance and ambience of the campus may very well be a point of attraction (and later long-term comfort) for prospective faculty. Make sure candidates have adequate time to spend touring the campus. If touring the fitness center is important, make sure it happens. If touring the library is vital, make arrangements. In fact, a thoughtful gesture would be to consult with candidates before the visit to learn what they would like to see, or whom they would like to meet.

A work environment is more than architecture and landscape. It's people. A thoughtful gesture in orienting potential faculty to campus is to link them with faculty who have similar interests and backgrounds. In fact, these people, who may or may not be part of the social work faculty, could be excellent tour guides. Alternatively, recently hired faculty, perhaps beginning their second or third year, can offer the perspective of a newcomer, and share their tales of adjustment as they walk around campus with faculty candidates. Informal chats may provide invaluable information that will help a candidate make an informed decision of whether to come on board or not.

Community Resources

Another environment outside of work is the community. Clearly, resources include social service agencies. The quality of local agencies, and the nature of their partnerships with the social work program for field internships and research projects are of critical importance to new employees. Additionally, there are other community factors to consider.

The campus may be part of an urban environment or part of a "college town," with businesses and activities that cater to students and faculty. Alternatively, the institution may be a "commuter campus," with few faculty or students living nearby. If a new hire is accustomed to living three miles from work, then the notion of commuting forty-five minutes (each way) in heavy traffic (a necessity since housing near campus is so expensive) may be viewed as having a negative impact on the quality of life. Whatever the situation, new faculty may want to know about housing, school districts, shopping, recreation opportunities, traffic, transportation, and the cost of living. Search committees may wish to build in extra time for prospective hires to tour the community, perhaps with a real estate agent. If possible, make arrangements for visitors to spend an extra night and day to experience local life *away* from the campus. Consider the advice of a social work educator with more than a quarter century of experience:

> Put together a packet of maps, community events, local publications, and housing options. If someone says, "I have a spouse," then do some networking in the community to explore employment options. Show interest in a spouse's career. Acknowledge that a *family* will be moving, not just an individual.

It is important to consider an applicant's family needs and to respect the future happiness of all family members, but this is often a delicate matter. Federal Equal Employment Opportunity Commission (EEOC) guidelines may limit the ability to ask potential hires about their families. A social work educator from the central United States made the following observation:

> [My state] offers no "partner benefits." Lesbians go elsewhere, where they can get better benefits. It's helpful to make contacts for spouses or partners, *but they need to bring up the subject first*, then the door is open. EEOC does not allow us to bring up marital status, race, or religion.

If a candidate does begin to talk about family needs, it is *definitely* in the best interest of the search committee to provide information about schools, facilitate contacts for employment opportunities, and provide information about family-oriented community activities. As discussed in chapter 8, major life decisions are heavily influenced by family needs. Few of life's decisions are more crucial than establishing a career and moving to a new location.

POST-VISIT REFLECTIONS

You've held an exit interview and accompanied your candidate to the airport. Within twenty-four hours, a phone call should be placed to let your candidate know how much you appreciated his or her visit. Be truthful. Be genuine. If you are working with a time line, share that information. But you may need to act quickly, especially if the candidate is a "hot" commodity. Three elements to consider during your post-visit reflections: goodness of fit, candidate enthusiasm, and sweetening the pot.

Goodness of Fit

It all boils down to this: a match between the needs of the social work education program and requisites for professional growth and development of faculty. Optimally, new faculty will fill gaps, bring new energy, and complement the strengths of existing faculty. A search committee should *not* look for someone who is "just like us." A search committee should look for someone who is willing to challenge established assumptions regarding the best way to deliver social work education.

Goodness of fit resists quantification. How do you know a new person will be able to meet the requirements (which may change mid-course) for tenure and promotion? How do you measure a candidate's willingness to work collaboratively? How does one predict how much fun it will be to interact with someone on a daily basis? Search committee members must give serious consideration to the questions: "Can I see myself working happily with this person for the next five, ten years or more?" and "Am I excited about what this new person will bring to our program?" Hopefully, the candidate is asking the same questions from his or her perspective.

Candidate Enthusiasm

A fair question to ask before both parties make an investment is: "On a scale of one to ten, how much would you like to join our faculty?" How excited is the candidate about coming on board? If a candidate is weighing other offers, the question may be difficult to answer, but the answer is critical. Ideally, neither party should have to settle for what seems like the best match at the time. Both parties should be genuinely excited. A degree of risk always exists; a perfect match is never certain. Mutual enthusiasm is a minimal requirement.

Sweetening the Pot

In a competitive market, what extra measures are you willing to take that will tip the scales in your favor? Are you willing to offer benefits or perks that existing faculty didn't receive when they came on board—such as a reduced teaching load that affords time to establish a research agenda? Are you willing to offer a truly competitive salary that may result in current faculty feeling resentful? Would you be willing to come up with a signing bonus of $2,500, knowing that existing faculty would complain? As competition grows keener, search committees need to be creative.*

As noted earlier, faculty searches are costly and time-consuming. Frequent turnover is not only disruptive, it is expensive. An expedited decision may be more costly in the long run. Offering a higher salary, or other benefits, may improve worker satisfaction and increase faculty longevity.

The success of a new hire cannot be measured by the signing of a contract alone. True success is a long-term affair. Faculty must feel welcome *after* the point of hire, if they are to be fulfilled professionally and make a significant contribution to the mission of the program. The next chapter will explore ways to keep faculty in place, while being productive and feeling content.

---

* Ideally, existing faculty would receive salary increases at the same time to avoid "salary compression."

Keeping the Grass Green

Faculty turnover is a normal development for every social work program. People retire, move on to other professional opportunities, or depart for reasons beyond anyone's ability to predict or control. However, searches are costly and consume time and energy. Chronic faculty searches hamper faculty opportunities to develop new curricula, produce scholarship, and engage in community service. Further, changes in faculty composition require a period of acclimation for all department members. Every time a new faculty member comes or goes, "family" dynamics change and the system balance is reestablished. Excessive departmental changes impact overall program stability.

"Keeping the Grass Green" refers to supporting new faculty after the point of hire (and not being tempted to consider alternative employment on the other side of the fence) (Kula, Glaros, Larson, & Tuncay, 2000; Wilson, 1995). As one subject commented: "Treat them right and they'll want to stick around." Respect for and cultivation of strengths will result in productive and happy faculty (Kanter, 2006; Peters & Waterman, 2004). Subjects were asked: "What does your department do to make new faculty welcome and sustain them after they are hired?" They were also asked: "Given available resources, what more could they do?" Chapter 12 is divided into six main parts: establishing a mind-set for sustainability; getting settled in the community; living a balanced life; establishing clear work expectations; gently launching a career; and providing intentional support for new faculty. The chapter also includes a section on "tenure and sustainability."

ESTABLISHING A MIND-SET FOR SUSTAINABILITY

The seeds can be sown at the end of a campus visit. As a veteran of thirty-five years suggested:

> Welcoming new faculty begins at the interview process, the campus visit, the way the agenda is set, *how* candidates are welcomed, personal escorts.

> At the exit interview there are two important questions: a) How did your day go? and b) What did you learn about the social work program?

The above questions deliver a message of welcome and support. The precise wording of questions at the end of an exit interview is not critical. Instead, the conveyance of respect for potential is paramount. We are all human beings who need to be touched by the care of our colleagues. We cannot simply throw our new colleagues into the deep end of the pool and see if they swim. We need to consciously nurture their professional growth and development.

As social work educators, we are obliged to adopt a perspective of strength, believing that all faculty (novice and seasoned) bring unique strengths to the academy. We need to presume that they are capable of achieving tenure, promotion, and above all, making a significant contribution to the education of future social workers. In order to achieve full potential, it is vital that we make new faculty feel welcome. A social work educator with nearly twenty-five years' experience offered the following advice: "Be collegial. Treat folks well, with respect and dignity. Listen to their talents. *Help them find and develop their voice.* Link them to resources. Link them to faculty outside of social work."

And in the words of one veteran of more than thirty-five years:

> Get them involved in projects related to student organizations, campus committees, and don't let them fail. You need to spend lots of time with them. *Expect success.* Be there for them. Every institution has its own quirks. Address problems quickly; head off trouble.

Simple gestures can go a long way toward acclimatization. Meet newcomers at the airport with flowers and perhaps a bottle of wine. Imagine what *you* would appreciate if you were entering a new chapter in your life. Let them know that you're genuinely glad they have arrived.

GETTING SETTLED IN THE COMMUNITY

Moving into a new community, unpacking, and living out of suitcases and boxes for a month (or three) while you become acclimated to a new job is not easy. Most new faculty appreciate their new colleagues offering a personal, caring touch by reaching out to help them get settled in a new environment. Consider this compendium of suggestions offered by subjects that will help new faculty adjust to a new setting:

> Give them a tour of the community, highlighting recreation, scenery, and transportation options. With enthusiasm, show them what you enjoy about living in [Collegetown, U.S.A.]

Help them with housing, be it an apartment rental or home purchase. Link them with a trusted real estate agent as needed.

Help them with physically moving in, unpacking, locating places to shop, eat, and the acquisition of services.

If a faculty member has children, bring the young ones age-appropriate gifts; help new faculty locate and compare schools and recreation options.

Invite them out for a meal at your favorite restaurant.

Call for "no particular reason" other than to see how they are settling in. Invite them out for a cup of tea.

"You have to go a little bit beyond 'Hey, how are you doing today.'" Socially connect them to the geographic and academic community!

LIVING A BALANCED LIFE

What do social work educators value in life? Achievement? Recognition? Money? Family? Relationships? Helping others realize their potential? Making the world a better place? Most likely all of these have a place in a balanced values system. But if we "knock ourselves out" building a long list of peer-reviewed publications—like so many notches on a belt—what is sacrificed in the process?

Subjects voiced strong concern that a vital component of work satisfaction was the ability to lead a balanced life. Professional success is certainly a component of a well-rounded life, especially for a dedicated social work educator. But time for reflection, time for nonwork activities, and especially time for family were mentioned repeatedly as key elements in leading a balanced life. A social work educator and administrator with three decades of experience articulated the importance of family:

> The piece that really makes the difference is if faculty feel you really care about their family. Let's say the parent of a faculty member dies in the middle of the semester. Immediately cover their classes. Give them the message that their family, their personal life is as important as their job.

From my own experience, I know the value of this support. Two weeks before the end of the semester in 2005, my mother's congestive heart failure became critical. I was unable to concentrate on end-of-the-semester responsibilities. Figuratively and literally, I needed to be somewhere else. I was reluctant to abandon my students and work-related activities, but I knew I had to make the journey. I flew 2,500 miles to be with her. I was able to be at her side when she died. While her passing was not unexpected, the loss was powerful and painful. In my fragile state, knowing I had the support of my colleagues made all the difference in the world.

Another social work educator, with twenty years' experience, offered sage advice for creating an atmosphere conducive to leading a balanced life:

> Have high expectations for yourself and your colleagues, but be reasonable about workloads. Social workers and social work educators are a dedicated lot, and vulnerable to giving *too much* of themselves. Sure, there's always more that can be done—but at what price? Burnout? Don't expect your colleagues to sacrifice downtime "for the good of the program." Don't encourage teaching course overloads; they have a way of becoming expectations. And don't take advantage of a colleague's willingness to please, or their fear of not attaining tenure or promotion, by assigning unreasonable amounts of work. Be considerate.

Subjects noted that living a balanced life does not occur by accident. New faculty benefit by being included in social events and non-academic fun. As an Academic Nomad noted: "Established faculty should go out of their way to be inclusive, professionally and socially." This requires a conscious and sustained effort—one that continues after the first few weeks. Don't let the effort lapse after the first "welcome" party. Continue informal lunches. As a veteran of twenty years noted: "Collegiality is built when folks share meals and downtime away from work."

"Southern hospitality" can exist anywhere.

ESTABLISHING CLEAR WORK EXPECTATIONS

Recall from chapters 5 and 6 that ambiguous work expectations do not promote faculty longevity. Moving targets, where the rules of the game change in midstream, lead to dissatisfaction. All faculty must perform "chores" that integrate to deliver a solid social work educational program. And while roles must adapt to the unpredictable vibrations of academic life, new faculty have a right to know what to expect in order to achieve professional success. The groundwork for clear expectations may be set during the first pre-hire interview. Expectations are later reinforced after a new faculty member comes on board.

For most new members of the academy, requirements for tenure and promotion are paramount. For many, especially those at R-I institutions, the phrase "publish or perish" is all too real. In the words of a social work professor of nearly thirty years: "When I began my academic career, someone said, 'Research is a queen, teaching is a rook, and service is a pawn.' Priorities and values were crystal clear." (Discussion on the impact of achieving tenure can be found at the end of this chapter.)

New faculty members are asked to participate and "volunteer" in many activities. As one social work educator with nearly twenty years of experience explained:

> To survive academia *and* maintain your sanity, you really have to be selective and learn when to say no. There's no end of opportunities for research projects, extra teaching, serving on committees [within the department and campus-wide] meeting with former students for consultation, and service in the community. But let's face it: some activities will look better on your C.V. than others when it comes to promotion and tenure. As social workers we give and we give. But if we give to the "wrong causes" too frequently, it may come back to bite us when we go up for promotion and tenure. Faculty have a right to know, *in advance,* which activities will help and which won't. There are only so many hours in the day.

GENTLY LAUNCHING A CAREER

Depending upon resources and protocol, it may be possible for new faculty members to have different, less-demanding workloads (compared to seasoned faculty) that ease their transition into academia. For example, subjects commonly reported institutionalized course releases that allow time and energy to establish research agenda. One subject with more than thirty-five years of experience commented: "We don't expect [new faculty] to do a lot of community service right off the bat. It's logical, given that it takes time to establish relationships." Another social work educator with more than twenty years of experience noted that at her university:

> We offer one-course reductions for the first year to allow new faculty to get their feet off the ground, and adjust to being in a new community. We have structured new faculty orientations. We check in frequently and ask "How can I help?" We share our syllabi and course materials. We show people the ropes; and create linkages across campus.

Subjects expressed concern that there be a conscious effort not to "throw new faculty into the fire." They voiced a need to "gently launch the careers of new faculty through nurturing." A social work educator with more than three and a half decades of experience articulated the need for nurturing well:

> New faculty must have reasonable schedules—economize time. Lead them to research dollars and release time. Have orientations for faculty at the resource center. Have them attend workshops on teaching effectiveness and building a tenure package. Allow lots of time for nurturing—guiding

> them through the academic rigmarole, especially during their first year. *Go out of your way to nurture* [italics added for emphasis].

The role of existing faculty is key; they need to give; they need to share. Ideally, there is a noncompetitive atmosphere where seasoned faculty welcome (and do not feel threatened by) promising new colleagues. The keys to success should not be hidden. As a veteran of thirty years noted: "Existing faculty should not be too entrenched. They must be willing to give up (and share) 'territory.'" Lead them to grants and other funding sources. Offer them coauthorship if they so desire. See launching a career as a collaborative effort. Offering helpful hints, and reaching out to faculty—especially new faculty—is almost always appreciated, and will help soften academic bumps in the road. One subject, with more than a quarter century in a relatively geographically isolated institution, voiced a need for mentoring new faculty:

> I've seen people come here and feel lonely. People don't reach out to them because of their own business, academic pressures, or family situations. Serious mentoring would help. Even dropping into their office, asking how they are doing would help. Find out what they're working on. Suggest ways you might be able to help. Or just *listen* to their needs and concerns. Offer to take them out to lunch. Imagine what would make *you* feel welcomed.

Assign newcomers to responsibilities that will enable them to flex their muscles. Always remember that new faculty members are hired for the strengths they bring to your program. Assume expertise. Assume excellence. Assume complementariness. Some social work programs employ a seniority system in determining who teaches required and elective classes. A hierarchical system may minimize arguments, but it does not belong in social work education. In the words of a social work educator with more than twenty years of experience: "Give them something in their area of expertise to teach." You hired them to drive, not idle in neutral until it's their "turn." In the words of one social work educator, it is vital to:

> Immediately include them in activities and responsibilities that are not just the stuff you don't want to do. Provide them with opportunities for engagement that will benefit the department *and* them for tenure—which may be the first thing on their mind. Socially connect them with the academic and social service community.

Social work educators worth their mettle will genuinely care about the professional and personal development of their peers. Sage advice comes from the leader of a program with three decades of social work education experience:

Push assistant professors to be involved. Provide mentoring. Have writing groups. The director should meet at least twice a semester to talk about the future. Make a point of visiting new faculty in *their* offices. It's surprising, the things you learn when you sit in somebody's office [analogous to a practitioner going to the client rather than the other way around]. The faculty visit—who comes to whom?—is a real indicator. Give priority to assistant profs for funding, travel, book reviews, and summer support. The piece that really makes the difference is if they feel you really care about their family. I'll give you an example: A parent of a faculty member dies mid-semester. Immediately cover her classes. Give her the message that her family and personal life are as important as her job.

PROVIDING INTENTIONAL SUPPORT FOR NEW FACULTY

During my first academic appointment, I noticed something was missing. Not once did the director come by my office (or call me into hers) to ask how I was doing, if there was anything I needed, or if there was anything I'd like to discuss related to my new job. How odd. At the end of my first year *I* set up an appointment to check in. But something didn't feel right; I felt like I was begging for validation. Had I landed in a sink-or-swim environment with no lifeguard on duty? It was then that I had an inkling of what later would be confirmed by subjects of this study: frequent and regular time with the director is vital, and formal mentoring is a prerequisite for new social work educator success and longevity. In the words of a social work educator with thirty years of experience: "Isolation [especially for new faculty] is the kiss of death." For deans and directors of social work education programs, spending time with new faculty, getting to know their needs, and responding to their requests is an excellent way of providing solid leadership.

A formal mentoring program is an excellent way of providing intentional support for new faculty. Subjects noted repeatedly (see chapter 6) how they wished they had experienced formal mentorship at the beginning of their academic careers. But with professional demands of their own, how do faculty find the time to mentor? One social work educator, with over thirty-five years of experience, is director at a program that incorporated an innovative mentoring program one year. Three new faculty began teaching in the same year, and a senior faculty member, *who received a course release to do so,* was assigned to be their mentor. She described the following mentoring activities:

> They held formal sessions for teaching strategies, promotion and tenure requirements, handling stress, workload balance, and socialization to committee responsibilities. They critiqued each other's papers, worked on co-authorship, and co-presented at conferences—all in a formalized process.

Subjects noted how important it is that the person serving in a mentor role *not* have hierarchical power or control over the neophyte faculty. Conscious personality "matches" are helpful. Optimally, a mentor will be a nonjudgmental confidant—someone who will provide a comfortable environment for expressing doubt or asking "embarrassing questions" without fear of repercussions, such as "What the hell am I doing here?" In addition to the activities noted in the previous quotation, a mentor may also make off-the-record classroom visitations (providing supportive feedback), assist with syllabi development, provide suggestions for workload/life balance, and link new faculty to critical resources such as information-technology support. A good mentor will unselfishly share resources.

National social work education organizations such as the Association of Baccalaureate Social Work Program Directors and the National Association of Deans and Directors of Schools of Social Work have recognized the importance of mentoring to support new faculty and those new to leadership positions. But support should not be limited to beginners. Social work, after all, emphasizes the importance of relationships. And in the immortal words of Bill Withers (1972): "We all need somebody to lean on."

TENURE AND SUSTAINABILITY

Tenure connotes job security, peace of mind, pride, recognition, a decrease in anxiety, and a sense of freedom that comes after mastering a significant rite of passage. Related to sustaining faculty is conquering the tenure hurdle. With only a handful of subjects *not* in tenure-track positions (four out of sixty-six), most subjects (sixty-two out of sixty-six) achieved tenure at an earlier point in their career.

They were asked how their achievement of tenure impacted their work. Specifically, they were asked how their "level of engagement" to their social work education program changed as a result of reaching tenure status. Their responses may have been influenced by the accuracy (and selectiveness) of their memory of an event that occurred ten, twenty, thirty years or more in the past. Thus, validity may be an issue. Reliability may also be an issue. Requirements for tenure "back in the day" were perhaps less rigorous compared to modern times. With many social work programs (and institutions of higher learning in general) raising the bar for scholarly activity, the pressure to "publish or perish" may be greater today.

Tenure and sustainability will be discussed from four points of view: how tenure changes academic life; positive aspects of tenure; negative aspects of tenure; and whether tenure is a spurious variable.

How Tenure Changes Academic Life

A veteran of fourteen years provided a colorful quotation: "Before achieving tenure, it scared the crap out of me. After, I was more confident, vocal, and had a sense of being an equal partner. I was no longer under scrutiny."

Provided a faculty member stays at the same institution, tenure is a one-time event. Once tenure is achieved, the preoccupation, time, and energy spent preparing a tenure file (and frequently a promotion file simultaneously) no longer exist. In theory, anxiety and fear diminish, and confidence is bolstered. A major distraction is gone, and energy is freed up to blossom professionally. And although new responsibilities may come with tenure (such as serving on committees that require tenure status), a shift in priorities becomes possible. A social work educator with thirty-five years of longevity recalled:

> I've come through this hoop, and *now* I can do some of the other things I'd like to do. It freed me up. It was a relief. Worry and time dissolve and my energy was transferred into other projects.

With the security of tenure comes freedom of expression. In the words of an Academic Nomad who has achieved tenure multiple times in his three-decade career:

> You have a safe voice in departmental and university decisions. I've seen too many junior faculty say: "I don't like this or that, but I can't say anything because I don't have tenure. I can't upset the department chair." With tenure, they can do what would have been risky before.

Although pressure to publish varies from one institution to another and standards (in terms of number of articles [or books], length of articles, notoriety of journals, etc.) are commonly ambiguous, the need to publish may be a powerful force influencing how non-tenured faculty members spend their time. One subject recalled an un-tenured faculty member "so preoccupied with publication that she didn't have much time for students." Another social work educator with three decades' experience recalled the following:

> Faculty pulled me aside and said: "Don't get involved with students and community; just write; don't waste your time on anything else. You have to publish." I ignored this advice. I didn't want to live like a cloistered monk. I did very well. But people get so anxious about tenure and promotion and doing the right things.

A certain amount of fear and anxiety is probably inevitable for most academicians. But as social work educators, we can do more to nurture new faculty. We need to believe in their ability to succeed and minimize bumps in the road. As professionals who espouse a strengths perspective, we can do a better job of retaining quality faculty.

Positive Aspects of Tenure

An argument against tenure suggests faculty will become *less* engaged once they have landed on the other side of the hurdle. The pressure is off, so they are free to take a more laid-back approach to work—perhaps showing up on campus less often, serving on one less committee, and missing an occasional faculty meeting. But sixty-two (four of the sixty-six subjects were not in tenure-track positions) social work educators told a more positive story. Tenure, they noted, can boost confidence. For example, a veteran of more than thirty-five years spoke:

> I think tenure is a *very* good idea. Many faculty will not be *fully* involved until they reach tenure. There's more identification with the institution, and leadership is more likely to emerge *after* tenure.

The general consensus among subjects was that engagement does increase with the attainment of tenure. One subject with more than a quarter century of experience observed: "My engagement level has *skyrocketed* because the scholarship pressure is off. I can do long-term projects. Having tenure frees up creative energy. I can take risks." And as if to punctuate this remark, a social work educator with more than three and a half decades of experience remarked:

> It's a lot of work and a lot of anxiety to become tenured. After, I was able to relax a bit. There is definite security, and feeling *accepted*, being part of the core faculty, becoming bona fide. *Before you're tenured you know you may have to leave, so you may be* less *engaged, and after you are* more *engaged* [italics added for emphasis]. You are no longer a visitor.

A common refrain among subjects was the relief from pressure and the ability to relax. If an article doesn't come in on time, it's not fatal, because tenure has already been achieved. As a veteran with fifteen years' experience explained:

> It's taken off the pressure: "Will I have this job next year?" I didn't expect this, but tenure reinforces the notion that I am a good teacher; that made me more confident institutions believe in me. That made me more

confident in terms of taking chances in the classroom; I have more freedom to experiment.

The liberation of creative energy was a common theme articulated by subjects. For many, the achievement symbolized reaching a higher rung on the ladder of professional development. As a veteran of three decades of social work education noted, when asked if her level of engagement had increased upon reaching tenure:

> It did. I became more stabilized and settled—and I could really think of what growth I wanted to give within the department, and myself, and not be worried about reappointment. It helped me to think about what would make me a more effective educator.

Again, subjects repudiated the notion that post-tenure life tempts professors to become less dedicated. As a veteran of more than thirty-five years commented: "I work harder *being* tenured. I'm more committed to the profession being tenured. I'm publishing more now being tenured. I have the freedom to be more productive."

Ironically, when faculty become tenured, they are free to become engaged in activities that don't add much weight to a tenure portfolio (i.e., activities other than publication). One quarter-century veteran of social work education commented on the joy of becoming tenured, and the opportunity to engage in other activities that make a difference in social work education:

> It was the best thing that ever happened to me. *Tenure meant that I could concentrate on the things I wanted to do* [italics added for emphasis], for example, recruitment of students, administrative activities. After tenure, my engagement level shot way up. I knew I could stay. It was a psychological boost.

Negative Aspects of Tenure

Although no subjects in this study admitted to becoming less engaged after they achieved tenure, some academicians subscribe to the theory that tenure does *not* strengthen the academic community. Indeed, tenure protects some people who should not be protected. Interestingly, everyone I interviewed knew *someone else* for whom the awarding of tenure was harmful. One subject, with over twenty-five years' experience as a social work educator and administrator, noted:

> Tenure isn't important to me. I don't believe in a tenure process. My level of engagement has stayed the same throughout my academic career. Whether I dig into my work or kick back has not been influenced by tenure.

But people who become dead weight after they reach tenure appall me. It's not right.

Surely there is a difference between "doing the minimum to get by" and being passionately devoted to one's work. Unfortunately, a system of tenure can "bring out the slacker" in some faculty. Most tenured faculty undergo some form of post-tenure review, but as one subject, speaking from the perspective of two decades of experience, noted:

> Post-tenure review is a good idea in theory, but from what I've seen, it does not influence the behavior or production of most faculty. It lacks teeth. There are no significant consequences. Perhaps if there were some merit increases involved—some way of measuring performance in a valid and reliable manner—with negative consequences for those who don't perform well, and positive rewards for those who do—then faculty could remain vital throughout their academic careers.

Is Tenure a Spurious Variable?

While little quantitative data are in this book, one statistic is telling: exactly half of all the interviewees (thirty-three out of sixty-six) maintained that the achievement of tenure did not significantly alter the way they approached work. After two years of analyzing subject responses, I remain skeptical of the veracity of their comments on this (*and no other*) topic. Were they *all* telling the truth? Were they being politically correct? Had they blotted out negative memories? Had they conveniently reframed their life stories? One subject, nearing retirement and with thirty years of experience, summed up the responses of many by stating:

> Tenure has had no impact on my approach to work. I've been a good worker since day one. Tenure did not make a difference to me. My commitment and performance have been at a consistently high level.

Another subject, with fifteen years of experience, spoke of jumping through the "hoop," but remained steadfast about his consistent level of commitment:

> Psychologically, yes, it did make a difference to become tenured. It was protection against punitive action: "You can't mess with me; you're not going to bully me around." But it's meant nothing to me in terms of level of engagement, because I have just one setting, and it's "full-on."

Allow me to be a heretic of my own research. What if tenure is a spurious variable, a canard? What if other employment-related factors are the cause of stress and anxiety? What if other factors influence the level of one's engagement? How does life-stage development influence one's attitude toward work in social work education (or any other field)? One subject with nearly thirty years of experience (and well into his sixties) offered the following thoughts:

> Tenure did not effect my work. However, the last three to four years I *have* become less engaged. I think what did it for me was life age and life stage. I'm in the process of reviewing my career. What are reasonable workloads? What are reasonable expectations? I am less engaged, no question about it. In the last three to four years—maybe longer—in part due to office relationships, in part due to winding down my career—balancing the needs of the program and family and personal needs. I'm a little burnt out with social work.

Disengagement may be viewed as a normal by-product of approaching retirement. Only one subject was interviewed (a month) after she had retired (the interview was actually arranged pre-retirement). After nearly thirty years of service as a social work educator, she offered the following comments:

> When I knew I was retiring last semester, I noticed I had not as much time and energy. It was time to pull away—time to pass the mantle. There was no grief, no adjustment. It was a relief to distance from college "changes" [turmoil]. There was no sadness. I retired on June 30 and went straight to [a different state] to be with my grandchildren for six weeks.

And another well-established social work educator, with thirty-five years of experience, offered related comments concerning retirement:

> As I face retirement, there is a certain pull-back. I'm less willing to become embroiled in what's going on institutionally—a disengagement of sorts. I'm to the point of wanting to pass the baton. It's a natural developmental stage.

Subjects noted that factors other than looming retirement decreased their engagement level. Spending time on family health issues such as caring for aging parents was cited as compromising performance at work. Perhaps the greatest source of anxiety, far outweighing tenure, and mentioned quite frequently among subjects, was "living through the culture of accreditation" (and reaffirmation)—the converse of *increased* engagement due to non-tenure factors, such as completing one's doctoral degree and the transformation in status from being a three-program department (e.g., sociology, criminal justice, and social work) to a school of social work. Achieving these milestones influenced many subjects to blossom professionally.

A final factor to consider when assessing engagement level is personal drive. I believe this is related to the passion that has sustained so many social work educators over long careers. Perhaps they have an extra dose of integrity, a strong desire to be productive, to feel good about themselves, and a genuine commitment to change the fabric of society.

The Pros and Cons of Longevity

In the 1960s, before the days of ubiquitous fast food venues, I worked at a restaurant with the moniker "Sid's" at the Brentwood Country Mart in Los Angeles. I cooked and sold hamburgers, tacos, and fries. A large sign on the wall behind where I stood announced to our customers: "Please be patient. Good food takes time to prepare." Does this analogy apply to the professional development of social work educators and social work education programs?

New academicians optimally enter the academy with at least a modest degree of competence and readiness to teach, conduct scholarship, and provide service. The question is: Like fine wine, do social work educators improve over time? If so, what factors contribute to healthy maturation?

Longevity is defined as the cumulative amount of time, measured in academic years, teaching full-time in one or more social work education programs. As noted in the introduction, the mean number of years for the sixty-six subjects was 25.58. Further, as noted on page 5, most long-term social work educators (n = 45, 68%) spend the majority of their career at only one social work program—either their *entire* career (n = 29, 44%), 90–99 percent of their career (n = 8, 12%), or the majority (60–89%) of their career (n = 8, 12%). Perhaps consistent with typical life-cycle patterns, most social work educators eventually "settle down."

Specifically, subjects were asked to share their thoughts on faculty longevity. In what ways might it benefit or harm a career, students, faculty, the department/school, or their institution of higher learning? Whether educators stayed in one program for an extended period, or taught in five or six different institutions (Academic Nomads), all sixty-six subjects had valuable ideas and stories to tell regarding the pros and cons of longevity.

Chapter 13 is divided into five sections: a conceptual framework; the pros of longevity; the cons of longevity; sustaining vitality throughout a social work education career; and a final word on longevity.

A CONCEPTUAL FRAMEWORK

At first blush, longevity may seem a reasonable goal. A social work program where job searches are a rare event speaks well for program stability and job satisfaction. Conversely, poor working conditions, administrators obsessed with power and control, colleagues with personality disorders, and mercurial work expectations (and limited resources) all may lead to frequent change of personnel. High turnover may also hamper program development and accreditation efforts. For those seeking a new position, and for those living with chronic faculty reconstitution, frequent turnover should raise a red flag.

Even with a wonderful working environment, clear and reasonable work expectations, excellent resources for professional development, and dynamic colleagues a certain amount of turnover is inevitable and predictable. Even given the best of working conditions, movement occurs. We may limit the frequency of turnover; we may prepare for its inevitability, but it is beyond our ability to control.

People retire. Retirement is not always a predictable event. The possibility of early buyout offers; unexpected personal illness; the need to care for an ailing relative, partner, or friend; or the diminishment of joy in academia all may lead to faculty turnover. As previously mentioned, with a large wave of baby boomers rapidly approaching retirement age, social work education must be concerned with sustaining a viable workforce. As one subject with thirty-five years of experience noted: "If everybody who is senior retired next year, there'd be a real lack of experience. Indeed, many social work programs are 'top-heavy' with senior faculty. The pool of models and mentors is diminishing."

Other reasons for departure include a better job offer with significantly higher pay and benefits, challenging new responsibilities, the opportunity to move into a leadership role, or the desire for a new adventure in a different geographic environment. Another factor to consider is the professional growth and development of one's spouse, partner, or family. Here is an example of a movement pattern for one subject's family:

> When I began my first academic appointment, it was understood that it was "my turn" to decide where we would move—although I certainly considered input from my family. I had three offers, so at least there were some choices. It's funny: if it were five years later or earlier, the choices would have been in other parts of the country. But I took what seemed like the best place at the time. When it was time to move again (my boss was a control freak), it was Lucy's [a fictitious name] turn. I became the "trailing spouse."

How much turnover is ideal? What can we do to limit its occurrence? What can we do to prepare for personnel changes? Chapter 13 explores facets of these questions. First, let's look at the advantages of faculty longevity.

THE PROS OF LONGEVITY

Subjects were quick to illustrate the positive aspects of faculty longevity. And while this is not a quantitative study, the positives outnumber the negatives by a wide margin. The pros of longevity are divided into thirteen categories: program stability and continuity; long-term vision and program development; the ability to see delayed outcome of teaching; loyalty, dedication, and pride that develop with time; institutional memory and accumulated wisdom; knowledge of "buried bodies"; hiring savvy; respect, status, and influence; long-term collegial relationships and friendships; benefits for students; financial security; stability for family; and leaving a legacy.

Program Stability and Continuity

More than a quarter century ago, Thomas Peters and Robert Waterman wrote a number-one national bestseller entitled *In Search of Excellence* (Peters & Waterman, 1982). The authors stress the importance of institutional memory as a key element in the success of an organization. In order to sustain institutional memory, at least a modicum of faculty longevity within a social work program is essential. In the words of a social work educator with fifteen years' experience teaching in the South:

> Knowledge of department [and institutional] history and traditions reso-
> nates with students. Students take comfort knowing that faculty have *in-
> vested their lives* in providing quality social work education for a particular
> program. It gives them reassurance.

Academia prospers when valued faculty, those who are engaged and productive, remain in the institution for an extended period of time. Beyond the advantages for students, faculty stability means a great deal to institutions because less time, expense, and energy are expended conducting faculty searches. Frequent turnover within a social work program may be the result of one or more of the following factors: a less than optimal working environment with difficult faculty (those who have not completed the work of adulthood*), poor organizational structure, ambiguous expectations, or poor leadership.

Faculty instability is not limited to a poor working environment. The quality of a social work education program in inextricably influenced by the caliber of its faculty members. Itinerate social work educators are less likely to enhance continuity and stability of social work programs. A veteran of more than twenty-five years spoke specifically to this point: "People want faculty that are going to stay. If you read a faculty applicant's curriculum vitae and see

* See pages 93–94.

movement from place to place—well, five schools in ten years raises all sorts of red flags."

In contrast, when a nucleus of core faculty remain intact, as noted by a veteran of more than twenty-five years:

> You have a chance to gel as a team; you have continuity. Teamwork and alliances take time to develop. You have curriculum consistency. There's less time spent hiring, training new faculty. It's like [social work] practice: frequent replacement impacts the quality of care.

Frequent searches inevitably take time away from faculty that could be spent advising students, developing curriculum, staying current with social work literature, and pursuing scholarly endeavors. Students suffer when faculty come and go. In the words of a social work educator with thirty years' experience:

> Stability improves the classroom learning experience. Over time, I've been able to establish what works and what doesn't work with students on my campus. I've been able to evolve intricate course outlines over time. Predictability is a big plus for students.

Long-Term Vision and Program Development

Significant contributions to a social work program take time. In the words of a veteran of three decades: "You have to put down roots and heart into a place in order to contribute significantly. If you can stay energized, see hope for the future, and potential for growth, then longevity is a good thing."

Think about being in the early stages of a career. How long does it take to learn the ropes and access resources? How long does it take to master the vicissitudes of academic advising (especially at the undergraduate level, with the elements of general education and liberal arts foundation requirements, and transfer credits)? How valuable would it be to collaborate with experienced colleagues who are willing to share their knowledge of program and institutional history? A social work educator with twenty-eight years of experience noted:

> To optimally develop a program you need to know its history, you need to have faculty who are skilled at obtaining resources, faculty who know the system. And faculty need tenure for stability to advance their careers and develop program loyalty.

Subjects stressed the importance of establishing ties to the practice community. One subject with twenty years of experience noted:

Faculty longevity helps boost our reputation among local and regional social service agencies. Positive working relationships do not develop overnight. This is especially true for our field faculty, who function as ambassadors for our program. Without their consistent maintenance of field placements, and the development of new internships, we would cease to be a dynamic program. Our field faculty have strong community links forged over time. Their high level of commitment and years of service are invaluable.

An important dimension of sustaining high-quality social work education program development dependent upon faculty longevity is the never-ending process of curriculum development and refinement. A good example is the reaffirmation of accreditation status that occurs every eight years. A program cannot resubmit the same document each time. There *must* be refinement, elimination of dated materials, and the addition of new relevant metrics, data, and curriculum changes. Preparing a self-study even a year or two before the document is due to the Commission on Accreditation is likely to create problems. A quality document takes time to prepare. Literally, years of planning, preparation, data collection, analysis, and implementation of change are necessary. In the words of one social work educator with more than twenty-five years of experience:

It's critical to have a core of experienced faculty available to constantly seek improvement and orchestrate accreditation—people with accreditation savvy and experience. Otherwise, you have stagnation and run the risk of losing relevancy to the profession and the practice community.

The Ability to See Delayed Outcome of Teaching

Think about student evaluations for a moment. Data are typically collected in the penultimate or final session of a class, when students are experiencing stress (or relief) with the onset of final exams or excitement with the prospect of a vacation. One thing is certain, they are still in school and have yet to apply the knowledge they have acquired in class to real-life professional social work. Students' assessment of the skill, knowledge, and practicality of what they have learned may not be valid when measured at the end of a semester. True student success is best measured after graduation, when students as professional social workers are able to apply their education by making an impact on clients, policies, and the fabric of society. Social work educators often experience the most meaningful validation years after students have left the classroom. A social work educator with more than twenty years' experience addressed the importance of validation:

> Students are the number-one driving force behind my love of social work
> education. On those days when I think I can't do it again, I watch my alumni.
> I watch them out in the community doing such wonderful things, becoming
> leaders, winning awards, and making a true difference in people's lives. I'm
> so proud of them. I've been at this long enough to see it happen time and
> again. And I know we must keep on doing what we do.

Shaping the lives of students, seeing former students succeed as professional social workers, and building a reputation on campus and in the practice
community are enhanced by faculty longevity. A heartrending quote from a veteran of over three and a half decades at the same program addresses this point:
"Overall, my longevity at [One-Place University] has been a good thing for me.
Students get nervous about change—'You're going to stay here until I finish my
degree, aren't you?' Who could turn down such a request?"

Loyalty, Dedication, and Pride That Develop with Time

The roots of attachment may take hold the first time an applicant reads
a job description. If there is goodness of fit between a social work educator
and a social work program, positive relationships develop with the passage
of time. Faculty become dedicated to program success and student achievement. A sense of loyalty grows and expands. As the years go by, a sense of pride
strengthens the roots of attachment. One subject with more than thirty-five
years of experience spoke of an esprit de corps that fuels pride in accreditation
self-studies and in the program.

With the passage of time comes comfort and security, the acquisition of
which many would not choose to re-create. In the words of a twenty-five-year
veteran: "Why would I want to start at another place where I didn't know
people? Besides, you get locked in with friends the longer you stay."

Dedicated long-term faculty may act as valuable ambassadors and mentors
for new and prospective faculty. They become reliable resources to forge ties
to the practice community. Seasoned faculty become conduits for new faculty
obtaining resources that enhance professional development.

Institutional Memory and Accumulated Wisdom

Institutional memory and accumulated wisdom are by-products of having
a historical perspective. Firsthand experience of multiple accreditation cycles,
changes in *Curriculum Policy Statements* published by CSWE enable seasoned
faculty to provide valuable perspectives regarding the evolution of social work
education. Program historians with the ability to shine a guiding light for junior
faculty are invaluable. An Academic Nomad with more than three decades of
experience described some of the benefits of institutional memory:

When faculty spend decades in social work education, especially true if it's at the same program, they provide a sense of history and maturity. They have more confidence navigating through the rough spots because they've done it before. They can see a budget "crisis" more realistically. They have more teaching experience and more patience with students. If a "tough" cohort comes through every four or five years, they don't take it personally. Their perspective comes with the passage of time—knowing the university system, the policies, the politics, and ways to cut through some of the red tape.

Experienced faculty know where to go to obtain resources, such as receiving assistance with grant writing, or gaining assistance in demystifying an arcane computer program. Perhaps there's a contingent of faculty members who are considering establishing a human services major that could compete with the social work program. Wouldn't it be helpful to have firsthand knowledge of past attempts to launch a program that might attempt to lure away your students?

Two social work educators, with thirty and twenty-two years of experience, respectively, offered the following perspectives on institutional memory:

It takes a long time to figure things out—to forge a path. You need to have a sense of history and institutional memory to build on previous efforts. It takes time to establish networks. But you can, over time. You can develop influence and respect. This is especially true for smaller programs, where you may feel threatened during a sagging economy.

Contributions over time—you can see them. You can see a program develop. You can grow and develop over time [programmatically and personally]. As long as you feel new challenges, [and] you stretch yourself professionally, then it's probably good to stay in the same place because you have all this accumulated wisdom—wisdom about things that aren't necessarily written down. You have a history of relationships. And it takes a while, on a university level, to be recognized for your contributions and what you might be able to contribute.

And then there are certain fringe benefits of longevity that don't immediately come to mind that transcend achieving academic excellence. A veteran of a quarter century remarked: "It's taken a while, but I've been able to acquire some of the best basketball seats in the arena."

Knowledge of "Buried Bodies"

Closely related to institutional memory and accumulated wisdom is the notion of "buried bodies," a term I was unfamiliar with prior to writing this book, but the meaning of which became clear after numerous references from a dozen subjects. Succinctly, "buried bodies" refers to the *real* history of program and institutional operations that lies beneath the surface, unbeknownst to the casual observer. These hidden truths are revealed over time. With revelation comes the ability to conquer barriers once thought insurmountable. In the words of a social work education veteran of nearly thirty years: "The savvy faculty member knows where all the bodies are buried, where the traps lay, who not to mess with, and who to butter up." Or in the perhaps more colorful vernacular of someone with more than thirty years' experience: "I know the system, who to call to help. I have buddies all over campus. I'm not going to step in a big pile of shit because I know how to avoid it."

Hiring Savvy

If you want to have a stable faculty and a social work program where faculty searches are a rare event (in contrast to a yearly standard activity), you must hire well. Creating the best possible match between employer and employee does not occur by chance alone. Conscious efforts on the part of job seekers (see chapter 10) and faculty search committee members (see chapter 11) are helpful in establishing and sustaining a stable, competent, and productive social work education program. Who among us, as an employer or employee, has not made an employment mistake? Who among us could not benefit by improving his or her hiring skills?

Hiring "well" is a complex enterprise. Hiring freezes occur when budgets are tight (as at the time of this book's publication). Salaries may not be commensurate with the local cost of living. Nevertheless, hiring savvy is often a positive by-product of longevity. Having seasoned faculty members on a search committee may make the difference between a good hiring decision and a poor one. Note the comments of a social work educator with nineteen years of experience, and a veteran of numerous searches:

> We've become more stable in recent years. It wasn't always so. Now we have fewer searches, the atmosphere is calmer. I like to think I've become savvier and make better decisions when it comes to hiring and retention. There's so much to learn at a university. It just takes time. You have to learn from your mistakes.

Respect, Status, and Influence

Assuming a certain level of engagement and productivity, longevity affords social work educators the opportunity to build a positive reputation on campus and establish critical connections with the social service practice community.

But the development of a campus-wide reputation and links with agencies does not occur overnight. In the words of a veteran of twenty-three years:

> Over time you establish relationships and strengthen them. You're recognized, you represent the community. That's one of the things about moving frequently; you don't get [the recognition]. By staying, you have more of a chance to leave a legacy. You establish continuity over time; you're reliable.

And speaking of creating a legacy, a veteran of twenty-four years noted:

> As the years pass, you realize you are really shaping the lives of students and building a reputation in the community. You build a legacy as "the go-to person" in specific curriculum areas. You could be known for your expertise in wraparound services for children and families. And if you stay long enough, you get to see former students blossoming in the community as professional social workers, many in leadership roles.

Perhaps a level above legacy status is becoming an institutional icon. Maybe this level is reserved for the thirty-years-of-service-and-above group. One subject with three decades of experience in the same department had this to say about the pros of longevity:

> As a field director, the positive connections I have established with the community are beyond value. I am a highly visible link between our social work program and the practice community. I have a positive reputation. I'm at the point where I'm teaching children of my former students. Icons are associated with the program in the eyes of alumni and community agencies. And we are a source of wisdom for newer faculty.

If you stay long enough, make valuable contributions to curriculum development, scholarship, and service to the campus and local communities, people notice. Experienced faculty bring wisdom to the program, the institution, and increase status and visibility on campus. They know how to rally for resources, even in a competitive atmosphere with lean budgets. "Campus clout" may become a positive by-product of faculty longevity. A faculty member for twenty years made the following relevant observation:

> As a mentor to junior faculty, I bring prestige to the university and the community. After I received my Trustee's Award, people paid more attention to what I had to say. It was similar to receiving my PhD—more recognition. You are the same person, but more people listen.

With recognition comes the power to influence program and campus policies. One becomes a symbol of accomplishment, an anchor of credibility, and a source of knowledge. Seasoned professors have the opportunity to forge a luminous identity (Becker & Carper, 1956; Becker & Strauss, 1956). Campus and community linkages developed over time pave the way to launch new programs and initiatives. A veteran of thirty years cited examples of her political power:

> My longevity at [Marvelous University] has been good. It takes time to understand political systems and build respect. As a social work administrator, I've been able to increase office space, acquire grants, add new programs, and create new policies. I have come to know the key players. I can exert influence where it is needed.

Another social work educator, with *more* than three decades of service at the same institution, spoke of the advantages of having built long-term networks on campus:

> I've developed the ability to establish relationships across campus. Through the years, I've learned how to navigate my way through the crossways of the institution. I can call someone in any department on campus and get the information I need. I can even get perks, like free football tickets.

Long-Term Collegial Relationships and Friendships

Recall the importance of family as a key ingredient in the recipe for worker satisfaction. A social work educator's colleagues are his or her family away from home (see chapter 3). Also recall that positive collegial relationships were identified as unexpected benefits of longevity (see chapter 4). In the words of a veteran of more than a quarter century:

> I'm not interested in running around and meeting a lot of people. I've hunkered down; I'm in a very manageable place. The pros of longevity are fairly obvious. You not only become vested in a retirement system, you build lasting friendships and connections with colleagues. And you have an opportunity to develop lasting collaborations with faculty you know and trust. Curriculum development and scholarly activities, especially in a noncompetitive environment, become enjoyable.

Benefits for Students

As an academician, it's a sweet reward when former students come to visit five, ten years or more after graduation to let you know how important a role you played in their professional development. Now imagine how rewarding it is from a former student's point of view to visit, now as a colleague, his or her former professor. As a social work educator with twenty-eight years' experience noted: "Students like the fact that there will be at least *somebody* they know when they come back to visit."

At the University of Alaska Anchorage, where I taught for twelve years, we had a motto: "We learn for life," a double entendre connoting that time spent at the institution enabled one to conduct a more productive life, *and* planting the seed for lifelong learning *beyond* graduation. A favorite professor may play a key role in lifelong learning. A social work educator with three decades of experience noted:

> [that he felt] . . . a responsibility to former students; it means so much to them to maintain that contact. I think of the value of mentors in my life. A relationship doesn't have to end after they receive their diploma. We're really all in this together.

As previously noted, when faculty demonstrate they have invested their lives in social work education by their dedication and longevity, students feel reassured. They have positive role models who offer hope for the future of society. According to a veteran of over thirty years:

> It's sad when there's not been enough faculty there long enough to give stability and long-term direction, and to be living historians. It's good for the program. It's good for the students. It's hard on students when faculty come and go on a regular basis. They legitimately wonder: "Who's going to help me with my advising? Who's going to teach the policy class next fall?"

Gone are the days when most students completed their undergraduate education in the space of four years. Increasingly, employment, care giving, and other time-consuming activities necessitate taking more (in some cases, far more) than four years to earn a degree. One subject with more than thirty-five years' experience nicely articulated the advantage of faculty longevity for students:

> Some long-term relationships are with students who are part-time, and it may take them upwards of ten or even twelve years to finish a baccalaureate degree—the longevity of faculty and the ongoing relationships can be extremely valuable. The days of four years in and out are long gone.

Financial Security

Retirement benefits amass over time, and they give social work educators a sense of financial security. A common scenario for subjects is to accrue 2 percent or more in lifetime retirement funds for every year of service. Let's say that at the point of retirement, one's years of service equal thirty, and the standard percentage is 2.5 percent. When the numbers are multiplied together, the retiree will receive 75 percent of an average of the three highest-paid years—for the rest of his or her life. Quite a nice benefit. Obviously, more years of service yield higher benefits. Many subjects reported looking forward to earning a lifetime reward of 80 to 90 percent of their salary for their "golden" years. Longevity literally pays off.

Moving to a new place of employment, especially in another state, may signal the end of an accumulation of years of service and beginning anew the process of vestment (see chapters 7 and 8). Consider the thoughts of a social worker with over two decades of service at the same location:

> I've been tempted with other job offers over the years. But as the years add up, I find I become less willing to move—even with a bump in salary. I've done the math as they say, and I don't think it's worth it. It could take another ten years to become vested again, and who knows what I'll be doing then? I'll *probably* still be teaching social work but—I know it may sound funny coming from a social worker, but I think I've become more conservative, at least financially. Money has taken on a new meaning over the years. I've got a safe and predictable retirement plan. For now, I'll play it safe.

Stability for Family

Not all forms of stability can be measured in dollars and cents. Moving to a new location with a partner and children is a major event, one that dramatically alters lives in terms of aspirations, friendships, school activities, community connections, and climate change. Note the thoughts of a subject with three children (in their teens at the time of the interview):

> I can't be selfish about my career aspirations. I have to consider my family's happiness. It wasn't always the case. But now with children and a spouse with his own career, I have to consider their needs. After-school sports, neighbors we like, and a safe, familiar community. It's really what I want for my family. They thrive on the stability. And besides, I've always wanted to raise a family in one place. It's not perfect, but I'd hate to leave. The idea of packing alone . . .

Leaving a Legacy

Go for that rocking chair with your name embossed in gold! Few might say it aloud about themselves, but longevity in social work education affords one the opportunity to leave a legacy. It's been said that as people enter the sunset years of their lives, they don't fear dying so much as they fear reflecting upon their time on earth and concluding that they didn't make a positive difference in the lives of others and society in general (Levine & Levine, 1989). Longevity enables social work educators the opportunity to make a positive difference. Fame may or may not be a by-product. A veteran of twenty-four years as a social work educator made the following observation:

> You do have a chance to build a legacy, to shape the lives of students. You can build a reputation at the university and within the community. People will come to rely upon you as a source of knowledge. The world can become a better place because of your efforts.

THE CONS OF LONGEVITY

If the shoe *doesn't* fit and you continue to wear it, someone's going to feel the pain.

Subjects were quick to mention the downside of longevity. When the goodness of fit between a social work professor and a social work program turns sour, everybody loses: the professor, other faculty, the students, and the program. A veteran of twenty years noted that faculty who "stay 'beyond their time' can suck the lifeblood out of a program." A cynical statement comes from a social work educator with more than thirty years of experience, and with tongue only partially planted in his cheek:

> No one should teach after forty-five [years of age]. You get all your education up to thirty-five, then spend the rest of your life trying to solve the world's problems with what you've got. Education should be a *lifelong* process, but the worst part of longevity is that people become jaded, lose their spontaneity, and lose their curiosity.

As previously stated, there are far less negatives than positives. Nevertheless, the cons of longevity are worthy of careful examination, because faculty who stay too long are deleterious to a high-quality social work program. The cons of longevity are divided into six categories: the negative impact of tenure; losing one's edge; disengagement; minimal salary increases; missed opportunity to experience other programs; and the need for "fresh blood."

The Negative Impact of Tenure

The pros and cons of tenure have been discussed in chapter 12. Recall that subjects maintained that the achievement of tenure did not significantly alter the way they approached work. Yet, I heard many stories of people whom subjects said they knew (miraculously, never themselves) who compromised their level of dedication after they became tenured, as if the arrow on the boat throttle was no longer pointed at "full steam ahead." After sliding into home plate and being declared "safe," some faculty become less enthusiastic. One subject with nearly thirty years of experience painted a disturbing image: "It saddens me to see people turn into a rock, collecting mold." Tenure has the negative impact of giving faculty permission to disengage. They may think: "Okay, you've done your seven years of productivity, now you can just show up for work and do a mediocre job. And don't worry; they won't fire you if you keep your head above water." Another subject, with more than a quarter century of experience, commented on the less than professional behavior of his colleagues after they bcame tenured:

> Some achieve tenure and go ballistic. Based on visiting over fifty programs [on accreditation site visits and consultations], I often identify one or more faculty who are less engaged—faculty who are off in their personal zone somewhere—following personal agendas, detached from the [social work education] program. How much of a private practice do they have? Can you be a therapist and a professor at the same time?

The downside of tenure is when faculty become less industrious. In the words of a veteran of twenty-five years: "People who stop being productive are a real scourge on the profession."

Losing One's Edge

Faculty who become too comfortable lose their sense of wonder, their appetite for new knowledge, and openness to different ways of knowing. The risk of cynicism and burnout may increase with longevity. Social work educators are aware of these risks, and some fear the change. In the words of two veterans, with nearly thirty and sixteen years of social work education longevity, respectively:

> The risk is becoming stagnant, complacent. The one guy in the department—please—he should get off his butt and do something sometime. It's a sad waste of humanity. If you've been using the same syllabus for twenty years—well, that's a bright red flag.

> I do know people who have been teaching the same way they did fifteen years ago. I find it hard to believe that their students find it exciting to be in those classes. A conscious effort to grow and develop is required.

Becoming too secure, losing one's edge, being stuck in old teaching methods popular a generation ago, and having a myopic attitude of "If it ain't broke, don't try to fix it" are all telltale signs. In the precocious words of an eleven-year veteran: "I want out if I depend upon telling students stories from thirty years ago." No one wants to become stale and lose relevancy to the *current* mission of social work and social work education. Consider this colorful image painted by a veteran of three and a half decades:

> The risk of longevity is that you become stale. I have a friend who's been here a long time and I kid him that he's shellacked his notes. I'd hate to become cynical. That [attitude] can become infectious and downright destructive.

No one sets out to become stagnant. And yet we see our colleagues losing their edge, especially in the latter stages of their careers. We may wonder how this happens. A veteran of twenty-four years offers the following cautionary comments regarding faculty who have lost their enthusiasm:

> The light goes out in their eyes. They stay in a rut. They are not going anywhere [note the double entendre]. It's comfort. It's security. They're not looking for a challenge anymore. They're coasting in stagnation. There's deadness. They've forgotten what it's like to feel passion in the classroom.

Disengagement

Closely related to losing one's edge is the notion of becoming disengaged. The risk of disengagement can increase with longevity. In the words of a social work educator with more than a quarter century of experience:

> Supervision after tenure and promotion is often a very murky affair. Their psyche may be drifting somewhere else and it's hard to supervise *that*. If someone doesn't show up for classes, you can fine them. For someone who does something unethical in the classroom, you can fire them. But for someone who becomes detached, faculty autonomy comes back and bites people in the ass!

I once knew a professor who gave the identical lecture *two weeks in a row*. Students swore the words were identical each time, as were the voice inflections and the pauses for laughter. And many of us have heard a story similar to the one told by this professor with thirteen years of social work education experience:

We've probably all had that professor who's stayed in the classroom and hasn't left, so he's telling stories and giving case examples from thirty years ago. He's still talking about AFDC [Aid to Families with Dependent Children] instead of TANF [Temporary Assistance for Needy Families, which replaced AFDC]. The danger of [staying] somewhere too long is you don't update yourself.

Minimal Salary Increases

One of the best ways to receive a significant raise in salary is for an academician to accept a faculty position at another institution of higher learning. If you remain at one institution for your entire career as a social work educator, don't expect significant raises. In fact, don't be surprised to see salary inversion, with new hires receiving *more* than you are currently making. As stated by a social work educator with more than twenty years' experience at the same program: "Administrations can put faculty in a box. They may take it for granted that you're not going to leave. Salary increases are minimal."

She makes a valid point. As years go by, loyalty, dedication, friendships, community obligations, family comfort, and environmental predictability lay down strong roots. Even with a certain level of job dissatisfaction, a faculty member may not choose to relocate (see chapters 7 and 8).

Even when working conditions are significantly less than desirable, and you are locked into what has earlier been identified as "Skinner Box raises" (see page 77), a higher salary at a new location may come with a non-monetary price. Comfort, familiarity, and the desire *not* to pack and unpack may discourage mobility.

Missed Opportunity to Experience Other Programs

If Academic Nomads are on one end of the "movement continuum," then social work educators who spend all of their careers at only one program are at the opposite end. Long-term faculty miss the opportunities "that might have been" to attain firsthand knowledge of how other programs operate. Perhaps by design, or perhaps due to circumstances beyond their control, they will have limited communication and experience with other educational institutions. Exposure to other social work programs is minimal. Again, as the years add up, change becomes more of a challenge. In the words of a veteran of more than two decades:

You may lose out on other opportunities by staying at one place too long. But it's difficult to leave. You become invested. And you ask yourself: "Do I really want to take on the challenges of *another* institution?"

The Need for "Fresh Blood"

The infusion of new talent is a pressing need for a dynamic profession. A social work faculty optimally should have a near-equal balance of new, mid-level, and senior members. With regard to longevity, if senior faculty dominate the playing field, new hires may be rare. Who, then, will challenge the old guard?

New blood brings in new ideas, passion, and vitality. Barriers once believed to be insurmountable are seen through fresh lenses. A social work educator with three and a half decades of experience, mostly at the same university, commented: "It would be *good* if we had more turnover at [Venerable University]. A lot of folks have been here a long, long time. That's not necessarily healthy."

Again, a strong program has a balance of junior, mid-level, and senior faculty. Maintaining this balance is an exercise in social engineering (e.g., challenging faculty who are "past their prime" to step down for the good of the program). Consider the analogy of a sports team made up of mostly veteran players near the end of their careers. The analogy is not perfect because we are comparing physical atrophy and mental atrophy, but the need for new approaches to work *is* appropriate.

Social work and social work education are dynamic professions. We must have injections of new talent in order to remain relevant. Consider the remarks of a social work educator with more than thirty years of experience:

> It would be tough on a department if *everyone* had longevity—because you don't have those new ideas and new eyes that challenge the status quo. New faculty bring social work education to a whole different level.

Speaking of freshness, one subject with twenty years' experience had the following story to relate:

> Newer faculty are often more technologically astute. I remember a member of our faculty; he was near retirement at the time. He was well known in the field [of social work education]—published up the wazoo. To say he was arrogant would be putting it mildly. He didn't know how to type! He talked down to the support staff, ordering them around as if they were lesser beings. He kept handing them near-illegible handwritten manuscripts. The irony was, he was completely dependent upon them. Needless to say, the support staff was dancing a jig when he departed.

SUSTAINING VITALITY THROUGHOUT A SOCIAL WORK EDUCATION CAREER

Many social work educators are productive throughout their entire careers. But if there is a genuine risk that faculty may come to rest upon their laurels after tenure, or become disengaged as they enter the latter stages of their careers, what can we do to sustain their vitality *throughout* their careers? After listening to the cons of longevity, as a researcher, I was hungry for a remedy, and to be honest, I needed a sense of hope for our profession. So I asked: "What can we do to stay fresh?"

What I learned is divided into ten categories: establishing a culture of renewal; a mind-set of responsibility to students; staying current with literature; engaging in faculty development; associating with dynamic colleagues; staying current with community practice needs; networking with in-state social work education programs; attending conferences; taking sabbaticals; and requiring serious post-tenure review.

Establishing a Culture of Renewal

Staying fresh does not occur by chance alone; it requires a conscious effort. As the mice in the motivational book *Who Moved My Cheese?* discovered, establishing a "willingness to change" culture is critical to job and life satisfaction. Hackneyed beliefs will not lead you to new discoveries (Johnson, 1998). How does a social work program develop and institutionalize a culture of renewal, humility, and openness to change?

An administrator's role may be key. A competent administrator will help faculty stay energized. Here are two examples given by long-term social work educators, both administrators, with twenty-six and thirty-six years of experience, respectively:

> [Successful] longevity is all about being stimulated, being actively engaged in what you believe. As an administrator, *I* must be excited, like the way I am about our new graduate certificates. I must also foster strengths, redirect energies to play to faculty strengths, so people feel valued. I must also be courageous and stand up to *unprofessional* behavior—hold people accountable.

> To offset the negative possibilities of longevity we *all* have to stay energized. Give people projects that enable faculty to feel there are critical stakeholders. Utilize their talents. Make sure they are serving the needs of something larger than themselves, the needs of the department. Promote an esprit de corps. Demonstrate pride in [accreditation] self-studies and pride in the program.

As competent social work educators, we can never know it all. We must stay hungry for new challenges and stimulation; actively search for new stimulation; sustain our passion; and look for ways to challenge ourselves, our students, and other faculty. Consider the thoughts of a veteran of more than a quarter century, when she was asked, "How do you combat stagnation? How do you keep fresh?"

> You must make an intentional decision, an effort to keep growing. Change your underwear and change your mind at least once a day, otherwise they both begin to stink. I don't know it all yet, so how can I *not* keep growing?

Think of how you are teaching today. Would it save time in the long run to just shellac your notes to preserve them for a class you'll be teaching ten years from now? A social work educator voiced wide-ranging thoughts about staying fresh:

> How do you stay vibrant? Seek new challenges. Constantly revamp course content and approaches to teaching. Avoid the rut of teaching classes the same way each year. Make a conscious effort. People and cultures change. Be responsive to political change. Stay in touch with community needs. *Don't marry yourself to work!* Have margins and boundaries. Don't put all your eggs in one basket. Students know if we don't live what we're teaching.

A Mind-set of Responsibility to Students

As social work educators, there are two basic questions we must ask ourselves: *What* are we working for? and *Whom* are we working for? The answer to the first question lies in our mission to prepare future generations for their professional roles. The answer to the second question, in conjunction with the first, consists of sobering words: we have a sacred obligation toward our students. In the words of a veteran of three decades: "If you don't love teaching, students will be bored to tears. We must continue to stay fresh."

As we established in chapter 3, social work educators are drawn to their profession by a calling and a dedication to change the fabric of society. A social work educator with more than thirty-five years' experience articulated this solemn responsibility:

> A conscious effort to grow and develop is needed. We must continue to develop and refine our worldview. We must stay attuned to cultural changes as our world becomes more diverse. *We have a responsibility for the future through our students. We are a conduit for our students.* [Italics added for emphasis.]

Staying Current with Literature

I often tell my students that they have a professional obligation to continue to learn *after* they matriculate from a social work education program. Similarly, social work educators have an obligation to stay abreast of state-of-the-art knowledge in their field. Staying current with relevant literature must be a normal activity, one which we build into our regular schedules. The last time I looked, no one had declared a publishing moratorium. New information keeps coming in and the number of journals continues to grow, but as a social work educator with three decades of experience remarked: "You've got to keep your skills current because it's a changing profession and it will pass you by." Staying current with social work–related literature is a great way to stay professionally connected. According to a veteran of more than thirty-five years:

> The key [to successful longevity] is to stay engaged with the discipline. Keeping up with social work and related literature is *so* important. The "state of the art" changes. What are the current challenges that are different compared to when you first began your career? How can you stay relevant? How can you protect your professional values?

Staying current with literature should not be limited to peer-reviewed publications, or journals with the words "social work" in the title. Changes in popular culture are not restricted to academic publications. One subject, with more than three decades of experience, suggested reading *Rolling Stone* and listening to today's popular music in order to stay attuned to the needs and experience of one's students. It's sobering when social work educators reach the point at which they are not only old enough to be the parents of their students, they are old enough to be their grandparents! Equally sobering is teaching the children of former students.

Engaging in Faculty Development

Faculty development connotes *active* involvement in one's professional growth and development. Intentional professional development makes a clear statement: "We will not settle for mediocrity." As social work educators we must be committed to lifelong learning, so we can forever teach our students how to make lives better. A social work educator with sixteen years of experience reflected: "Every semester I try changing my classes a bit. It makes me grow as a social work educator." Attending trainings and workshops helps, especially in the area of information technology, where change and innovation are frequent. Consider being computer savvy a professional obligation. Teaching can always improve. Meaningful post-tenure review would be helpful.

Two more subjects, with twenty and thirty years of experience, respectively, add other useful suggestions:

> How do you stay fresh and prevent burnout? Should you "vote someone off the island" every five years? Do in-services, provide recognition, give faculty resources; give *older* faculty a chance to do something new. Perhaps provide funding to attend an international conference to revitalize them. Why are [institutions] so punitive with travel money? It's their demise!

> The *best* course to teach to stay fresh is policy because it *doesn't work if you keep it the same every year.* Change is constant. Try new things each year. Create new activities. Take on a new class or a class you haven't taught in ten or more years. Or look at your program and ask: "What's the next step?" Force yourself to try at least one new activity in *every* class you teach *every* semester. But don't just change for change's sake. Be responsive to student needs.

Associating with Dynamic Colleagues

Relationships among faculty can be divided into two realms: social and professional. Depending on events and daily activity—and the moods of peers—personal and professional contact with colleagues may be a source of pleasure, pain, or somewhere in between. Consider the comments of a subject with almost twenty years' experience:

> All things being equal, I'd rather spend my time with colleagues who are excited about their work, and willing to exchange ideas. They are not competitive. Being knowledgeable and articulate helps too, but what *really* matters is: Is this someone with whom I can have a mutually stimulating discussion? Can we spur each other on? These are the people I want to spend time with. They make coming to work a joy.

Sometimes dynamic colleagues are no further away than across the hall or in the office next door. You may find that the most dynamic faculty reside in your own program. But don't limit yourself. Consider the words of a faculty member with just over twenty years of experience:

> I do enjoy faculty members in my department, but there are some who I would not want to spend time with unless it was absolutely necessary. I assume I'm not alone here. I compensate, if that's the right word, by hanging out with faculty from other departments. They are top-notch colleagues,

and some have become close friends. We can challenge each other's ideas, review each other's manuscripts, and talk about the craziness of academic life.

Fruitful longevity requires sustaining passion. One can nourish passion by finding new challenges. An open exchange of intellectual passions with colleagues is a viable gateway to professional growth and development.

Staying Current with Community Practice Needs

In 2009, I conducted a needs assessment. It was completely voluntary. Neither accrediting agency nor administrative directive required that I collect data. I simply wanted to check in with regional social service agencies to make sure our graduates would meet the needs of the practice community, now and in the future. To agency leaders, I provided a copy of our curriculum, including course descriptions, and a list of all the elective courses we had provided for the previous three years. I asked for the following input:

Describe what you believe to be compelling social work education curricular needs now and in the future.

What knowledge and competencies are graduates of social work education programs lacking today?

Looking over our list of elective courses we have offered during the last three years, what ideas do you have for additional topics? Are there any topics that no longer appear relevant?

Not only did these efforts enhance public relationships with social service agencies, they are likely to strengthen the partnership between practice and academia. New elective courses that emerged from this particular needs assessment included: "Working with Military Families," "Crisis Skills in Social Work," "Wraparound Services," and "Social Worker Safety."

My colleagues had a wide range of suggestions for staying current with practice community needs. One subject with over thirty years' experience advised: "You can't sit around and wait for community members to seek you out. You must *look for* ways to participate in the community." Subjects considered service to the community as a moral obligation to the professions of social work and social work education. Ideas brought forth by subjects ranged from joining local social service agency boards to going out with child welfare workers on home visits to lobbying for or against initiatives at their state legislature. As subjects were quick to point out, social work education must be a profession responsive to a dynamic society.

Networking with In-State Social Work Education Programs

"Well we all need someone we can lean on" (Jagger & Richards, 1969). Communicating with other social work programs in your state (or in less-populated states or your region) may be mutually beneficial for all parties concerned. Some states, such as California and New York, have statewide public educational systems that exist under the same rules and regulations. In Massachusetts, for example, all social work programs are obliged to abide by the same union contract. In the words of one respondent with more than two decades in social work education:

> It just makes sense for us to compare notes. Sure, we compete for students; that's inevitable. But we also share similar challenges. We really need to pool resources, strategize about effective ways to work with administrators, and share ideas that will prepare our students for current and future workforce needs. I also appreciate the camaraderie I receive from my in-state colleagues. I think we instill pride in each other. As social work educators, we really need that. I attend regular statewide meetings for social work directors. It has a powerful, reassuring impact on how I approach work.

Attending Conferences

I conducted fifty of the sixty-six interviews for this study in person at state (New York), regional (Mississippi–Alabama), and national (BPD and CSWE) conferences. In one three-day span, I conducted twenty-two interviews. I realized the essence of why I attend conferences: feeling the passion and the power of social work education from Florida to Alaska, from Maine to New Mexico, from Texas to Minnesota, and the territory of Guam gives me strength. United we influence the very fabric of society.

Sustaining vitality throughout one's social work education career requires not just leaving your office; it requires getting out of town. It requires a live exchange of ideas with social workers and social work educators from other parts of the country, and if you are fortunate, other parts of the world. Subjects who attend conferences report returning to their home institutions with new ideas for teaching strategies and assignments, and reinforcement from their peers. Consider this statement (especially appropriate for mid-career social work educators) from a social work educator with twenty-nine years of experience:

> You can get very comfortable—in a rut—leading to burnout, doing the same things over and over. You can stop looking for ways to be creative. This is one reason we make it a point to go to BPD every year—to discover new ways to be turned on to social work. You can get too comfortable

when you've been somewhere too long. When you go to conferences, you can *look for ways to challenge yourself, students, and faculty.* Change can be positive. We *need* periodic renewal and communication with other programs. We can share experiences: "We tried this and that." The results may be good or bad, but they get people thinking and working toward improvement.

Taking Sabbaticals

Few professions are afforded the benefit of a paid sabbatical leave.* Sabbaticals allow social work educators an opportunity to immerse themselves in in-depth research or other scholarly activities (I used a sabbatical leave to collect and analyze data for the book you are now reading). Perhaps more important, sabbaticals may be viewed as a valuable time for renewal and an opportunity to reflect upon the meaning and future of one's life and career.

Consider the notion of a "micro-sabbatical." Imagine you have a full day to work on an article you are writing. Bathroom breaks and meals aside, it is unlikely you would work a solid fifteen hours without taking a break to walk around the block, read your e-mail, or engage in some other diversion from the task at hand. If the notion of a micro-sabbatical is valid, you would be more likely when you return from your intermission to dive back into work with re-newed energy, increased productivity, and even new ideas. Now extend this no-tion to six months or a year away from the academy. You may very well have the opportunity for increased activity and new ideas on a grand scale. One subject, with over three decades of experience, went so far as to propose mandatory sabbaticals:

> The worst part of longevity is that people get jaded, lose their spontaneity, their curiosity, and their creativity. We could minimize this by *requiring* faculty to take sabbaticals *and* having less time in between sabbaticals, like five years instead of seven. We should enforce conditions of sabbaticals like showing evidence of productivity. If we did this, then longevity would be an excellent thing.

Requiring Serious Post-Tenure Review

As discussed in chapter 12, there are pros and cons to tenure. One of the cons is that some faculty are at risk for becoming less engaged and less

---

* Most institutions of higher learning offer sabbatical leave for full-time faculty. Sabbatical compensa-tion varies across the nation. A typical example would afford a faculty member a year off every five to seven years, with anywhere between one-half to two-thirds wage compensation. Another option may be to take a half year off with full wage compensation. Not all institutions offer sabbaticals, and not all faculty take advantage of sabbaticals.

accountable for the quality of their performance. Subjects lamented that the "shield of protection" made it difficult to dismiss tenured faculty even if their teaching was subpar and their level of disengagement from academic responsibilities was pernicious. Yet subjects were equally adamant in their belief that serious post-tenure review, with negative consequences for poor performance, would be beneficial to the quality of social work education. Listen to the ideas of a veteran of twenty-eight years:

> There must be serious post-tenure review—something with teeth—something with consequences that keeps faculty accountable to the students, program, and university they serve. Perhaps faculty who have become deadwood should be *required* to have extra professional development assignments, or be required to teach a class or two that they have never taught. Or perhaps they could learn a new foreign language that would enhance cultural competence.

And consider this quote from a participant with two decades of experience:

> Working with dinosaurs can suck the lifeblood out of a program. One remedy is genuine post-tenure review. People have to take stands against substandard tenured faculty. It's a moral imperative. We can't afford to tolerate it.

But like the weather, everyone talks about serious post-tenure review ("with teeth"), but no one does anything about it. Regular evaluations of teaching, research, and service may be in order. "Fading" faculty could be provided with guidance, suggestions, and referrals to help rejuvenate their careers. Better still, as a preventive measure, they could be involved in regular mandatory professional development activities throughout their careers, *before* they reach the point of decline.

A FINAL WORD ON LONGEVITY

In deference to the topic of this chapter, determining if longevity is good or bad camouflages a more important question: Are social work educators able to maximize their potential? Quoting the sage words of a social work educator with well over three decades of experience:

> Longevity may not be the issue. Significant positive impacts may be made in short *and* long stints. People have been in one place a long time or a short time and have been disasters. It depends on the person, values, commitment to students, and the institution's willingness to support student

and faculty growth. The political climate [of the institution and the program] may have a tremendous impact.

Some institutions will "chew you up and spit you out." There is no glory in trying to outlast another faculty member or administrator who has not finished the work of adulthood (see pages 93–94). Even with the best of preventive medicine and conscious effort to stay fresh, the original goodness of fit may deteriorate over time. In the words of a colleague with twenty years of experience: "Some institutions can burn you out. You become embittered, always feeling judged. Sometimes if you're judged in a negative way, it can really stick in your craw."And that's not good for anyone.

In contrast, you may find your "true home" and feel fortunate to spend the majority of your career in a nurturing environment. Reading *Career Reflections of Social Work Educators* may improve your chances of finding the best fit. But there are no guarantees. For some, your fate may be "the luck of the draw," or circumstances beyond your control. But five years, fifteen years, or thirty-five years—does it really matter? Perhaps we should give less attention to the number of years we serve, and more attention to the quality of service we give.

References

Anastas, J. W. (2006). Employment opportunities in social work education: A study of jobs for doctoral graduates. *Journal of Social Work Education, 42*(2), 195–209.

Barnett, E., Gibson, M., & Black, P. (2003). Issues in education: Proactive steps to successfully recruit, retain, and mentor minority educators. *The Journal of Early Education and Family Review, 10*(3), 18–28.

Becker, H. S., & Carper, J. (1956). The elements of identification with an occupation. *American Sociological Review, 21*(3), 341–348.

Becker, H. S., & Strauss, A. L. (1956). Careers, personality, and adult socialization. *The American Journal of Sociology, 52*(3), 253–263.

Beckerman, N. L. (2002). New faculty: Reports from an orientation program. *Arete, 26*(1), 92–96.

Brown, D. G. (1967). *The mobile professors.* Washington, DC: American Council on Education.

Brown, P. M., Rice, A. H., Angell, G. B., & Kurz, B. (2000). Faculty hiring practices in social work education: A national survey. *Critical Social Work, 1*(2), 1–11.

Capell, R. G. (1979). Changing human systems. Toronto, Ontario, Canada: International Human Systems Institute.

Cartledge, G., Gardner III, R., & Tillman, L. (1995). African Americans in higher education special education: Issues in recruitment and retention. *Teacher Education and Special Education, 18*(3), 166–178.

Childress, C. (2001). *Can a fast growing work environment decrease employee retention?* Unpublished master's thesis, Cardinal Stritch University, Milwaukee, WI.

Council on Social Work Education (2007). *Statistics on social work education in the United States: 2004.* Alexandria, VA.

Council on Social Work Education (2008). *Curriculum policy statement.* Alexandria, VA.

Erikson, E. H. (1997). *The life cycle completed.* New York: Norton.

Feld, S. (1988). The academic marketplace in social work. *Journal of Social Work Education, 24*(3), 201–210.

Fogg, P. (2006). Young Ph.D.'s say collegiality matters more than salary. *The Chronicle of Higher Education, 53*(6), A1, A11–A12.

Frankl, S. N. (2003). Strategies to create and sustain a diverse faculty and student body at Boston University School of Dental Medicine. *Journal of Dental Medicine, 67*(9), 1042–1045.

Goleman, D. (2006). *Social intelligence.* New York: Random House.

Harvard Graduate School of Education (2006). *New study indicates faculty treatment matters more than compensation.* Retrieved October 3, 2006, from http://www.gse.harvard.edu/news_events/features/2006/09/26_faculty

Henry, E. C., Caudle, D. M., & Sullenger, P. (1994). Tenure and turnover in academic libraries. *College & Research Libraries 55*(5), 429–435.

Jagger, M., & Richards, K. (1969). *Let It Bleed.* Abkco Records.

Johnson, S. (1998). *Who moved my cheese?* New York: Putnam.

Jung, C. G. (1954). The psychology of transference; Fundamental questions of psychotherapy; From the practice of psychotherapy. In *The collected works of C. G. Jung,* translated by R. F. C. Hull. Princeton University Press as Bollingen Series XX: Princeton, NJ.

Kanter, R. M. (2006). *Confidence.* New York: Random House.

Karger, J. H., & Stoesz, D. (2003). The growth of social work education programs, 1985–1999: Its impact on economic and educational factors related to the profession of social work. *Journal of Social Work Education, 39*(2), 279–295.

Kula, K., Glaros, A., Larson, B., & Tuncay, D. (2000). Reasons that orthodontic faculty teach and consider leaving teaching. *Journal of Dental Education, 64*(11), 755–762.

Lemire, L. M. (2007). *The undercover wounded healer: The role of personal therapy in being a clinical social worker.* Master's thesis, Smith College School for Social Work, Northampton, MA.

Levine, S., & Levine, O. (1989). *Who dies?: An investigation of conscious living and conscious dying.* New York: Random House.

Lewington, J. (1999). Canadian universities are losing top professors to U.S. institutions. *Chronicle of Higher Education 46*(4), 1–6.

Logan, N. S. (1997). Promoting the recruitment and retention of minority faculty. *Journal of Dental Education, 61*(3), 273–276.

Maeder, T. (1989). Wounded healers. *Atlantic Monthly*, January.

Magen, R. H., & Emerman, J. (2000). Should convicted felons be denied admission to a social work education program? Yes! *Journal of Social Work Education, 36*(3), 401–405, 411–413.

Mahroum, S. (1999). Patterns of academic inflow into the higher education system of the United Kingdom. *Higher Education in Europe, 24*(1), 119–129.

Matier, M. W. (1985). *Factors influencing "star" faculty attrition at institutions of higher education.* Doctoral dissertation, University of Oregon (Educational Policy and Management), Eugene, OR.

McBride, S. A., Munday, R. G., & Tunnell, J. (1992). Community college faculty job satisfaction and propensity to leave. *Community/Junior College Quarterly, 16,* 157–165.

Munuchin, S. (1974). *Families and family therapy.* Cambridge, MA: Harvard University Press.

Nelson, C. (1997). The real problem with tenure is incompetent faculty hiring. *Chronicle of Higher Education, 44*(12), 4–5.

Nouwen, H. (1979). *The wounded healer.* New York: Image.

Peters, T. J., & Waterman, R. H. (2004; 1982). *In search of excellence.* New York: HarperCollins.

Peterson, E. (2006). Examine hidden costs before changing jobs. Retrieved May 16, 2006, from http://bankrate.com/nsc/news/pf/20030428b1.asp

Phillips, R. (2002). Recruiting and retaining a diverse faculty. *Planning for Higher Education, 30*(4), 32–39.

Regher, C., Stalker, C., Pelech, W., & Jacobs, M. (2001). The gatekeeper and the wounded healer: Challenges for admissions decision makers in social work. *The Clinical Supervisor,* 20(1), 127–143.

Richardson, J., & McKenna, S., (2002). Leaving and experiencing: Why academic expatriate and how they experience expatriation. *Career Development International, 7*(2), 67–78.

Russo, R. (1997). *Straight man.* New York: Random House.

Satir, V. (1967). *Conjoint family therapy* (Rev. ed.). Palo Alto, CA: Science and Behavior Books.

Satir, V. (1972). *Peoplemaking.* Palo Alto, CA: Science and Behavior Books.

Scott, N., & Zeiger, S. (2000). Should convicted felons be denied admission to a social work education program? No! *Journal of Social Work Education, 36*(3), 405–411.

Tabachnick, S. E. (1992). The problem of faculty relocation. *Academe, 78*(1), 24–26.

Wilson, R. (1995). Finders, keepers? Recruiting and retaining minority faculty members challenges Old Dominion U. *Chronicle of Higher Education, 41*(38), A13–A16.

Wilson, R. (2000). Columbia expands into educating children as perk for its parent-professors. *Chronicle of Higher Education, 46*(49), A14–A16.

Wilson Schaef, A. (1992). *Beyond therapy, beyond science.* San Francisco: Harper.

Winter, P. A., & Kjorlien, C. L. (2000). Community college faculty recruitment: Effect of job mobility, recruiter similarity-dissimilarity, and applicant gender. *Community College Journal of Research and Practice, 24*(7), 547–560.

Withers, Jr., W. H. (1972). *Lean on me.* Sussex Records.

Zeiger, S. J., Hobbs, R., Robinson, M., Ortiz, L. P., & Cox, M. J. (1999). The impact of expansion: Adding an MSW program to an existing BSW program. *The Journal of Baccalaureate Social Work Education, 5*(1), 27–44.

Zeiger, S. J., Ortiz, L. P., Sirles, E., & Rivas, R. (2005). Organizational development continues: Adding an MSW program to an existing BSW program. *The Journal of Baccalaureate Social Work Education, 11*(1), 40–57.

Index

KEY TO COVER PHOTOS

1	Lynne Adkins	34	Ann McAllister
2	Sally Alonzo Bell	35	Aaron McNeece
3	Freddie Avant	36	Ann Meyers
4	Jackie Azzarto	37	Emily Meyers
5	Frank Baskind	38	Linda Moore
6	Gerald Berman	39	Murali Nair
7	Luther Brown	40	Larry Ortiz
8	Pamela Brown	41	Michael Patchner
9	Kathy Byers	42	James Piers
10	Mary Campbell	43	Jean Quam
11	Graciela Castex	44	Tim Rehner
12	Barbara Chandler	45	Robert Rivas
13	Brenda Armstrong Clark	46	John Rogers
14	Vivian Dames	47	Alvin Salee
15	Judith Davenport	48	Joe Schriver
16	Virginia David	49	Jack Sellers
17	Eddie Davis	50	Paula Sheridan
18	Tammy Faux	51	Brad Sheafor
19	Jerry Finn	52	Debbie Simpler
20	Jody Gottlieb	53	Elizabeth Sirles
21	Kay Hoffman	54	Marshall Smith
22	Jane Hoyt-Oliver	55	James Stafford
23	Ruth Huber	56	Andrea Stewart
24	Grafton Hull	57	Paul Stuart
25	Mitch Kahn	58	Anne Summers
26	Karen Kirst-Ashman	59	Mary Ann Suppes
27	Connie Kledaris	60	Mary Swigonski
28	Rebecca Leavitt	61	Billie Terrell
29	Twyla Lee	62	Rebecca Turner
30	Alice Lieberman	63	Katherine VanWormer
31	Donna Macintosh	64	Sue Wein
32	Cheryl Mathews	65	Linda Williams
33	Carl Mazza	66	Jackie Winston